AC/DC

ALBUM BY ALBUM

BY MARTIN POPOFF
WITH
RICHARD BIENSTOCK, PHIL CARSON,
MARK CICCHINI, RICH DAVENPORT,
DAVE ELLEFSON, MIKE FRASER,
JAY JAY FRENCH, MICHAEL HANNON,
PAUL KEHAYAS, ROBERT LAWSON,
JOEL O'KEEFFE, PHIL RUDD,
ROBERT SIBONY, MARK STRIGL,
BRAD TOLINSKI, BILL VOCCIA,
AND SIMON WRIGHT

VOYAGEUR
PRESS

Brimming with creative inspiration, how-to projects, and useful information to enrich your everyday life, Quarto Knows is a favorite destination for those pursuing their interests and passions. Visit our site and dig deeper with our books into your area of interest: Quarto Creates, Quarto Cooks, Quarto Homes, Quarto Lives, Quarto Drives, Quarto Explores, Quarto Gifts, or Quarto Kids.

First published in 2017 by Voyageur Press, an imprint of The Quarto Group, 401 Second Avenue North, Suite 310, Minneapolis, MN 55401 USA. T: (612) 344-8100 F: (612) 344-8692
QuartoKnows.com

Voyageur Press titles are also available at discount for retail, wholesale, promotional, and bulk purchase. For details, contact the Special Sales Manager by email at specialsales@quarto.com or by mail at The Quarto Group, Attn: Special Sales Manager, 401 Second Avenue North, Suite 310, Minneapolis, MN 55401 USA.

10 9 8 7 6 5 4 3 2 1

ISBN: 978-0-7603-5374-5

Library of Congress Cataloging-in-Publication Data

Names: Popoff, Martin, 1963- author.
Title: AC/DC : album by album / by Martin Popoff.
Description: Minneapolis : Voyageur Press, 2017. | Includes index.
Identifiers: LCCN 2017024505 | ISBN 9780760353745 (hc w/jacket)
Subjects: LCSH: AC/DC (Musical group)--Criticism and interpretation. | Rock
   music--Australia--History and criticism.
Classification: LCC ML421.A28 P66 2017 | DDC 782.42166092/2--dc23
LC record available at https://lccn.loc.gov/2017024505

Acquiring Editor: Dennis Pernu
Project Manager: Jordan Wiklund
Art Director: James Kegley
Page Design: Renato Stanisic
Layout: Kim Winscher

Printed in China

CONTENTS

INTRODUCTION

There's something amusing about the second book I've done in this cool drunken kitchen party *Album by Album* series being about all things AC/DC, where first time out, the subject was fussy math rock pioneers Rush. The music of these two legendary bands couldn't be further apart philosophically—within our classic hard rock bubble, anyway—but it's heartening to realize there's a huge overlap in the fan bases. Millions of people love Rush and millions of those same people love AC/DC too. I think that's testimony to the fuzzy lovability of both bands.

Back on planet work, however, I found the prospect of constructing the AC/DC book a bit more daunting, given that, at first blush, it seemed like there was less to talk about, certainly fewer nooks and crannies to the music. How wrong I was, for once I gathered my army of AC/DC experts, I quickly realized that we could talk and shout and laugh about Angus, Malcolm, Brian, and Bon endlessly. And it often seemed like we did, given how much interview footage I ultimately had to choose from and could not stuff between the pages of this action-packed love letter to Australia's greatest export.

There were so many plots and subplots, from the weird formation of the band to its closed-shop ethic, from the inevitable assault on Europe and America to the hiring of new producers, from the shocking death of Bon Scott straight into one of the biggest selling albums of all time, leading to a level of fame, infamy, and legendary status very much anchored in that first album crowed and cawed by an unknown Geordie named Brian Johnson.

What I love about this book, and the reason I think you're gonna dig it, is the enthusiasm of the speakers and their ability to convince us that there is indeed a lot to talk about with this band famous for "making the same record over and over again." At the massive and commercial end of the catalog, their words will have you revisiting records you thought you knew top to bottom. More intriguingly, their instruction and exposition will bring you new appreciation for albums to which you might've paid cursory notice and then forgotten, like *Powerage*, *Fly on the Wall*, *Ballbreaker*, *Stiff Upper Lip*, and their likely last release, *Rock or Bust*.

That's really what I love the most about this series: this delivery of an enriched and educated viewpoint, not only from us to you, but also from these guys to me in real time as I wrote it. I had all manner of things pointed out to me that I never would've considered as I talked to these cats. And as soon as the interview was over, out came the CDs, finger on the fast forward or rewind buttons, in search of a fresh revelation about what Angus does at the twenty-eight-second mark.

So there you go. This AC/DC fan (who was introduced to the band in 1977 with a domestic Canadian copy of bought at Kelly's in Winnipeg, Manitoba, while on a cross-country family vacation) . . . well, I found myself plowing through the catalog yet again, which has never really been an issue, because I've always been a regular listener of this band. After all, I'd say pretty much unarguably that AC/DC has got to be one of the top handful of goodtime party bands ever concocted. Whether it's drinking, socializing, jogging, gyming, driving fast, or just at those thorny times when a pick-me-up or attitude adjustment is called for, nothing slakes one's thirst like *Powerage* or *Highway to Hell*.

So pour yourself a stiff one, and come on in. Step on up and clink drinks with seventeen—eighteen, if you count this author—dedicated fanatics just like yourself, each with his own story about when he first stuck his finger in that socket (yes, there are no gals—though oh how we tried to find some). Don't be shy; join in the debate—while writing this, I could almost hear you pounding your fist on the bar, either in agreement or spoiling for a fight. Here's hoping that out in the pubs and clubs I get to hear from you which of these guys you thought was full of crap and which seemed to be reading your very thoughts, confirming what you were sure that you alone understood about those mysterious Young brothers and the happy and healing headbanging they conjured.

—*Martin Popoff*

ISSUE VARIANCE NOTES: Issued only in Australia. Not to be confused with international versions of *High Voltage*, although "She's Got Balls" and "Little Lover" would be included on those records.

SIDE 1

1.	Baby Please Don't Go	4:50
2.	She's Got Balls	4:51
3.	Little Lover	5:37
4.	Stick Around	4:40

SIDE 2

1.	Soul Stripper	6:25
2.	You Ain't Got a Hold on Me	3:31
3.	Love Song	5:15
4.	Show Business	4:46

All songs composed by Angus Young, Malcolm Young, and Bon Scott except "Baby Please Don't Go" (Big Joe Williams) and "Soul Stripper" (Angus Young and Malcolm Young)

Personnel: Bon Scott—lead vocals; Angus Young—lead guitar; Malcolm Young—rhythm guitar, lead guitar, bass, backing vocals; Rob Bailey—bass (in band but limited playing on album); Peter Clack—drums (in band but performs on "Baby Please Don't Go" only). Session appearances: George Young—bass, rhythm guitar, backing vocals; Harry Vanda—backing vocals; Tony Currenti—drums (session drummer but plays on all tracks except "Baby Please Don't Go")

Released February 17, 1975

Recorded at Albert Studios, Sydney, Australia

Produced by Harry Vanda and George Young

HIGH VOLTAGE

with **RICH DAVENPORT** and **ROBERT SIBONY**

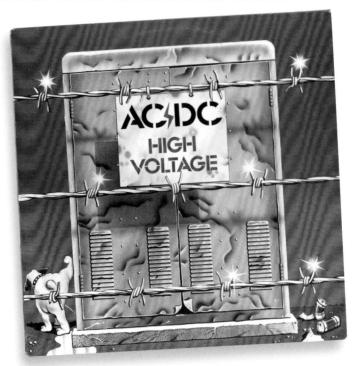

Did the most loved band in the whole darn world ever hafta pay their dues? I'd say the answer is yes. Fact is, when AC/DC ambled onto the Australian scene in February 1975, clutching their mom-approved debut album, *High Voltage*, they had only been a band for a little over a year, with their new lead singer Bon Scott joining a mere month before the album's taping in October 1974.

But there was quite a bit in place already. Older brother and co-producer George Young had already been a pop sensation with his band the Easybeats, which he shared with Harry Vanda, who came along and co-produced *High Voltage* with George. As well, George was already in tight with Ted Albert from the decades-old music industry Albert family, and so a record deal was soon in the offing, along with the opportunity to record in a new state-of-the-art studio.

The end result of having these ducks in a row was a slight and scrappy record that most AC/DC fans throughout the ensuing decades knew little about, outside of two tracks, "She's Got Balls" and "Little Lover," which would be included on the international debut record for AC/DC, also confusingly called *High Voltage*.

It's for good business reason the voltage was kept low, with most of these songs evading wide release. And it's not that the record's collaborative contributions were objectively bad. It's just that what would become one of the most identifiable sounds in rock was still in its formative stages, if fairly moved along with "She's Got Balls," "Stick Around," "Soul Stripper," and, if you'll buy into bald-faced boogie as part of AC/DC's later identity, "Show Business."

As Malcolm told me in a hotel room interview (the day after the band's historic 2003 SARSstock concert in Toronto, alongside Rush and the Rolling Stones), there was a clear reason the band played songs such as "Show Business" and "Baby Please Don't Go." "The kids were just like that on the pub scene," he explained. "Some of these pubs hold fifteen hundred, two thousand, and they wanna rock out there. And the boogies, they could understand those straight enough. . . . It was like, 'Give us a boogie! Give us a boogie!' So everyone

OPPOSITE: The Australia-only *High Voltage*.

BELOW: The Australia-only release of *High Voltage* was a slight but scrappy record, helped along by the co-production of the experienced George Young and Harry Vanda.

played a boogie. You know, we used to like Canned Heat from way back, and we would just jam on stuff, around their ideas at the time, and we'd put a bit of boogie into our own material. But we were always into the blues and the rock 'n' roll stuff. We grew up on it. We had older brothers who were into Chuck Berry and Little Richard and Jerry Lee Lewis and we grew up as kids hearing that. You know, it's in us. And we just tried to emulate that, these guys, with their feels, and get it really rockin' and then keep it going."

Additional to its deliberate roots rock premise, the whole of the *High Voltage* album was expertly recorded and solidly played, the team making deft use of the studio's top-notch equipment and Harry's and George's production know-how. But even these somewhat advanced songs were AC/DC Lite, somewhat average, filler if one must be harsh. Elsewhere we got a frantic version of "Baby Please Don't Go," very much in the Ted Nugent and the Amboy Dukes vein. "You Ain't Got a Hold on Me" is another song one might arguably add to the bank of tracks comprising the roots of AC/DC proper. And, sure, "Little Lover" aligns with "The Jack" and "Night Prowler." But gosh darn right off the path is "Love Song," which is as close to a ballad as the band would ever get, offering amusing glimpses at the pasts of both George and Bon, the two seasoned elders.

It's almost as if George and Harry and Malcolm were grasping for something specific, something that didn't exist, a sonic worldview that kept flashing by just outside their peripheries. Eagerly and enthusiastically, and through sweat and ambition, they would be rewarded for their efforts. Soon they would have more than enough incendiary punk-but-not-punk songs to present when the possibility of an international label deal became real. Ergo, there goes almost all of *High Voltage*, not into the vaults, although in the pre-Internet information age, they may well have. *Jailbreak '74* would remedy some of that, as would the *Backtracks* box set of 2009, but as history stacked up, *High Voltage* remained the red-headed stepchild of the catalog, the shot heard only Down Under, foretelling a rock 'n' roll thunder that would soon shake the planet.

POPOFF: To start with, AC/DC actually had quite a bit going for them right off the bat. This wasn't just a bunch of kids banging around and putting out an indie record. They had producers, a label, a great studio to work in, even roadies and a tour bus.

SIBONY: No, you're right, and it all starts with George Young, the older brother of Angus and Malcolm, who was with the Easybeats, who were a pretty big band in the mid-sixties, influencing guys like Bruce Springsteen and David Bowie, believe it or not. So he and Harry Vanda, who was Dutch, had that band together coming up in the immigrant experience in Australia, with another Dutch guy, and George, whose family had recently arrived from Scotland, and even a drummer from Liverpool, Snowy Fleet. And they produced a lot of stuff and actually wrote and produced that big hit, "Love Is in the Air."

Anyway, what happened with Vanda and Young, as a production team they went to Europe and were in England for a few years. J. Albert & Son was a big music store in Australia and Ted Albert was one of the young guys, and he wanted to get into rock and start producing. His great granddad had this music store, which opened in 1902, which started after they moved to Sydney from Switzerland in 1884, and started off fixing watches and clocks. And it's a major music store. I mean, we're talking, classical . . . they made pianos, giant organs. And they sold music too, records, and they got into publishing and radio broadcasting and eventually owned a bunch of radio stations.

In 1973, they built a state-of-the-art studio in this place called Boomerang House, which is a house owned by the Albert family. And that begins the association with Young and Albert. And the early AC/DC records were produced under Albert Productions and EMI Australia. Ted Albert did that to lure back Vanda and Young, back to Australia. And he basically made them an offer they couldn't refuse. So they went there, and they were basically staff writers and producers for Albert Productions.

And, you know how it started? They were, of course, friends of Ted's, and Ted came over to the house one day to meet George about something, and, of course, the two kids, Angus and Malcolm, are downstairs playing in the basement, and Ted says to their father, "If they ever want to do something, call me." So that was the beginning of it. So you're right, they were in a pretty established place, here with Ted, who was basically the outcast of the family, going into rock 'n' roll. But that's how it all started.

Pre-Bon, pre-Phil, and pre-Mark . . . Chequers, Sydney, early 1974.

POPOFF: And why, given Australia's pop sound—much of it at the hands of George and Harry—does this new band have this sort of slightly post-fifties rock 'n' roll vibe?

DAVENPORT: Yeah, well, Australia was a little bit like catching up musically in the sixties, but they did get there. Obviously, the first major band was the Easybeats, with George Young on guitar. And Angus and Malcolm obviously looked up to him as their older brother, not only musically, but I think the way they conducted the business of the band. George's outlook on the music business was that they were severely ripped off when they were in the Easybeats. So his experience shaped the brothers' outlook on the business.

But back to the sound, in terms of early seventies, the Australian pop rock and pub scene was coming into its own. Now, it was different from English pub rock; that was a disparate scene with everything from sort of country rock with Brinsley Schwarz to more bluesy bands with Dr. Feelgood, whereas the Australian pub rock sound was much harder-edged and a lot more bluesy. You had guys like Lobby Loyde,

The Easybeats, seen here in London in 1968, featuring Malcolm's and Angus's older brother George (far left) on guitar, were one of Australia's first major bands. Malcolm and Angus obviously looked up to him not only musically, but for the way he conducted band business.

who had a band called the Coloured Balls, and Buffalo—they were a heavy band—that featured Pete Wells from Rose Tattoo on bass. Billy Thorpe & the Aztecs were a sixties band, and then they re-emerged in the early seventies; they were very influential. And, obviously, pre-AC/DC and Rose Tattoo, Buster Brown, for Phil Rudd and Angry Anderson.

So the sound is very hard-edged, and they were playing these huge "hotels," they called them, but they were like a big pub room, a much bigger room than you would get in an English pub. These were like spit and sawdust places where you had to really impress the crowd and knock them out with rock 'n' roll. That's what we want. So that environment was a big part of shaping that sound.

Now the band really was inspired by a lot of straight-ahead rock 'n' roll: the Stones, Free, Rod Stewart, a lot of blues stuff, Little Richard, that kind of thing. So they've got that rock 'n' roll sound there. But the key to them developing their sound was George. Various people who were in the studio for the first album have all pointed to the fact that George was guiding them and getting them to cut the fat off any of the riffs and songs and just chop them down to the essentials.

Malcolm's guitar sound was pretty much half the band, and you can hear a Stones influence in there. But I think he was influenced by George as well, his style of playing, in terms of stripping the songs down. Not to say that George did everything, but he was very instrumental in getting them to strip off the extraneous bits. And if they came up with anything that didn't sound like what they had done before, he'd say, no, stick to what you're good at.

POPOFF: *High Voltage* **was produced by both Harry and George. What was Harry's role?**
DAVENPORT: That's a tough one. I know that they were very, very close, because they were in the Easybeats together. From what I've read of the Angels and Rose Tattoo, it's always Harry and George, and Harry did that and George did that. With AC/DC, it tends to be more George being hands-on, possibly because of the familial relationship as the older brother. But AC/DC don't tend to mention Harry as much, to be frank, and I don't know why that is.

POPOFF: Whoever was responsible for what, they sure managed a good production sound, especially when it came to the guitars.

(continued on page 16)

Victoria Park, Sydney, 1974.

(continued from page 13)

SIBONY: Yes, and you can hear that loud and clear on both the soloing and the riffs on "Soul Stripper" and "She's Got Balls," where Angus is already as good as we'd know him for later—he's absolutely already the iconic lead guitarist we know him as today, at twenty years old, especially on "She's Got Balls."

And how these guys produced, and how they did guitars, was amazing. They went around to all the clubs in Australia, looking for bands. They listened to some of the records these bands made and when they went to see them live, it was like, this is not the same band. They didn't capture it. So the great thing about George and Harry was that they were both guitarists for the Easybeats, and the songwriters, so they used that knowledge to establish that live guitar sound of AC/DC and get it onto a record. Even today that guitar sound still stands out—you can still use that guitar sound today. You know how hard it is to capture energy in the studio? Well, they did it with AC/DC; you could feel it off the records.

Harry was the lead guitarist in the Easybeats—he was the Angus to Malcolm, right? And he was pretty schooled in music and the two of them made a great songwriting team. They were two young kids, eighteen years old, who were in Australia as immigrants who hung out in the sort of migrant camps they had and started doing music. And their parents were very supportive too—remember, George was a major rock star before AC/DC. The whole family played. There were eight brothers and sisters. Even Alex, the older brother, fifteen years older than Malcolm, played on some of the records that Vanda and George produced. So everybody thinks AC/DC was just a garage band that luckily hit it big. But it's not like that. They were very well schooled in music and of course in the music business because the brother had already gone through it and was already a major star already in 1966 with "Friday on My Mind."

POPOFF: What have you ever heard about what the atmosphere was like in Albert Studios?
DAVENPORT: Well, everybody who I've either interviewed—and I've spoken to the guys from the Angels and I've read interviews with Angry Anderson and stuff with the guys from AC/DC—they all point to George and Harry as being a very efficient production team, very hands-on, quite driven. I've never read anybody criticize them and say that it was terrible, that they really overworked us. Mark Evans mentions that they were all about capturing the performance. The band would play pretty much live, with some overdubs. And the story about Angus's amplifier catching on fire, on

The band poses for *High Voltage* promo stills in the studio of photographer Philip Morris.

one of the tracks on *Let There Be Rock*, Mark mentions if you listen to "Hell Ain't a Bad Place to Be," if you're a stickler for tuning, the guitars were slightly out of tune on that, but they just went with the performance. George and Harry said, no, you've got that, you got the feel there, let's leave it.

POPOFF: And what was the studio itself like?

DAVENPORT: It was big enough for the band to set up live in the room, but I don't think it was a huge room. Mark Evans mentions that he and Angus and Malcolm would be in one room, and then there was a door taken off another room, so you can see through to Phil in the next room. And then they would work on the backing tracks, and Bon would work on his vocals over the top. They'd kind of literally taken the door off the hinges so they could see through, and from what I understand, they would just play through a back line of amps and pretty much go for it live.

POPOFF: How does *High Voltage* balance the traditional while suggesting something new?

SIBONY: That whole record, they take really common guitar licks and they just change them slightly to make it their own, mainly by adding bit more melody and offering modern chord changes. They had this magic of doing that. George made them realize that it's all about the hook, and even the guitar line had to be a hook. It's not only about the vocals, but it's about the guitar too, which also had to pull its weight and provide a hook.

POPOFF: There's a bit of mystery about who plays what on *High Voltage*. Can you sort that out a bit for us?

DAVENPORT: On drums is a guy named Tony Currenti, who runs a pizzeria in Sydney. And he moved from Italy to Australia in the late sixties. At the time, AC/DC had Bon on vocals. He had not long since joined. He'd been with the band a few months. And they had a guy named Rob Bailey on bass, and another drummer named Peter Clack.

Now, what happened, when I interviewed Tony, was that he said that he knew Vanda and Young. He had been in the studio working on a session with Jackie Christian & Flight, the band that he was in, and they said, "Look, can you stay behind?" They obviously liked his drumming. Tony was saying that they told him that Peter Clack had taken an inordinate amount of time to try to lay down a drum track and they wanted to move on quite quickly and get things done.

So Tony said that at the time he came in, "Baby Please Don't Go" was recorded, and that was with Peter Clack. But the rest of the tracks that were on *High Voltage* were Tony on drums. And he said that they recorded eight songs over four nights. He already knew Bon Scott, because he had been in a band a few years previously, in the early seventies, when Bon was in Fraternity, and sort of got quite friendly with Bon, and they had a chat and a drink together at the bar.

And George Young brought Tony into the recording studio session, and when he opened the door to the studio, he recognized Bon. And he said that that was really good at making him feel at home and comfortable, and Bon was making him feel welcome, making him a cup of tea [*laughs*]. That helped him settle in and get cracking with it, really. He also said that the first night it was Rob Bailey playing bass, and then the next three nights were all George Young. So quite a lot of the bass lines were actually played by George on that first album.

POPOFF: What would make them cover "Baby Please Don't Go"?

DAVENPORT: It makes a lot of sense. I know they are blues fans. Now, obviously, I don't know this, but I have a feeling that they were fans of Them, Van Morrison's very raw R & B band. Because, no disrespect to AC/DC, but the riff for "Jailbreak" is very, very close to "Gloria" by Them. And there are very few AC/DC songs where you could say, oh, that sounds like another riff. But that is one of them. The other one I would think of, offhand, is "Beating Around the Bush," which was like a speeded-up version of "Oh Well" by Fleetwood Mac. And "Ride On," which has a similarity to "Jesus Just Left Chicago" by ZZ Top.

Other than that, obviously, there's twelve bars that sound like Chuck Berry, but it's their version of "Baby Please Don't Go" that shows their boogie roots, tied in with the blues roots. And they maybe had heard the Van Morrison version before, I figure. If you listen to the original Muddy Waters version, it's about half the speed, and Them give it a fair kick up the bum and speed it up, and then AC/DC did it a shade faster than that.

BELOW: Sheet music for "Baby Please Don't Go," 1975. Was their cover of the Big Joe Williams chestnut inspired by Van Morrison's Them?

BOTTOM: Three-track German promo, 1975. "Baby Please Don't Go" and "Jail Break" [sic] b/w "Soul Stripper."

They put their own stamp on it, it's like an ascending chord sequence in the middle, and there's like a question and response with Bon and Angus on guitar. And there's a kind of a trademark thing at the beginning, the riff that people associate with "Baby Please Don't Go"—Angus and Malcolm play in octaves. Malcolm plays the low octave and Angus plays the high octave, and he would occasionally do that on riffs throughout the career. Bon's ex-wife Irene told me that Bon told her second husband they were planning to record a cover of "Gloria" as a B-side, when they met! This was around *Highway to Hell*.

"A complete anomaly." "Love Song (Oh Jene)" was AC/DC's first official single with Bon. The B-side, "Baby Please Don't Go," is what radio stations ended up playing.

POPOFF: But other bands helped establish and then push the mandate, correct?

DAVENPORT: Yes, and actually, "She's Got Balls" is probably one of the first songs that has that relentless driving riff style. So on that original Australian *High Voltage*, the bare ingredients of AC/DC are there, although some of the songs, for me, don't have quite the attack that the later material has, and that would be placed firmly into *T.N.T.* I mean, "Stick Around," good song, but it doesn't quite kick in as much as they do on some of the later stuff.

And "Little Lover" is quite slow. You've got things like "Love Song," which is really different for AC/DC, a complete anomaly, because it's quite intricate and fiddly, and it starts with triplets and arpeggios and things like that. I would imagine that's the kind of thing that George Young would've guided them away from. Also, lyrically, Bon is singing more love songs, more generally singing, and less of the lascivious stuff that he is known for.

Although there's "She's Got Balls," and "Soul Stripper" has his trademark kind of sauciness about it. But again, "She's Got Balls" really has that relentless driving power that AC/DC is known for, so that's a really good pointer to what they became. And "Show Business" sort of prefaces "It's a Long Way to the Top." I think the first lines are *You learn to sing/ You learn to play/Why don't the businessmen/Ever learn to pay?* That's perhaps a trial run at exploring the things that Bon later develops with "It's a Long Way to the Top."

POPOFF: So we were learning about Bon.

SIBONY: Sure, and all his struggles. But he overcame it and became the ultimate rock star, didn't he? Or if not rock star, grinding, working musician.

He lived the life; there's no two ways about it. Angus would say, "I could come home from a gig at three o'clock in the morning, and Bon is like, 'Okay, one more drink.'" He would not stop. But I just loved his attitude. He was a really fun-loving guy and would come across like he just really liked life and wanted to take advantage of everything. But it also seemed like he knew that he didn't have a long time to live. He was on that road and he didn't care. He lived that lifestyle and you could hear it in his lyrics.

High Voltage international (bottom) and European (top) cover art, 1976.

POPOFF: But even on *High Voltage*, AC/DC were as much about the guitars as anything Bon would be on about, right?
SIBONY: Yes, and you've got to give the brothers a lot of musical credit, you know? They had the same manager as Aerosmith at one time, David Krebs, who said, "Joe Perry had nothing on Angus." Which summed it up. Joe was the guitar god, whereas Angus, just because of his silliness and his little boy act, was never really considered a serious guitarist.

Although in terms of composition, Malcolm was the guy who wrote most of the licks and was the leader of the band. Originally, Angus wasn't even in the band, and Malcolm got him in the band to play lead. Malcolm had a great line. He said that working on leads interrupted his drinking [*laughs*]. But if you listen to the records, it's beautifully done. They stereo'ed it really nicely, with Malcolm on one side representing the low part of the frequencies while Angus takes care of the high part. Exactly like George and Harry did in the Easybeats.

POPOFF: And the pattern is set, and a sound is born, right here on the tracks comprising *High Voltage*.
SIBONY: But the beauty of it is that at the base, it's common pentatonic blue stuff. But the way Malcolm turns it around, and what he does rhythmically to it, makes it his own. There's no really explaining that kind of magic. I mean, everybody loved AC/DC as far as my memory is concerned, growing up. If you look at the history, everybody loved them. And at the root, they were just a great party band. Somehow, they took that party and barroom mentality and made it work in a stadium, which is so rare.

ISSUE VARIANCE NOTES: Issued in Australia only; however, the international debut of the band, called *High Voltage*, issued in April 1976 in the United States and the following month in Europe, contains seven of nine tracks, the exceptions being "Rocker" and "School Days." The international *High Voltage* adds two tracks from the Australian issue *High Voltage*, namely "She's Got Balls" and "Little Lover."

SIDE 1

1. It's a Long Way to the Top (If You Wanna Rock 'n' Roll)   5:15
2. Rock 'n' Roll Singer   5:04
3. The Jack   5:52
4. Live Wire   5:49

SIDE 2

1. T.N.T.   3:34
2. Rocker   2:49
3. Can I Sit Next to You Girl   4:12
4. High Voltage   4:02
5. School Days   5:23

All songs composed by Angus Young, Malcolm Young, and Bon Scott except "Can I Sit Next to You Girl" (Angus Young and Malcolm Young) and "School Days" (Chuck Berry)

Personnel: Bon Scott—lead vocals, bagpipes; Angus Young—lead guitar; Malcolm Young—rhythm guitar, backing vocals; Mark Evans—bass; Phil Rudd—drums, percussion

Released December 1, 1975

Recorded at Albert Studios, Sydney, Australia

Produced by Harry Vanda and George Young

T.N.T

with RICH DAVENPORT and ROBERT SIBONY

Folks tend to look at AC/DC's second album, *T.N.T.*, as the record on which the band's trademark sound is codified. That argument only goes so far, with "The Jack," "Rocker," "Can I Sit to You Girl," and the cover of Chuck Berry's "School Days" sitting just as far to the left as three-quarters of the first album and one-third or so of the third record, *Dirty Deeds Done Dirt Cheap.*

But sure, the rest of this charmingly twee album works to establish the band's open architecture and almost hypnotic sense of repetition—instantly, in fact, with "It's a Long Way to the Top" and "The Rock 'n' Roll Singer," on which Harry Vanda and, more so, George Young, and then Malcolm Young, propose a new form of mere abstract art, namely music that puts ambition and ego aside. It's almost a dare to the critics to empty their minds and embrace the Zen, or perhaps punk rock's aural nihilism before punk rock even existed.

The embrace of almost nothing continues blissfully, sublimely, with "Live Wire," "T.N.T.," and "High Voltage," the tightest suite of songs from a style standpoint. Flip the mirror, and *T.N.T.* is the manifestation of everything set in motion at the hands of Vanda and Young in terms of building of an Australian pop and easy-listening landscape, funneled through the fidgety hands of what may as well have been four schoolboys and their ersatz other older brother, the troublemaker of the family, Bon Scott.

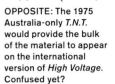

OPPOSITE: The 1975 Australia-only *T.N.T.* would provide the bulk of the material to appear on the international version of *High Voltage*. Confused yet?

BELOW: *T.N.T.* worked to establish AC/DC's almost hypnotic sense of repetition—perhaps punk rock's aural nihilism before punk rock even existed. Here the band plays at another sort of nihilism at the 1975 photoshoot for the "Jailbreak" poster.

Malcolm and Harry waiting to go on. Opera House Concert Hall, Sydney, June 1974. Malcolm did double duty with headliner Stevie Wright, whom Vanda also backed.

Back to the original premise. The pre-headbang head nod of AC/DC, its central idea, its Sweet-and-Slade-meet–Status Quo, one might say is spread across the first three albums. And then, really, the next three have such strong personalities of their own, I'm ready to throw up my hands and propose that the most belabored "trademark AC/DC sound" is in fact the one spread across every last Brian Johnson record from *Back in Black* to *Rock or Bust*. In other words, the AC/DC of the Bon Scott years is in fact not to be denigrated as a bunch of the same, but as a potpourri of curios, as evidenced here in *T.N.T.*'s glam and boogie and blues.

We must praise *T.N.T.* for repeated hammering home of a remarkable "so old it's new" sound, as more like accidentally stumbled upon through the likes of the debut's "Soul Stripper," "Stick Around," and most instructively, "She's Got Balls," the mention of which brings up a point of housekeeping that we may as well deal with right here: for those who might be a bit confused by the existence of the *T.N.T.* album, six out of its eight tracks were chosen to comprise the international version of what was called *High Voltage*, the band's first album issued internationally. In other words, as far as North America and Europe were concerned, AC/DC debuted in May 1976 with a record called *High Voltage* that had very little to do with the band's Australian debut of the same name. The international *High Voltage* is every song from *T.N.T.* except for "Rocker" and "School Days," both swapped out for "Little Lover" and "She's Got Balls."

In this light, AC/DC was forced to make their awkward introductions to the world with what was essentially their 1975 record, while they ran around bumping into each other all excited about their third record . . . which wouldn't hit America until 1981.

POPOFF: To start, what kind of record do we get with *T.N.T.*? The band seems less derivative than on the debut, wouldn't you say?
SIBONY: Sure, I think *T.N.T.* established the AC/DC sound and is one of their greatest albums. It shows how simple the songs could be, but so powerful. And I think what they really understood back then, George was really adamant about making sure that with Angus and Malcolm, any guitar licks, they would have to go to the piano and actually play it and be able to sing it. You know, similar to the "old gray whistle test" from the Brill Building, which was like a song factory and publishing house.

They called it the "old gray whistle test" because the older office workers and cleaning staff, they'd test the songs out on them and if they were whistling it the next day, it was a hit. Or they would go to the elevator and ask anybody on that elevator to listen to that song, and yeah, if they could whistle the melody back, it had the chance of being a hit and they would work on it. And George thought that way.

Victoria Park, Sydney, September 1975.

So something like "Rock 'n' Roll Singer," the riffs and licks are not complex, but they are very melodic; makes me think of Keith Richards. And myself, being a session drummer, and having played these songs as a kid in so many bands in the seventies and then eighties, people think what Phil Rudd is doing is so simple, but it's not. A lot of guys can't play like him.

He understands space, and that's what made AC/DC the perfect stadium band. It sounds big because they don't play too much. In fact, first time I saw them, in Toronto, they sounded so loud. Boston and AC/DC were the loudest concerts I'd ever been to. I mean, just so stupidly loud [*laugh*] and great energy. In fact, I even remember them louder than the headliner because there's something about their sound. Aerosmith almost had a softer, more refined sound, and the edginess of AC/DC sort of added to the decibel level. It's almost a psychological thing. But no, *T.N.T.* is so full of classic AC/DC songs, it makes the debut almost a throwaway.

POPOFF: To be fair, the debut is not even particularly the real band, with session musicians and whatnot, right?
DAVENPORT: Yes, this is the first lineup with Mark Evans in place and Phil Rudd had come in on drums. So by the time they were making *T.N.T.*, they had a lot more gigs under their belts, and I think the band had gained confidence by playing live. From what I understand, Bon took to AC/DC like a duck to water, but I don't think he had that much time to sort of bed things in by the time the first album was being recorded.

But by the second album, things are a lot more defined, they've got one album under their belts, and I get the impression that they've sharpened the essential aspects of what they do. And this points to George's guidance. But they broke themselves in on the road and got to the essentials of what they were, and so it's a much more assured album. But George was very hands-on in the studio, even playing bass, and Mark would have to watch and learn, which he was happy to do.

And yes, as Robert says, Angus and Malcolm and George, the three of them sat at a piano. They would come in with the basic riffs and ideas for the songs, and then George would strip it down and help them define the structure on a piano. And Angus said he would even make it sound like Mantovani or something like that, and if the arrangement worked on a piano, then they would go in and build it up with the band from there. And so the combination of that and the definitive lineup and the live experience—seeing what went down well—combined to make a record that was more crystallized, clearly formed, and defined.

POPOFF: And they were looking a lot less embarrassing on stage as well, right?
DAVENPORT: Yes, they'd ditched the glammy image, the last vestiges of that were hanging about. If you look at the video with Dave Evans from the original version of "Can I Sit Next to You Girl," he is wearing like flowery sleeves, almost, on his shirt and Malcolm looked like one of the Rubettes, with like a satin jacket [*laughs*]. And Mark Evans says he was

When he joined the band in 1974, Bon had already been around awhile, first in Aussie bubblegum pop group the Valentines (seen here), then in the country-rockish Fraternity.

FRATERNITY

PHILIPS

MY OLD MAN'S A GROOVY OLD MAN
THE VALENTINES

NICK NACK PADDY WHACK   EBENEEZER · GETTING BETTER

"It's a Long Way to the Top" sheet music and US promo single, both 1976. Bon's backstory up to his joining AC/DC.

given a satin jacket to wear when they first started. So that was stripped off, and they started to dress as they were, apart from Angus as a schoolboy.

SIBONY: Yes, they had the tights and top hats and the eyeliner and makeup—the drummer, specifically—and then Malcolm went around to see some bands, and all the bands started to do that. So he was like, screw that, we're not doing that, we're going back to T-shirts and jeans. Because they didn't want to be glam rock; he didn't want to be a part of that. Which took a lot of guts in that era, with David Bowie and Genesis and Queen and all that, to actually go against it and say forget it and make it work somehow. But they drifted away from that anyway, because the glam thing didn't sit well with the rough crowd they were playing to.

POPOFF: One thing I've always appreciated is how the record begins virtually like a concept album, with two pretty involved five-minute tracks—"It's a Long Way to the Top" and "Rock 'n' Roll Singer"—that are almost autobiographical, on the part of Bon.

DAVENPORT: I'd say they were very hard-won lyrics for Bon Scott. I interviewed his ex-wife, Irene Thornton, and she told me in so many words that Bon had actually lived every word of both of those songs. I get the impression that the two songs, in that particular order, make a lot of sense. "It's a Long Way to the Top," that's the backstory; it's his life up to that point. And then "Rock 'n' Roll Singer," that speaks of him having finally gotten the right band in AC/DC, and sensing that it's finally happening for him.

Because he's quite a bit older than the rest of the guys. He is in his late twenties already and had been around for a while. Bubblegum pop with the Valentines, and then he'd been in another band, Fraternity. For me, the thing that really informs "It's a Long Way to the Top"—this is what Irene was telling me—Fraternity had moved to London as a band in 1972, and they were a real hot property in Australia. They were a little bit bluesy, but very laid-back, a little mellow, a bit like the Band, sort of country rock, and they'd done really well in Australia.

But when they moved to England, there were like eighteen people living in a house in London, including pets and small children, wives, girlfriends. They were literately living cheek to jowl, and they were all very excited. The manager paid for them to go over. They had all been living in this commune in Australia together, and I don't know if they expected to do the same thing, but the musical landscape had moved on. When they arrived, it was all glam rock. And this sort of country rock stuff was seen as old hat. And they had a lot of, unfortunately, very disappointing experiences playing live and it just didn't really seem to catch on.

Irene mentioned that she and Bon had just gotten married and they went over there and everybody was very depressed, and the dream they had of going to England and London had gone bad. These bands he'd come from, it just fell completely flat, and it unfortunately killed the morale of the band.

Although one thing that did happen during this stint, Fraternity, who I think had changed their name to Fang at that stage, they played on a bill with Geordie, Brian Johnson's band. And Bon did actually remark on how impressed he was with the singer. That story has grown to the point where I've read an interview with Angus where he said, "Bon said should anything happen to me, he's your man." Which I don't know whether that's true. But he did see Brian play live.

Anyway, they moved back to Australia, Fraternity fizzled out, and Bon was very much seen as the old man by that stage in the pop industry, seen as washed up. He'd had a long past in rock 'n' roll, even by his mid- to late twenties, and the relentless drag of gigs and not really getting anywhere, I think that's reflected in a few of his songs like "It's a Long Way to the Top" and then later "Ain't No Fun Waiting Around to be a Millionaire."

But sure, these two songs together, he knew exactly what he was talking about because that was his path. It'd taken a long time. You know, there are lots of songs about partying written by hard rock bands, but this was a completely different side. AC/DC had songs that celebrated music, but this was like the reality of what it was like to be in a band.

So you go from that stage, to "Rock 'n' Roll Singer" and Bon has finally found his niche, he's being himself in this band. You see the videos of the Valentines, they're all wearing like turtleneck sweaters and big bell-bottoms, and they've got songs like "Nick Nack Paddy Whack" and "My Old Man's a Groovy Old Man." It's like a sendup for an Austin Powers movie. But once he joined AC/DC, that was that. There was a bit of playful intimidation from the brothers, "Come on, old man, show us what you can do," but he just went for it. And I think at that stage in his life, he's got nothing to lose, so he really did go for it. So that song kind of celebrates where he is at that stage in his career, finally a "Rock 'n' Roll Singer."

POPOFF: Both are examples of songs that are just driven by this rock-solid rhythm section. How about a little more on the philosophy there and where it comes from?

SIBONY: You've got to realize, George and Harry were pretty innovative, because they started doing tape loops a long time ago. And this has a lot to do with the AC/DC sound. Tape loops had been around since the fifties, but they really perfected it. And what it is, you've got a quarter-inch tape, and basically let's say they record the drummer and they take the tape and splice it together and it goes in a loop so it plays over and over again exactly the same.

The Bee Gees did this in Australia too, although that was in the sixties. But people don't realize, a lot of the disco hits were drum loops. Because they knew that drummers were so . . . they couldn't get them to play simply without sticking in a fill. George hated drummers, so he actually started playing drums, playing the simple beats and then looping them and doing layers of them in the studio. Their big hit with John Paul Young, "Love Is in the Air" is a tape loop.

I really think this philosophy got across to, or was pressed upon, Phil. Because he doesn't do a lot of fills, and that's what's beautiful. When you think he should do a fill, he doesn't. And I think that has a lot to do with George saying no, keep it simple—it has more effect. And he's right, it does. It's really hard to get drummers to do that unless they're professionals. These guys are all kids and wanna play, right? It must've been a major task to get Rudd to play the way he does. But it worked, because that's the sound of the band.

And AC/DC, people talk about the repetition and the hooks; well, looping is the definition of repetition and it's good for the emphasis of the hook. You look at all our music today—it's all loop-based. Which is sad, but it's the way it is. But with

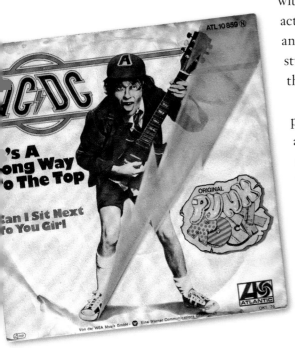

"It's a Long Way to the Top" b/w "Can I Sit Next to You Girl," Germany, 1976. The latter had received a previous somewhat more subdued release in Australia, performed by the Youngs with Peter Clack on drums, Rob Bailey on bass, and Dave Evans on vocals. Note the "Original Punk Rock" tag.

AC/DC, a good hook is played over and over again. They do that so well and can do it without boring their audience.

So, yeah, to me, Phil Rudd was an important part of that nucleus of AC/DC responsible for their sound, with his understanding of space and time, and how he lays back. He's not a metronome; he lays back a little bit. People try to play like him and it's not as easy as it looks. What makes a great drummer is they make songs feel good.

POPOFF: **Looking at some of the other tracks here, "Can I Sit Next to You Girl" has a bit of a history.**

DAVENPORT: Yes, the single of that song was the first AC/DC release they'd come out with, but that was the lineup with Peter Clack on drums, Rob Bailey on bass, Angus and Malcolm and Dave Evans on vocals. It was released as a single, and there's an Australian film about delinquent kids at school and it's featured in that, the single version of it. And it shows some kid having a bit of an air guitar session to the song. If you listen to the original, it starts off with a much gentler intro, a sweeter guitar tone from Angus. It's essentially the same song, but as he goes on, it doesn't quite have the attack. It wasn't as heavy as it became. And there's a strange kind of echo effect on the chorus as well, which was stripped off the Bon version, which is much more direct, hard-hitting, and streamlined.

POPOFF: **And we've got the cover of "School Days" here, but for what it's worth, "Rocker" could have been a cover as well, given how completely boogie rock it is.**

SIBONY: Angus was a big Chuck Berry fan. His whole thing with the running around back and forth, that's from Chuck Berry. He listened to tons of Chuck Berry and you can hear it in his guitar. It's all taken from that, and they just put their own twist to it.

"The Jack" is one of the traditional roots songs here as well. Although the lyric, Malcolm had gotten a letter from some female fan on the road,

"T.N.T." b/w "I'm a Rocker," Australian pressing, 1975. Angus and Malcolm showing their love of Chuck Berry on the B-side.

and she claimed that he gave her venereal disease. That's what the song is about. And then he went to get checked out and he didn't have it. But it's common slow twelve-bar blues. But they make it their own—that's what makes them great. Like the Rolling Stones, like Zeppelin, they take the blues and make it their own.

DAVENPORT: In my mind, I relate "Rocker" to "Show Business" from the debut. It's kind of a not serious, partially autobiographical lyric by Bon. He describes the clothes, blue suede shoes, and he mentions a V-8 car. That conjures up almost a 1950s American kind of image, and then he talks about tattoos, so you know it's about Bon [*laughs*]. It's a mix of that with the slightly autobiographical. And it's also a fast twelve-bar as well, with a very fast solo by Angus.

So that song sums up part of their early sound, taking that twelve-bar blues influence and turbocharging it with so much energy, creating a precursor to faster songs like "Riff Raff." They don't have too many faster ones. "Let There Be Rock" is quite fast as well, but a lot of the songs are a much steadier tempo.

POPOFF: Of course the title track is one of the record's classics. In fact, it's one of the most enduring early songs, given that it's played in football stadiums and stuff.

DAVENPORT: Yeah, and Angus did the *Oi, oi, oi* part for "T.N.T.," which makes the song so perfect for that.

SIBONY: And you know why was Angus doing that? Just to keep time when he was showing George the guitar line. That's the only reason he did that, and George said, "We're keeping that." Yeah, that was just a fluke. Which most great things are. Great song—doesn't it relate to exactly what AC/DC is about? That electricity and that explosive performance? It's almost like that working-class mentality, where you give two-hundred percent all the time, no matter what.

DAVENPORT: Yes, and another thing, Mark Evans mentions that the riff was a bit more elaborate when it first started, and George shaved bits off and made it more staccato. Because if you listen to an AC/DC riff, the punctuation and the kind of staccato nature of it, a lot of the riffs don't necessarily come in four beats to the bar. On the one you've got the drums laying down four on the floor, but I think a key part of that song is the guitar riff, specifically Malcolm—he's playing off that and around that. Keith Richards does that a lot. But Malcolm has that sort of slightly punchier version of that sound. So

"T.N.T.," with the spaces between the guitar stops, I think that's a key riff for them. And it maybe shows George's influence.

And again, it builds up. One thing with AC/DC, there's a lot of simplicity in the music, but the arrangements are often quite . . . "intricate" is the wrong word, but they're very well thought out. They're not just *thump, thump, thump* all the way through. If you listen to "T.N.T.," it comes in with the chords and then it builds up. If you listen to the way that the bass comes in, he's playing on different beats than the rhythm guitar. There are like little bass fills in between the chords, and then the choruses have all of them hammering away together. But there's a lot of dynamics in there. It's great on the stage. "Live Wire" is a brilliant example of that as well.

SIBONY: It's nice that you mention his four on the floor—bass drum on one, two, three, and four, like Ringo Starr—because that's a great thing about a lot of the songs. You hear it used, although not always, in "It's a Long Way to the Top," "Rock 'n' Roll Singer," "Live Wire," "T.N.T.," "High Voltage" . . . pretty much everywhere. It's subtle on some of these, and he moves in and out of it. A lot of drummers can't really do four on the floor well and make it sound rock versus making it sound disco. There is a talent to doing that. Rudd made it work with this kind of rootsy hard rock stuff.

POPOFF: As Robert mentioned, *T.N.T.* also includes "The Jack," which is in the wheelhouse of "Little Lover" from the debut.

DAVENPORT: Absolutely, and although it's slow, I mean, I've seen arenas full of people almost headbanging to that song. A key element of the song is Phil Rudd's drumming, because he hits it so hard and yet it's so minimal. But he really nails the groove. And you know it's Phil Rudd playing when you hear him. He's got his own clear and definable style, and he drives along so well along with Malcolm's rhythm playing. And, in particular, "The Jack" has kind of tempo that a stripper, I could imagine, performs her art to. It's a relentless rhythm and there's space in the song, which is a key thing in their riffs.

The vocal melody that Bon comes up with is very catchy as well. It holds the attention and raises the song from a humdrum, slow twelve-bar that has the potential to lose people's attention. If you listen to live versions, you will see there's a dirtier original lyric, which got cleaned up for public consumption [*laughs*]. I actually prefer the clean lyric because I think it shows his saucy double entendre humor at its best. And some of the card-playing metaphors are so well thought-out: *All the cards were coming/From the bottom of the pack/And if I'd known what she was dealing out/I'd have dealt it back.* I mean, blatant lines also, like *She was holding a pair* [*laughs*]. I think the clean lyric is more accomplished.

I want to mention Angus's solo as well. Because, without being too technical, he moves between the standard blues scale, which is the minor pentatonic, and the solo actually starts out on the major pentatonic. There are courses these days on how to blend the minor and major pentatonic, and he does it effortlessly. He starts with a major, he goes to the minor afterward, and he plays around the beat. I think it's one of his best solos. And it was quite an accomplished thing to do. It's easy to forget how young he was at that time. He would've been around twenty.

SIBONY: Yes, twenty going on sixteen. They actually billed him as sixteen years old, and George once even joked that we'll tell everybody he's nine years old. You know, it worked for PR. They said he was born in '59, but he was actually born in '55. And they played up the schoolboy thing, with that uniform that was actually sewn by his sister. She had said something like, "You're going to be a schoolboy all your life." The idea was sparked when she would see him come home from school and run straight to his room and practice his guitar while still in his school uniform.

They tried everything before they came up with this—Zorro, Superman, a gorilla outfit. But Malcolm thought the schoolboy outfit was the perfect gimmick. Angus said an interesting thing about it once. He said that if you are going to wear something like that, you have to keep moving all the time so you don't get hit with various "missiles" from the crowd, and so there he is, in constant motion for the rest of his life, on stage, right?

But if you look in the gatefold of *T.N.T.*, there's these little police file cards on each guy, and Angus is played up as the only one still in school. And then, it's interesting, on the international version as *High Voltage*, they carry over the idea, only now it's little color pictures, live shots, instead of what were essentially mug shots on *T.N.T.* But again, there's a warning letter from Angus's headmaster at school, saying he can't stop eating chocolate bars and Smarties—which is true, Angus was a raging chocoholic.

POPOFF: And we mustn't forget, this record has bagpipes!

DAVENPORT: Yes, Mark Evans says that that was a suggestion by George, and then Bon said he'd been in a pipe band. What he neglected to mention was he'd been a drummer in the pipe band. Mark goes on to recall the recording session where he said it was like a Scottish Rubik's Cube. They spent about four hundred dollars, which was a big expense at that time, for the band starting out. He got a set of bagpipes, and it took a lot of shouting and swearing to assemble them, and then Bon basically couldn't really play them [*laughs*] because he'd been a drummer in this pipe band.

And Mark mentions him, Phil, and Malcolm just blowing into the chanters, the pipes, the three of them, to get this bagpipe to work. And what happened in the end was it was so sporadic and patchy, George got a little bit of bagpipe music that was usable and then looped that. It was all this expert tape editing.

And when they played it live, again, Bon didn't play that well. And from what I understand about bagpipes, there's like this underlying drone, and you played the melody on top of that. Because Bon was struggling, he used to use a backing tape of the . . . I can't remember if it was the drone part or the melody part. But one or the other was on the backing tape and Bon would play the other part. It was unreliable, and it ended up, they had an argument backstage, and the sound man, quite a large chap, threw the backing track cassette against the wall and smashed it apart, so it kind of put the kibosh on that.

ABOVE: "High Voltage" b/w "Soul Stripper," Germany, 1976.

TOP: "High Voltage" b/w "It's a Long Way to the Top," Portugal, 1976.

ISSUE VARIANCE NOTES: The international version of *Dirty Deeds Done Dirt Cheap* was issued in Europe in 1976 and in the United States and Canada in 1981. The international version deletes "R.I.P. (Rock in Peace)" and "Jailbreak" and adds "Rocker" (from the Australian album *T.N.T.*) and "Love at First Feel," a track not included on any of the band's Australian albums.

SIDE 1
1. Dirty Deeds Done Dirt Cheap   4:13
2. Ain't No Fun (Waiting 'Round to Be a Millionaire)   7:31
3. There's Gonna Be Some Rockin'   3:17
4. Problem Child   5:46

SIDE 2
1. Squealer   5:18
2. Big Balls   2:40
3. R.I.P. (Rock in Peace)   3:36
4. Ride On   5:53
5. Jailbreak   4:41

All songs composed by Angus Young, Malcolm Young, and Bon Scott

Personnel: Bon Scott—lead vocals; Angus Young—lead guitar; Malcolm Young—rhythm guitar, backing vocals; Mark Evans—bass; Phil Rudd—drums

Released September 20, 1976

Recorded at Albert Studios, Sydney, Australia

Produced by Harry Vanda and George Young

DIRTY DEEDS DONE DIRT CHEAP

with RICHARD BIENSTOCK and BILL VOCCIA

Whether *Dirty Deeds Done Dirt Cheap* was rejected for US release due to Atlantic's issues with production or Bon's vocals, one can consider it a career setback. But it's also understandable on another level: their US and international debut, essentially *T.N.T.* rechristened *High Voltage*, reflected AC/DC's beloved DNA more than the strident, adventurous *Dirty Deeds*.

Strident and adventurous, to be sure, but what is also included is the very basic and regressive boogie premise that is missing

from the international *High Voltage*, and which harkens back to the original Australian *High Voltage*. In other words, *Dirty Deeds* feels like the record that should have come after the band's first album and before their second album, *T.N.T.*

To be sure, "Dirty Deeds Done Dirt Cheap," with its daringly spare arrangement, along with the similarly unappointed "Problem Child," "Squealer," and "Jailbreak," present the beloved unemployed, hands-in-pocket version of the band. Elsewhere, there's a reach-around to the band's Chuck Berry roots, with "There's Gonna Be Some Rockin'" and "R.I.P. (Rock in Peace)," and then the epic and almost conceptual "Ain't No Fun (Waiting 'Round to Be a Millionaire)." There's the stealthy "Ride On" alongside the notorious "Big Balls."

I've always looked at *Dirty Deeds* as a record of peaks and valleys, one where George Young essentially threw out his rulebook, with the band not stripping everything down, with the band repeating themselves, with the band ignoring the very real and magical fact that they had found their distilled essence on *T.N.T.*

Perhaps some of the scatter and texture of *Dirty Deeds* is due to the mid-process journey to the UK, where the possibility of global success beckoned.

But alas, the band had to return to Australia to finish the album, having scrapped music they tried to make away from cozy home.

In any event, there's a sense of wisdom on Atlantic Records' part with respect to their approach to the American market. The glued-together *High Voltage* would make sense, as would *Let There Be Rock*, but *Dirty Deeds*, despite being halfway there, was also halfway neither here nor there.

POPOFF: Why do people like AC/DC? And more so, what qualities do they possess that are inherent on *Dirty Deeds Done Dirt Cheap*?
BIENSTOCK: As somebody who grew up loving hard rock and heavy metal, I felt that beyond the great riffs and the great songs themselves, that there was such a lack of humor and personality in the music. And AC/DC has that in spades. The Bon Scott years—I mean, forget about it; it's pretty out there and in-your-face. But even the Brian Johnson years, they were just a funnier band, while also having all those classic metal tropes. They could also be frightening, aggressive, heavy, and angry, if you look at it that way. But they had this extra element. The obvious stuff is Angus in a schoolboy outfit, but it went beyond that. The songs were witty—often in sort of a dumb way —but they made you laugh and they took you to another place where I felt that a lot of these other bands just weren't able to go.
VOCCIA: From the very beginning they had a successful formula and style; they really created their own unique sound, in my opinion—you know an AC/DC song within the first few seconds. There's a lot of early rock 'n' roll groove to it. And for them to continue on through all the years without changing their formula, right up to the latest album, because it works for them . . . that was smart.

POPOFF: And so here they are, up to their third album, how have they changed? What advances have they made beyond *High Voltage* and *T.N.T.*?
VOCCIA: The original *High Voltage* was their first endeavor in the studio, and there was a lot of early writing going on. I don't think they'd really quite found themselves yet on that album. They had matured greatly on *T.N.T.* and I'd say the contrast between *T.N.T.* and *Dirty Deeds* is minimal. Those albums are really quite closely related, especially in terms of production, with Vanda

OPPOSITE: Bon Scott onstage in London, late 1976. AC/DC had humor and personality in spades, especially during the Scott era.

BELOW: Because the band was touring and trying to break outside of Australia, *Dirty Deeds* became more of a "road album"— recorded in bits and pieces, thus contributing to its immediacy.

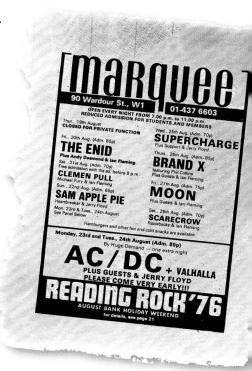

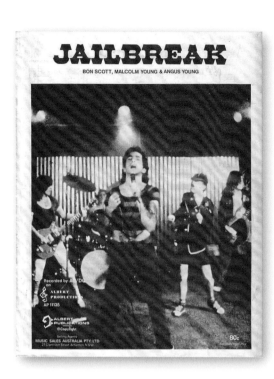

JAILBREAK

BON SCOTT, MALCOLM YOUNG & ANGUS YOUNG

Recorded by AC/DC
on
ALBERT
PRODUCTIONS
AP 11135

ALBERT
PUBLICATIONS
©Copyright

Selling Agents
MUSIC SALES AUSTRALIA PTY LTD
27 Clarendon Street Artarmon N.S.W.

80c

ABOVE: "Jailbreak" sheet music. Included on the original release, this stellar track curiously was left of the 1981 international edition.

OPPOSITE: Mal and Ang lock in at the Marquee Club, London, May 12, 1976.

and Young adding nice touches like the background vocals in "Dirty Deeds" and the *oi*'s in "T.N.T.," just to add a little extra creativity, as well as a bit of a shout-out or sing-along kind of thing to use in live performances. But I know *Dirty Deeds* wasn't well received at the time it came out. The band was trying to get into other markets, trying to break into the United States and break internationally, trying to get airplay, but the album was rejected by the label in America, where it wasn't issued until after they had broken with *Back in Black*.

BIENSTOCK: From my understanding, *Dirty Deeds* is the first record for them where, although they haven't been to America yet, they have been touring more and making more of a road album, I guess you could say. Where they're trying to find the time and the space and the places to actually get in and record, as opposed to just being home and making a record. And that probably contributes a little bit to the immediacy in terms of the songs. And they probably have a better idea of what's going to go over live and how the songs function, what people are looking for from them. It feels a bit more focused to me, and more like the AC/DC I think of. It's straightforward—you're kind of getting it all right up on the surface. That's what I've always liked about it.

POPOFF: Sure, and we're really starting to hear that classic AC/DC guitar tone, especially on the title track, "Problem Child," and "Jailbreak." How do Angus and Malcolm get that sound?

BIENSTOCK: As a guy who comes from the whole *Guitar World* magazine background and all that, the AC/DC tone is, for a lot of people, me included, the holy grail of hard rock tone. But at the same time, they're not a band that really talks about it too much. With AC/DC, you could easily say that, well, Malcolm is playing his Gretsch through a 100-watt Marshall and Angus is playing his SG through a 100-watt Marshall and you'd pretty much be right.

As far as *Dirty Deeds* goes, the intricacies are not well known, but Malcolm basically does have that one Gretsch that he played. Angus had a few different years of SGs. I know his main one was a '68, which I would

assume was what he was using on there. But he also has a '64, although I'm pretty sure that came into the picture much later on. So if I had to guess—and I feel like a lot of times, that's what people are doing on those early AC/DC records—it's probably his '68 SG through a 100–watt Marshall head, and Malcolm with his Gretsch Firebird through a 100–watt Marshall head. And as far as I know, they weren't effects pedal people, ever, unless you've heard different. With them, it's pretty straightforward. That's one of the beautiful things on the AC/DC tone: it's not that overdriven. It very well could just be the amp cranked until it's breaking up.

POPOFF: What are a couple of your favorite tracks on the record and why? "Problem Child" was obviously deemed good enough to be put on the international edition of *Let There Be Rock*.

VOCCIA: Right, "Problem Child" was originally on *Dirty Deeds*. The Australian version of *Let There Be Rock* had "Crabsody in Blue," which got swapped out for "Problem Child" [on 1977's international version], partly because it was part of their live set, and maybe they felt that it was more radio-friendly or commercial for the international market. It's one of my favorites of the catalog. As an AC/DC tribute band guitarist, that's always one of my favorites to play live. Lyrically, it's Bon talking about Angus; Bon always used to say that Angus is a problem child. But it's just a nicely paced, solid rock song.

BIENSTOCK: "Problem Child" is just a classic, iconic, early AC/DC song. People tend to sort of put it on Bon, like, this is his life and blah blah blah. I never really felt that way about the song. It's him just telling another kind of classic, like, rock 'n' roll rebellion story. I never saw it as being about Bon or anything like that.

Musically, that's your standard Angus type of riff, where it's like—and I'm just thinking off the top of my head—A to E and then A to D. It's like, you have that tonic chord, then it goes down and then goes back to the chord and then it goes out. If I sat here and thought about it, there's a million AC/DC songs that have that sort of chord structure.

POPOFF: How would you contrast what Malcolm and Angus are doing differently there? Because this seems to be a classic case of Malcolm to the left, Angus to the right.
BIENSTOCK: Sure, yeah, first of all, there's that tone. If you tear into it and listen, on some of these albums you can kind of separate the left and right speaker and all that. Malcolm definitely has a bit of a tighter, cleaner tone. Angus's, I guess you could say, is grittier. In reality, it probably has just a little more treble in it, while Malcolm's is a little bassier and muffled. For the most part, on a lot of the songs, they actually just play the same thing. But Malcolm, again, plays everything a little bit tighter, a bit more on the beat and more exact. Every riff he is going to play is exactly the same while Angus plays a bit looser. Angus's tone is closer to what someone like Slash did later on, more on the treble side. If you separated Slash and Izzy on *Appetite for Destruction*, Slash's tone on his own doesn't necessarily sound so great, because it's a little piercing and maybe a bit overdriven. But it kind of rounds out and fills in that part of the sonic picture. And that's the way Malcolm and Angus work together as well.

Advertisement from *Sounds* magazine, November 6, 1976.

POPOFF: At the other end of the spectrum from something like "Problem Child" is some pretty simple and rootsy boogie rock, like "There's Gonna Be Some Rockin'" and "R.I.P. (Rock in Peace)." Where does that side of their game come from?
VOCCIA: A lot of it was an influence from their brother George Young and his band the Easybeats, and just having that musical influence within their own household from a very young age. So it was old, early roots rock 'n' roll, Chuck Berry, the influence of the Easybeats, blues. Although they were trying to come up with a more direct

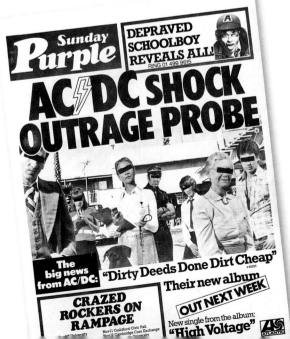

THE NASHVILLE
Corner Cromwell Road / North End Road
(Adj. West Kensington Tube) 01-603 6071   Free

Thursday, 22nd April
STRANGLERS
+ THE SNAKES   £1.00

Friday, 23rd April
101'ERS
+ SEX PISTOLS   £1.00

Saturday, 24th April
**MAX MERRITT &
THE METEORS**   50p

Sunday, 25th April
DIVERSIONS   Free

Monday, 26th April
AC DC
(ANTIPODEAN PUNK EXTRAVAGANZA)   Free

Tuesday, 27th April
PLUMMET AIRLINES
+ BLOKES

hard rock version of that, not aiming for that genre, like say Buffalo with their Deep Purple and Black Sabbath influence, but by just turning up the guitars to get that tone. So, yeah, starting with original R & B, Chuck Berry and John Lee Hooker, and then just driving the amplifiers to come up with that sound. So you see a lot of those riffs, back and forth, like A/B chords, in songs like "There's Gonna Be Some Rockin'" and "R.I.P."

POPOFF: Which, as Malcolm told me once, learning that stuff was a case of survival—if you wanted to get through your set down at the pub without being physically removed from the stage.

Antipodean Punk Extravaganza. The Nashville Rooms, London, spring 1976.

VOCCIA: Yeah, that could be part of why they were doing that. They were playing those types of working-class clubs in the early days, with a lot of booze going around; they're catering to that type of crowd for sure. They're also showing up with little tiny Angus running around like a schoolboy. I've read accounts that say they got laughed out of the place a lot and things like that. But once they saw him perform and run around like a crazed maniac, they changed their mind pretty quickly. Plus, there was good interplay between him and Bon Scott, who has more of the macho style and stage presence. It must've been quite a sight to see in the early days.

BIENSTOCK: I would imagine that's partly the case. You go in there and you've got to grab people's attention from the get-go, and that's probably a good way to do it. Australia turned out some pretty hard-rocking bands.

Basic fifties rock structure. "Dirty Deeds" B-side "R.I.P. (Rock in Peace)," Australia, 1976.

POPOFF: Richard, where do these boogie-rock songs on *Dirty Deeds* sit with you?

BIENSTOCK: "There's Gonna Be Some Rockin'," to me, is kind of a throwaway on the record. I don't feel like that song adds much to the experience. In the early days of AC/DC, they had a few songs like that, and that one is a little too mid-tempo and laid-back for my tastes. I almost feel like it doesn't go anywhere. And given the different versions of that album, that might've been one of the ones I would have chopped off instead of "Jailbreak," which is an amazing song.

"R.I.P.," here in America, none of us knew that song for decades to come. Again, it's another one where it's pretty straightforward, with that kind of basic fifties rock structure to it. The title is an obvious play on words, but not in an impressive way. So it's another one that's perhaps a throwaway. But when I heard it years and decades later, it was interesting to hear something I hadn't heard before.

POPOFF: But the rest of the record, you're quite a fan of.

BIENSTOCK: Absolutely, and a great place to start is with the title track. One of the things that I love about that record more than a lot of the other records is it really puts a lot of emphasis on the vocals. And not just Bon

Scott, because *Dirty Deeds* has great background vocals, which is something AC/DC doesn't get so much recognition for. But starting with the title track, I love the background vocals on that, the way they do the *done dirt cheap*. It's a twisted, almost animalistic and sort of ugly approach, but it works perfectly. It's aggressive and almost feral, and yet also very youthful—they sound sort of adolescent. And of course, Bon is great on it.

As well, Angus's solo is truly iconic at this point. I mean, people really know that solo. It's one of those that he plays pretty much note-for-note when they do the song live. And yet the thing about it is, it's actually a pretty terrible solo, in a lot of ways [*laughs*]. I mean, that sort of run that he does up the neck at the end of the solo, with the open string and the fretted notes, is kind of awful. He sort of frets out at the end of it and there are some clams. And they've left them in there. That's just the way it is. He starts off very strong, and you can feel him almost kind of losing it at the end. You can feel him kind of struggling to hold onto the end of the phrase—and he barely does.

And the thing I love about it, you go and see him live now, thirty-five years later, more than that, and it's still the same thing. Sometimes it sounds like he's barely going to make it through, and that's the way it is. That's the way they recorded it and that's the way he does it. So it's this weirdly iconic bad solo.

VOCCIA: The "Dirty Deeds" solo is great [*laughs*]. I always loved "Problem Child" and "Squealer." Angus let loose a lot more here than he does nowadays, in so many ways. He was full of energy, and trying to play as crazy as he could. Songs like "Squealer," "Whole Lotta Rosie," "Let There Be Rock" are some of the greatest guitar solo songs ever made. And it's all Angus. On the original *High Voltage* album, Malcolm did do some high lead work on a couple of the songs. But after that, he pretty much stuck to the rhythm guitar parts and let Angus go for it.

POPOFF: Are you surprised that "Dirty Deeds Done Dirt Cheap" has become a sports area staple?

BIENSTOCK: That's the thing with AC/DC—almost any song could work in that respect. Clearly, there's nothing in the lyric that lends itself to the sort of "rah rah, go team" type of thing. But it's got this great sing-along quality to it, as does every AC/DC song. It's got those nice big chords and the spacing between them, so it works well over a shitty arena loudspeaker. It's not going to be awful; you can still figure out what's going on. Plus,

it was one of those songs that came out at the right time, at least here in America, after they were already a massive band. It's a song people heard a lot at the time even though it wasn't a new song.

Part of the reason AC/DC work so well as an arena band is that they do have these big spaces in between these big chords. You know what it's like hearing a thrash band in an arena—you can't tell what's going on. And AC/DC is the exact opposite of that. It's got a lot of space and a lot of air in it.

POPOFF: And of course live, there's always Angus and his manic soloing to help bring forward a few chuckles. What he does up there kind of reminds me of Frank Zappa and his approach to guitar soloing. Like, guitar solos are innately stupid, so here's a parody of a guitar solo.
BIENSTOCK: I would agree with that, yeah. It's in the playing itself, but to bring it back around, there's a huge parody in the way that he physically does his guitar solos, in particular, the way he does his guitar solo spot on stage for the past thirty years or whatever. Not really the striptease part, but when he's getting down on the ground and he's spinning around on his back. It's so over the top, but it's not just that it's over the top—it's also sloppy and jerky in a way. He looks far from glorious while he does it—he looks like a sweaty mess. And there's nothing fluid or really guitar hero about it. But at the same time, that's the way it's received by the fans. He gets the cheers and people love him for doing that. But you're exactly right—it's almost a parody of what these guys do.

Backstage after a gig at London's Marquee Club, August 1976.

POPOFF: And as we've alluded to, *Dirty Deeds* comes out in the fall of '76 in Australia, and then slightly altered in Europe in the winter of the same year, but not until March of 1981 in the United States and Canada.

VOCCIA: Right, and *High Voltage* was the first record for Europe, followed by *Dirty Deeds*. They originally went into the studio in the UK to do some recordings, but then they ended up scrapping that whole project. That's when they did a few of those other tracks that weren't even released on the album. And then later on, they decided to do the album recording back in Australia, at Albert Studios, where it took only like a couple of weeks—likely rushed due to the touring commitments they had. They were constantly on the road, trying to get results, trying to get themselves where they wanted to go. And so yes, but this point they had played in both the UK and mainland Europe.

POPOFF: And they were in danger during that time as being viewed as part of this new punk movement too, correct?

VOCCIA: Yeah, that was actually a problem for them. They didn't want that. Then again, at certain times, they did use that to their advantage to get gigs. But overall they didn't want to be grouped into the same category as the punk rock bands. It was something they didn't think they were. But the German Atco "It's Long Way to the Top" seven-inch has a big ol' "Original Punk Rock" logo on the picture sleeve.

OPPOSITE: The Marquee Club on Wardour Street, London, August 1976.

BELOW: The 1977 UK maxi single *Grab a Hold of This One* featured "Dirty Deeds Done Dirt Cheap," "Big Balls," and "The Jack."

POPOFF: I suppose there's no question that the most notorious song in the record is "Big Balls."

BIENSTOCK: Sure. I feel we have to talk about that one, which is infamous for obvious reasons. The first time I heard it, like most Americans, was in the early eighties, after *Back in Black*. And the lyrics to that song caused no end of glee. I was seven, eight years old, so we all loved it. But I remember, what really shocked me about that, again, was not so much what he was singing, but really the sound of Bon's voice. People knew *Back in Black*, with Brian Johnson, when this record came out.

Now Bon always sounds like Bon, but for some reason, on "Big Balls" he *really* sounds like Bon. And I remember

hearing that first line to the song, *I'm upper, upper class high society*. And he's so mangled and garbled on that, I remember thinking, "Are they serious? Like what the hell is this?" You know, not even so much because of all the balls stuff. But more like, there's no way that's a real singer. And it was.

So I feel like that song is the most exemplary of how wild his voice is; that's the best example of how really bizarre and unconventional a frontman he is. For all everyone talks about the lyrics, it's not any more lascivious, and maybe even less so, than a song like "Sink the Pink" or "Given the Dog a Bone." But it's juvenile, so that was the appeal of it. But for me, the sound was the point, rather than what he was saying.

POPOFF: Now, even though "Ain't No Fun (Waiting 'Round to Be a Millionaire)" is part of that boogie tradition, there's enough going on there to make it interesting, including that nice picking through the chord in the intro and the chorus.

VOCCIA: Sure, and even though "Ain't No Fun" is a very repetitious song and it goes on really long, it's just a great story, with Bon's tongue-in-cheek lyrics. It's always been one of my favorites on the album, again, saved by the storyline plus by the tempo picking up at the end. And Angus and Malcolm are playing these different things in that song; they're not playing exactly the same parts.

BIENSTOCK: If I really think about it, that's not a common Angus Young type of riff. It's actually a little more melodic than you usually get from him, and a little more sort of chimey actually. It's a little unusual, especially in that period of AC/DC, to hear him do something that has so much melody in it.

Not to move away from what you're saying, but again, this is one I love for Bon more than anything else. It's a great lyric. In those early stages, you get a lot of songs about being poor and trying to make it. "Ain't No Fun" is in a similar tradition to "Long Way to the Top," but it's less hopeful-sounding. Maybe it splits the difference between "Long Way to the Top" and "Down Payment Blues," which is totally depressing. It's in the middle there, where the guy's got the financial troubles of "Down Payment Blues," but he's also got some possibility of becoming a rock 'n' roll millionaire—but it's a long way to the top. So he's in purgatory. And Bon's really good at the silly little throwaway lines like *patches on the patches on my old blue jeans*. He's got his nine-to-five working woman to take care of him, and he's not necessarily proud of it, but that's the way it goes.

POPOFF: The poverty and grittiness of this song is surely better represented by the original crudely drawn album cover than it is by the arty Hipgnosis one, which most of us know.

VOCCIA: I think the original is the perfect album cover for the title—*Dirty Deeds*. You've got Bon and Angus on the front, in the pool hall. Bon is flexing his arm tattoo and Angus is skulking in the background, holding his two fingers up, which is essentially F-you in Australian. Then you have the other band members on the back—Phil Rudd with the pool cue, Malcolm with a beer can. It's got this badass-looking "don't mess with us" attitude.

BIENSTOCK: I always found the two covers interesting too, because I feel they can color how you see the music. I mean, I almost see it opposite. There's this very cartoonish element to what AC/DC do. With the original cartoon album cover, you can view the songs through the lens of being a sort of glammy, sillier version of hard rock. Whether it's "Problem Child" or "Dirty Deeds," you can almost view them as Slade-type songs. But the Hipgnosis cover, with the bars over the eyes, adds a sort of darker, more sinister feel to all of it, and makes it sound more like gritty hard rock. I don't think the original cover would've worked in America. We don't have that kind of humor that goes along with the music.

No Wuckin' Furries. The Nashville Rooms, London, spring 1976.

POPOFF: *Dirty Deeds* includes what is possibly the band's quietest and mellowest song, "Ride On," which is in the tradition of all their near-ballads.

BIENSTOCK: Yeah, for sure, and that's a case where that actually is a great Angus solo, definitely soulful, as is the whole song. He's doing what you would expect to happen in that song, but it works. His phrasing is great, the way he bends notes and holds his intonation is great, and it's got a real feel to it and, as usual, great tone. It sounds like he's really playing from the heart. People talk about how that song sounds a lot like ZZ Top's "Jesus Just Left Chicago," and it really does. I've never heard them comment on that. Even down to tone—AC/DC never used a clean tone like that otherwise, or at least not going all the way through the verses. And it is pretty similar to the clean tone in the ZZ Top song.

"Squealer" and "Ride On" contain probably the two best solos on the record. And the interesting thing about the "Squealer" solo is that the first few notes, and then the phrasing, are exactly the same as the "Dirty Deeds" solo. Like the way he comes in from the chorus, and when he goes into that solo part, he attacks it exactly the same—same notes, same phrasing. And the difference is, of course, as you were saying before, the "Dirty Deeds" solo is the one they remember. But the "Squealer" solo, in my opinion, is a much better one [*laughs*].

POPOFF: And "Squealer" has that busy bass line, which is unusual for AC/DC.
BIENSTOCK: Yeah, it's a great song, and it's got that great funky bass line, as well as, again, the awesome background vocals. I love the way they attack that. The weird thing about that song, though, is that it's a pretty decrepit song lyrically [*laughs*]. It's dark and sort of mean in a way that Bon usually wasn't. And I think people recognized that about the song. People don't love it in the way that maybe it deserves to be loved, because it's kind of a nasty song. Against AC/DC fashion, it's a very humorless song. Bon could be dirty and sort of sexist and misogynistic and all that, but there was always an undercurrent of playfulness. But "Squealer" is unusually dark.

POPOFF: I suppose one surprise omission that was on the original, that we didn't get on our 1981 version of the album was "Jailbreak."
BIENSTOCK: Oh, for sure. "Jailbreak" is awesome. I don't know why that was left off. It's one of their best early songs. For AC/DC, it's a little more theatrical than they usually got with that whole middle part and the spotlight and the machine gun firing and all that. It has that video too, which is totally ridiculous. It's another one of those songs where you can see it as menacing and aggressive, or you can see it as totally camp, depending on how you view these things. It's just a great Angus riff, a great tune, and another one where I just love the background vocals. There's something about that period, the way they were doing the backup vocals, where it was so nasty and dirty and adolescent and awesome.

POPOFF: Finally, there was the controversy in America about issuing *Dirty Deeds* right there in the gap between *Back in Black* and *For Those About to Rock*. The whole thing was blamed for the latter selling a mere four-times platinum versus *Back in Black*, which sits now at double diamond, an astounding twenty-two-times platinum.

BIENSTOCK: It's clearly a classic record company move. *Back in Black* is massive. They don't have a follow-up ready. If you can put out a bit of extra product, who's not going to take advantage of that? I've never really heard the band say much about it, but I can't imagine it's something that they wanted to come out, when they were just sort of re-establishing themselves. And in America, probably a lot of people thought that they were just a new band, thinking Brian Johnson was the guy who was always there. This was definitely going to be confusing, because not only is it a different singer, but also the music doesn't sound the same either. And the album cover is weird and doesn't even have the real logo on it.

VOCCIA: You could look at it one way or the other. AC/DC were the biggest band around at the time with *Back in Black*. *Dirty Deeds* also catapulted into the charts just as quickly as *Back in Black* and sold tons of copies. It definitely helped the band, I would say, as far as the popularity was concerned at the time. So it worked out in a good way, versus, you know, if they would've waited, then maybe *Let There Be Rock* would've sold more copies.

Then again, *For Those About to Rock* went number one in the United States. It was the very first really hard rock album to reach number one in Billboard. So that was a pretty good achievement. Despite that, sure, *Dirty Deeds* was released, and some people were saying it could've affected the sales of *For Those About to Rock*. But maybe the releasing of *Dirty Deeds* got more airplay for the band. "Dirty Deeds," the song, was all over the radio, and maybe that got the band more fans rather than having an adverse effect on sales.

Because Atlantic rejected the album, American listeners weren't treated to *Dirty Deeds* until the band had already broken in the states with *Back in Black*.

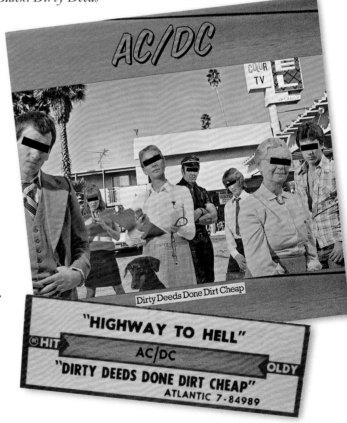

LET THERE BE ROCK

with **PHIL CARSON, MICHAEL HANNON, JOEL O'KEEFFE,** and **PHIL RUDD**

ISSUE VARIANCE NOTES: The US, Canadian, and Japanese versions of *Let There Be Rock* delete "Crabsody in Blue" and add "Problem Child" from *Dirty Deeds Done Dirt Cheap.*

SIDE 1
1. Go Down   5:17
2. Dog Eat Dog   3:30
3. Let There Be Rock   6:02
4. Bad Boy Boogie   4:18

SIDE 2
1. Overdose   5:47
2. Crabsody in Blue   4:39
3. Hell Ain't a Bad
   Place to Be   4:12
4. Whole Lotta Rosie   5:25

All songs composed by Angus Young, Malcolm Young, and Bon Scott

Personnel: Bon Scott—lead vocals; Angus Young—lead guitar; Malcolm Young—rhythm guitar, backing vocals; Mark Evans—bass; Phil Rudd—drums, percussion

Released March 21, 1977

Recorded at Albert Studios, Sydney, Australia

Produced by Harry Vanda and George Young

Fingers in the socket, AC/DC fulfilled the promise of showered sparks implied on previous sleeves wrapping records of modest means. The songs on *Let There Be Rock* may not have been written with appreciably new and improved acumen and architecture, but the molten production values of the thing immediately catapulted the band onto a different rock 'n' roll power grid. From this point on, AC/DC would become viable late seventies competitors, rather than rubes from the outback still celebrating the British blues boom of the sixties or, even worse, original rock 'n' roll from the fifties.

But one can only go so far with such rudimentary sounds. *Let There Be Rock* was the author's first AC/DC album, and his fourteen-year-old ears loved the band instantly but always in a protective way—like they were mentally a bit vulnerable. In other words, we humored them the way all of us tacitly agree to give the Stones a pass. To one already steeped on Sabbath, Purple, Priest, Aerosmith, and Deadly Tedly, AC/DC was a bit unstudied, not much more than Kiss without makeup. Still, I do recall myself and the buddies deeming *Let There Be Rock* only the second album since Rainbow's *Rising*, in the history of rock, with no ballads, every song heavy start to finish, even though "Problem Child" (mine is a Canadian issue) was suspiciously twee and almost broke the streak.

The impression over the decades? *Let There Be Rock* is AC/DC's Volume 4, juiced with glorious distortion but a bit menacing and off-putting. And let's face it: the songs are relentless, allowing little space for the listener to catch one's breath, like Status Quo with a full head of steam, and yet still built on various hard-headed permutations of the boogie rock plod.

OPPOSITE: *Let There Be Rock* Aussie cover art, 1977.

BELOW: *Let There Be Rock* catapulted the band onto a different rock 'n' roll power grid, 1977.

LEFT: Malcolm backstage at the Palladium, New York City, August 24, 1977. Afterward, the band did a surprise set at legendary New York punk club CBGB.

INSETS: *Let There Be Rock* didn't even need an anthem like "Whole Lotta Rosie" to put it over the top. Dutch pressing, 1977.

Personal faves are the tracks in the cracks, like "Go Down," "Bad Boy Boogie," "Hell Ain't a Bad Place to Be," and "Overdose," but the whole thing just trundles through the desert like a tank generating a dust storm of death. One need not even rely upon twin frenetic anthems "Let There Be Rock" and "Whole Lotta Rosie" to put the record over the top. In fact, through sheer dint of laser-focused execution and drunk-with-power production, AC/DC proved more than capable of transforming songs that were every bit as spare as those on *T.N.T.* into a collection of eight sonic juggernauts capable of pasting any "blue jean army" of the seventies to the back wall of any hockey barn once the band had begun their inevitable assault on America, specifically July 27, 1977, four months into the reign of this incendiary platter that matters.

POPOFF: Phil, having signed the band to Atlantic, set the stage for us. Where was AC/DC in their career with *Let There Be Rock*?
CARSON: Sure, well, to back up a bit, I thought they were really solid, straight-ahead rock 'n' roll, and actually the first thing I saw was a Super 8 film of AC/DC doing "Long Way to the Top," with Bon Scott blowing away on the bagpipes, and I thought it was a really great presentation. And when I made the deal with them, I arranged for them to come over from Australia to England to do this particular tour, and that's why I made the deal.

I thought it could work. AC/DC were a great rock band, and I compiled the album *High Voltage*. I just took six tracks from *T.N.T.* and two from *High Voltage*, and that was the record released by Atlantic everywhere other than Australia. That was the first impact that they had, and they started to make some good ground in England. America really didn't catch on, except for one or two specific DJs on the East Coast. And then they delivered *Dirty Deeds*, which I thought was a pretty good album with some good things on it, particularly the title track, but the guys at Atlantic in New York rejected it. And I did not reject it. I put it out, because I thought it was a very good record.

They had to release *Let There Be Rock*, because by the time the band delivered it, I had sold quite a large number of *High Voltage* and *Dirty Deeds* throughout Europe. And the band was beginning to get a groundswell in America in spite of the poor decision-making process at Atlantic in New York at that time. So they had to release it. You know, they still didn't hold AC/DC in particularly high regard at that point, and it's only because of the dint of sheer hard work that those guys put into what they do, in touring, that it worked. If it'd been left to Atlantic in America, to do it on their own, it would've been a miserable failure. But fortunately, the band put the effort into it, as did the rest of us working at the label outside of America.

RUDD: I don't know, they're all kind of written sort of to a schedule. You've got a big deal with a big record company, they want this, they want that, boom, boom, boom. So, you've got to keep coming up with it, you know? We did what we liked, and when we liked it, we let it out.

POPOFF: And what kind of record is *Let There Be Rock*? Is there a reason, for example, that it is so powerful compared to the earlier records?

RUDD: I don't really know, mate, because at that point, I was just along for the ride; I was just a youngster. But George and Malcolm were just fuckin' mega-dudes when it comes to doing what they do. I just sort of followed their lead and they didn't ask much of me, and I didn't have a lot to give, to be honest. But *Let There Be Rock* . . . we were always a reaction band. I mean, I saw Angus tip a jug of beer over a guy's head one day who just sat there looking at us. Just couldn't get a rise out of this guy. He was just tapping on the table and everyone was fuckin' watching him, and Angus picked up a full jug of beer and tipped it over the guy's head [*laughs*] and the whole crowd went nuts. That was at the Station Hotel in Melbourne, which is a sort of "cool" gig, you know, sort of too cool to be clapping and be all enthusiastic, you know?

HANNON: That album was an awakening for me. See, I was a Kiss kid, then I heard AC/DC. Just blew me away. It would still be years later until I discovered Motörhead, who never got pushed in the States. But yeah, AC/DC, I didn't think anything could touch it. I saw the *Let There Be Rock* tour in Wheeling, West Virginia, and they opened up for UFO. *Let There Be Rock* was my first AC/DC album. The first song I ever heard from them

(coninuted on page 62)

Waring Abbott perfectly captured Angus's frenetic energy with this multiple exposure at New York City's Palladium, August 24, 1977.

(coninuted from page 59)

was "Overdose." They played it on the Wheeling radio station, and I bought the eight-track tape of it. And on the eight-track tape, it's a different version of "Overdose" than there is on the album. There's lead guitar on it and the intro is longer. But it's funny, they were both American versions I had. The Australian version I have now, the one that has the black cover with the hands just playing guitar, that's the guitar player from Buffalo. But I have both the American eight-track and the American vinyl, and they're different mixes.

But to me, it's a more powerful album, sure, but also more serious, and with some longer songs. Because they were kind of known as a teenybopper band at first. If you look at those old videos, they're doing songs like "Show Business" and stuff, and Bon would wear the red-and-white striped coat and they were kind of a poppy, glammy-looking band at first, certainly when they had the singer before Bon, before they got really filthy and dirty [*laughs*].

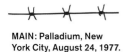

MAIN: Palladium, New York City, August 24, 1977.

INSET: Print ad, 1977. The first use of the word "grungy" to describe rock 'n' roll?

POPOFF: **What would be an album highlight there for you?**

HANNON: The title track, for sure. Great storytelling lyric there. I mean, *black man had the blues*—that's where

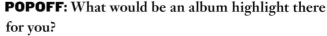

ous, Grungy, Distasteful, , Wretched, Putrid, Taste- oud, Raw, Nauseating, Vile, inable, Disgusting, Rotten, gnant, Crass, Rude, Pecu- alacious, Slimy, Perverted, icable, Yucky, Raunchy, Re- ve, Revolting, Crude, Gross, ge, Primitive, Primal, Porno- hic, Sleazy, and Wonderful.

C/DC has the last word.

LET THERE BE ROCK
AC/DC

AC/DC. "LET THERE BE ROCK."
Their latest album from
Atco Records and Tapes.

Produced by Vanda and Young for Albert Productions.

rock 'n' roll came from. It's a cross between the blues and country western. And *white man had the schmaltz*, and the money to put it together, to get the recordings out. And between the two of them, they created rock. It's great. And I guess they did the video for that song, and Bon broke his ankle. In the video, where he jumps off the stage, he fell on it and popped his ankle. And the guitar solo, it's that sixteenth note thing that Angus does later on "Playing with Girls" and "First Blood." And he just keeps going on it. He does it on "Bad Boy Boogie" too; it's the same sound—one note repeating. He just makes it ring more and more as it goes on by just opening up on the string.

POPOFF: **What did George Young and Harry Vanda bring to the table as producers?**
CARSON: George was a very good record producer, but I didn't have much to do with George. I was working the band, not the producer. For a manager, they had Michael Browning, who I felt was very dedicated, an excellent guy to work with. They also had a good agent, both in Europe and America, and they would work. They were all very good about the way the band went about its business.

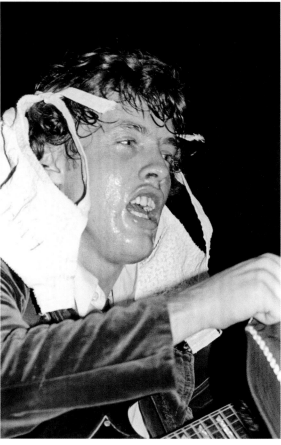

Angus being a problem child at the Palladium, New York City, August 24, 1977.

RUDD: When it comes to just the feel, George is the feel master. There's just something about George. When he plays bass, he always gets the song along, but subtly; he's a fantastic bass player. And, I mean he did a lot of stuff in Australia with Harry Vanda. Back then, they had hit after hit after hit after hit. They were just pouring 'em out. And they were great. But it was a little in-house thing, is the way they liked to do it. They weren't a band that was going to come out and show 'em what was going on. They were a radio band. We tried to get George to play bass, for quite a while, in the band. But he had already been through it with the Easybeats and stuff.

HANNON: On that one, produced by Vanda and Young, they were playing loud as they could and just really going for it. Like they did a live show— well, now do it again. And that's what they said they did—made it sound like a live band. And you can tell they went for it, and if it had a good feel, they kept it. It didn't matter if it slowed down here and there, or the tempo went up, or even if it was out of tune. If you listen to "Hell Ain't a Bad Place to

Be," there's a guitar way out of tune on that song. It's really, wow, you can hear that waver. But it just, it had the feel and the vibe.

O'KEEFFE: This is the guitar album. I mean, *Powerage* is a big guitar album, but this is where AC/DC became the AC/DC that we know today. This is the one that really did it—it's a serious album. It kicked the world in the balls. People heard that and went, "What the fuck is this?!" I mean, up until this point, there'd been, you know, "Dirty Deeds" is a great song, but there are some songs on there that are more like Chuck Berry, kind of just sitting back. And this is like a volcano went off. You start out with "Go Down," and automatically, straightaway, you hear the amps buzzing and the hum in the fucking preamps and the desk where it's being recorded. The tape machine's distorted, just straight at you and then it's boogie as hell.

They really got a lot of boogie on this album; this album is the sound of Australian pub rock 'n' roll, from start to finish. You hear this in Rose Tattoo and the Angels. You hear really similar tones in the kick and the snare, and in the guitars. In a similar way, in the sound of the room as well, and even in Bon's vocals. It would be the same mics, the same fucking desk, the same room that gave you the Angels and gave you Rose Tattoo—I guarantee it.

POPOFF: What about Angus and Malcolm when they played together? What was the magic of their sound?

CARSON: Malcolm was a solid rhythm player. Without him, that band wouldn't have sounded the way it did. And Angus, he's a very strong blues-influenced guitar player.

RUDD: He's a unit on his own, Angus. There's no one like Angus. What would you call him? He's just so fucking awesome he doesn't know what to do with himself. He's pretty fucking good, mate; that's all I can tell you. He's a great guy to play with live and an exceptional player in the studio. But as with everybody in AC/DC, it was all maniacs, you know, spill all over the stage if we had to, to get it done. Angus will do anything, mate. He'll do fucking anything, and he will do it well. He's pretty much the man.

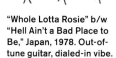

"Whole Lotta Rosie" b/w "Hell Ain't a Bad Place to Be," Japan, 1978. Out-of-tune guitar, dialed-in vibe.

Das rock. The Markthalle
in Hamburg, Germany,
October 4, 1977.

O'KEEFFE: Well, in terms of these guys on rhythm guitar, if you take "Hell Ain't a Bad Place to Be," they're playing the full chord on the intro, like an open G-D, G-D, G-D, A. And then on the main riff, they're down here on the fifth fret, and the sixth and seventh . . . no, wait, fifth, seventh . . . sorry, I'm actually not a musician. So it's open string, open string on the A string. And then on the D string, he'll be playing D5, D4, D5, D4, D5, D4, then D5, D7, D7, D7 with the open A [*sings it*]. It's just a different way of playing it.

Mal's got a thicker, heavier sound, cleaner sound, taking up a different end of the sound, whereas Angus is over here. It's a little bit . . . not looser, but it's got a bit more character and groove to it. Whereas Mal is locked into a certain groove and he stays there. Angus is okay to move around with it. So if he's a bit earlier or a bit late, it's cool, because his brother has the fort held down. What that does, it makes it sound bigger. And if the guitars aren't perfectly in tune—which they hardly ever are with AC/DC, but they are with each other—that also makes it sound bigger. It's weird, but the guitar sound on this album is the best they ever had, that's for sure.

POPOFF: And they're not distortion pedal guys, right?
O'KEEFFE: No, no, Angus has a fifty-watt Marshall JMP amp he's been using since then; it's the same one he uses for everything, pretty much, for solos, from what I've heard. But they're always bringing amps in, trying

different things out. But the Angels, you know that song, "Take a Long Line"—AC/DC sold their amps to the Angels. That's why "Take a Long Line" sounds like *Let There Be Rock*, and that's why *Powerage* is a very different sound—because they're all brand-new Marshalls. It's because they sold the fuckin' money amps to the Angels in 1977.

POPOFF: "Bad Boy Boogie" is, unsurprisingly, the closest thing to a true boogie on *Let There Be Rock*, although "Go Down" and "Whole Lotta Rosie" and even the title track for that matter go there as well. Why is there so much boogie in the Australian hard rock bands of the seventies?

O'KEEFFE: I grew up in it, and growing up with it, I don't think of it as a blues or boogie, even though I know it is. I don't think of it like that because it's its own thing, but that's where it comes from. Australian pub rock 'n' roll is very meat and potatoes and it's derivative of where it comes from. It comes from bands like The Who, ZZ Top, and Free—bands that were doing it before it really emerged here, those certain simple rock 'n' roll guitar blues bands. Then they got it out to Australia. We'd hear the simplest stuff and the best stuff that was coming from the US and the UK; that would translate to us and then we'd put it together in a big mixing bowl.

And if you play a Chuck Berry song in Australia in the seventies, it's still kind of cool, where it might not have been as cool in the US or UK. It's like, "What are you playing? This is twenty years old. We need to move on." But in Australia, we hadn't. We were still catching up. It's not like now, with the Internet and everything. So that sound connected with the people. With the working-class people, you've got to give them something that's going to get them moving. And, yeah, we drink a lot in Australia. So you needed something that they could sing to by the time you get the second chorus and they've never heard the song. They should know it. It should be that obvious.

RUDD: I don't know, Australian bands had a colonial sound, and there had been a few pioneers, Aussie pioneers, guys like Matt Taylor, that just had a real sort of *bumpa bumpa* thing about them, you know? There's no . . . it's not too fancy in Australia. We play it sort of straight. And I mean, AC/DC were particularly looking to keep it straighter than anyone else, you know? And it worked out really well. We've had some massive audiences. You remember Toronto Rocks, don't you, Martin?

POPOFF: Oh yeah, absolutely. In fact, I interviewed Malcolm in the hotel the next day. Probably Toronto's most historic concert of all time, and a career highlight for the band as well, I take it.

RUDD: It was, it was. It was a stunning crowd. It was the second . . . it was the biggest show in North America or history, wasn't it? 485,000. It did well. But yeah, us bands from Australia hit them over the head. When AC/DC went to Europe, we hit 'em all over the head. That's all we did, pretty much. We hit everyone over the head, let's face it. And they got it [*laughs*]. Sometimes you have to knock them over the head, Martin, before they get the idea. You're waiting for something to happen, but it's already happening.

POPOFF: Phil, what did you bring to the band from a drumming standpoint?

RUDD: I don't really have any inherent or inside talents or capabilities. I just sort of swing at them and see what happens. Everyone considers me to be the engine room of the band. The rhythm section is sort of nailed down by me. That's probably what I do best. I just nail it down, brother. I just keep it nailed down. I'm not about more chops.

POPOFF: And what about Bon? How did he help shape the band's character?

RUDD: Bon was a poet. And I don't know whether people realize that. Bon was really quite a guy. He had a lot of poetry in him; he saw the world his way and wrote about it, in his inimitable way. Sometimes a bit, you know, not in the way you'd like to explain it to your mom, but still with a sly kind of cheeky smile. Bon was a star. And he had a bloody good attitude.

HANNON: Bon was great. Here's the thing, starting with Kiss, I must've been into not really caring, or knowing, what those lyrics meant, what a "love gun" was and stuff. I was just rocking, singing lyrics, didn't even know what they meant, didn't even care even though I could memorize them. Same thing with AC/DC. But Bon's lyrics were a lot more adult to me, and the band looked more like scary rock dudes. I got to see Bon live on two different tours, but you saw very few pictures of them. You would see that regular picture of them, like they only had one 8×10 shot.

But Bon's words were more authentic and they made Kiss sound really wimpy, I thought. I was a fourteen-, fifteen-year-old. Those lyrics were filthy, "Big Balls" and stuff like that, but I did know they were filthy. "Whole Lotta Rosie" was about that big woman that he had sex with, from

Tasmania, big girl. It's like, what the hell?! In fact, that was the song they played on the radio in my area after "Overdose," which was like the first one they played on radio all the time, and then it was "Whole Lotta Rosie."

POPOFF: We got our FM out of Spokane, and I'm pretty sure it was "Problem Child" that got the most play there.
HANNON: That song, of course, is from an earlier session, but I thought it fit perfectly. It wasn't until I moved up to Columbus, Ohio, and got an import of *Dirty Deeds* that I realized that; I had no idea. And then I found out there was a song on *Let There Be Rock* called "Crabsody in Blue," and they wanted to get rid of that goofy song to make it a full-on rock album. That song made AC/DC look more in line with punk, I think, and it's like Atlantic wanted it all to be abrasive. Whatever the case, "Problem Child" was a better fit.

POPOFF: Joel, what's your assessment of "Crabsody in Blue?"
O'KEEFFE: Ah yes, a song about getting crabs in the back of the car, in the back of the tour van. Bon sang it like they could see them walking across the seat. That's a great song, classic. I don't know if he was drunk in the studio or what, but that's just pure fucking Bon Scott character. It's what sells that song. You get any other singer in the world and it wouldn't work—you would forget about it. It's like "She's Got Balls"—only Bon could do that. So that was on our Australian version, but you got "Problem Child," which was recorded for *Dirty Deeds*. That's why it sounds so different, poppier in fact. I suppose Atlantic thought it got overlooked on *Dirty Deeds*.

POPOFF: How would you characterize Bon as a lyricist on here?
O'KEEFFE: These are different lyrics for them. Normally they're singing about Bon's latest night on the town or big fat women or whatever or rock 'n' roll, but on something like "Dog Eat Dog," they're really singing about how hard it is to be in the world—it's a dog-eat-dog world out there. They don't touch on things like that very much, but when they do, they fucking nail it. And then something like "Problem Child," you can see that they would've been on tour or something, and Bon would've gone, "Angus is a fucking problem child." Put it down in the black book and then put the lyrics down. I think the way they wrote the songs, Bon would have a lot of stuff, and then they'd get it all out, and then they'd sit around and throw in whatever ideas, and boom, there's the song. They say in all the books that Bon was sort of

the elder. I mean, he looks older in the photos as well. But he was young enough in character that it didn't seem like that when they were on stage. But he had the experience of being in a couple of bands by the time.

POPOFF: Around this time, 1977, punk was all the rage. Phil, did you guys pay much attention to that scene? Were you ever marketed as, or confused for, a punk band?

RUDD: None of us were into that. AC/DC weren't a punk band. We were a rock band. You know, if there was anything going down on our side, like, we would be in. We would play *and* fight, you know what I mean? [*laughs*] We were that sort of band, a no-bullshit band. We just . . . we weren't offending anyone. We would just sort of carry on with it. But the confusion, that came from that "antipodean punk rock extravaganza" label they put on us, that came out before the Sex Pistols and all those guys—we were just a little stroppy bunch of fucking midgets, you know? And we just looked like the punks, and that's where that sort of came from. And the obsession with punk that followed after that, that came from Malcolm McLaren and the Sex Pistols, all that stuff on King's Road. It started as a fashion and it turned into an attitude.

HANNON: They kind of were marketed that way here and there. If you look at those old press clippings, the first tour in Europe, they're called the new punk sensation from Australia and stuff like that. That was the label that was kind of getting used, and Malcolm and Angus, said, essentially, "No, that's bullshit; we're a rock band. Those punk bands can't even tune their guitars."

POPOFF: It's funny, but speaking of punk, after Rainbow's *Rising*, this record and the Sex Pistols albums were the only two albums we had as kids with no mellow songs on them.

HANNON: Yeah, I noticed that too. It's like, *Let There Be Rock* just keeps kicking ass and I love that. There was no such thing as a band like that. *Rising* had keyboards, and to me that equated with wimpiness; I know that sounds simple or stupid, but as a kid, that's what I thought. But with *Let There Be Rock*, it was rock solid all the way through. Even my heroes, Kiss, had ballads like "Hard Luck Woman" and "Beth" and poppy things like "Tomorrow and Tonight" and "Christine Sixteen," and when they started wearing fur, I fucking took my Kiss posters down. Ted Nugent was always kicking ass, but even Ted would have those mellow songs like on his first album, "You Make Me Feel Right at Home"—I never made it all the way through that fucking song as a kid, playing it in my room. I didn't want to hear that crap. And then *Free for All* had "I Love You So I Told You a Lie" and "Together." It's like, "What the fuck, dude?!" But AC/DC just kept kicking ass and I loved it, because to me there were no bands like that. Not until Motörhead.

O'KEEFFE: I agree. Look, from start to finish, every single song is as iconic AC/DC as the last one. And to this day, they're still playing "Dog Eat Dog," "Let There Be Rock," "Hell Ain't a Bad Place to Be, "Whole Lotta Rosie," and "Problem Child." Fully five songs off an eight-song album, that they're playing today. Five! That's more than they play off *Back in Black*. That's more than they play off *Highway to Hell*. It's my favorite AC/DC album, but besides that, that right there is the sign of a great album. If I had a few beers, I could tell you a whole lot more. For example, the specifics of "Let There Be Rock" . . . you can hear the finger hitting the strings. There is that much detail on it. It's just so good. There will never be another *Let There Be Rock*.

The December 9, 1979, *Let There Be Rock* tour date in Paris spawned a concert film released in 1980.

POWERAGE

with DAVE ELLEFSON and PAUL KEHAYAS

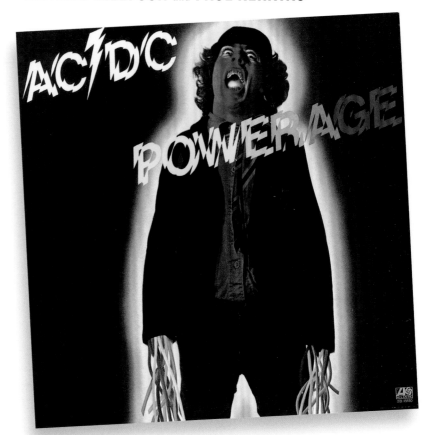

ISSUE VARIANCE NOTES: The European version of *Powerage* features an earlier mix than the subsequent US, Canadian, and Australian mixes, including minor performance differences. Initial European copies of *Powerage* included "Cold Hearted Man" but not "Rock 'n' Roll Damnation." Later issues contained both. Australian, US, and Canadian issues included "Rock 'n' Roll Damnation" but not "Cold Hearted Man." *Powerage* was the first AC/DC album where the cover art was the same across all territories.

SIDE 1

1.	Rock 'n' Roll Damnation	3:35
2.	Down Payment Blues	6:20
3.	Gimme a Bullet	3:00
4.	Riff Raff	5:14

SIDE 2

1.	Sin City	4:40
2.	What's Next to the Moon	3:15
3.	Gone Shootin'	4:05
4.	Up to My Neck in You	4:58
5.	Kicked in the Teeth	3:45

All songs composed by Angus Young, Malcolm Young, and Bon Scott

Personnel: Bon Scott—lead vocals; Angus Young—guitar; Malcolm Young—guitar; Cliff Williams—bass; Phil Rudd—drums

Released May 5, 1978

Recorded at Albert Studios, Sydney, Australia

Produced by Harry Vanda and George Young

More casual and charming than the menacing record before it, *Powerage* is many a fan's most beloved of the catalog, as it is your intrepid author's. Indeed, in terms of volume, it's a match to *T.N.T.* and *Dirty Deeds*, although that's where the comparisons end.

The author's indulgent memory concerns carting home the fresh-off-the-presses Canadian red vinyl issue on the back of his bike on a blazing summer day, hoping to beat warpage as he clocked the four miles, long winding hill included, home to his parents' living room hi-fi for inspection. But another memory is of "Rock 'n' Roll Damnation" being the advance single to radio, and me and my buddies cringing with concern that the scowling, pool cue–swinging black 'n' blue bruisers who made *Let There Be Rock* had summarily gone pop, maracas included. Love the song like a big bottle of happy pills now, but at fifteen, that chorus was blasphemy, entirely too cheery compared to what came before.

And then there was "Gone Shootin'," "What's Next to the Moon," "Gimme a Bullet," and "Down Payment Blues"—tracks that were walled off or politely paid little mind until the heavy metal barriers came down some time at university.

In fact, *Powerage* helped knock down those Doors and Joy Divisions, just as much as Pink Floyd, Yes, and Marillion did, for this was the work of a band now comfortable in their own skins, second-guessing nothing, making no apologies for being more simple and rock 'n' rollsy than they had ever been, or at least since the debut.

And even the "heavy metal" on the record sounded like the work of guys who after the show might be changing your tires and wiper blades. "Sin City" was heavier of title (and placement: lead track, side two) than of riff, but "Kicked in the Teeth" and especially "Riff Raff," the latter featuring a note density new for the band, became the new high school anthems inspiring bad deeds behind the backstop.

Is there some rose-coloring going on due to this being my first AC/DC record in the position of knowing the band like an old pair of shoes? Possibly, although the searing summer of its arrival in Trail, British Columbia, and the fact that the vinyl was glowing red . . . a fifteen-year-old metalhead didn't need to go to the hot production or the electrocuted Angus on the cover to imbue this record with sun-burning powers.

And so *Powerage* sits, not so much glowering like *Let There Be Rock*, but glowing like the lights at a backwoods roadhouse, inviting passersby to clink drinks and swap tales with the local bikers

OPPOSITE: The first AC/DC album to be released nearly simultaneously and with the same sleeve art in all markets.

BELOW: By 1978, AC/DC were producing "heavy metal" that sounded like the work of guys who might be rotating your tires or changing your oil after the show. This shot was captured at the fifth Day on the Green festival at Oakland Coliseum, September 2, 1978. AC/DC shared the bill with Ted Nugent, Blue Öyster Cult, Journey, and Cheap Trick.

and farmers. Somewhat of a shame, intensifying the nostalgia factor—and through no fault of the band, really—it would never feel this intimate again, with AC/DC soon becoming no less than a small yet immutable corner of worldwide consciousness forever. Amen.

POPOFF: **To begin, Dave, what was your first introduction to AC/DC?**
ELLEFSON: I grew up on a farm, six miles north of a small little town, three thousand people, Jackson, Minnesota. And the whole town was set up to support the farming industry. But at one point, a local musician who had country bands, he and his wife started up a store on Main Street that had records, and I guess probably eight-tracks, cassettes, and some musical equipment. For me it was *If You Want Blood (You've Got It)*, the live album from the *Powerage* tour. A lot of fans in my generation, my age group, we discovered groups by way of their live albums: Kiss, *Alive!*; Grand Funk; Rush, *All the World's a Stage*; *Frampton Comes Alive!*; and AC/DC, *If You Want Blood*. Seeing Angus stabbing himself with the guitar, and then flip it over, on the back, he's laying on the stage dead with the guitar neck in his back, it was like, "Dude, I have to have this album [*laughs*]." Shortly after, I bought *Powerage* and then *Let There Be Rock* in that music store.

POPOFF: **What did you think of *Powerage*?**
ELLEFSON: Well, again, I discovered the band on a live album, and then I go back and start doing my research and look into the history, and I saw the band live on the *Powerage* tour, then I saw them on late-night TV on *Midnight Special*, I believe, with "Sin City." First of all, "Sin City" was awesome, although I always wished they had better bass guitar production [*laughs*]. I kinda wished they had better record production, which then later happened with *Highway to Hell*, with Mutt Lange. But as a bass player, it caught my ear how simple it was, because simple becomes effective. And I also would come to appreciate Ian Hill in Judas Priest for having a similar approach as these guys.

As AC/DC got more famous, the bluesy nature of their music became more streamlined and they would use simpler riffs. And as the guitar parts were the defining parts of their songs, the rhythm section of the bass on the drums would start to become less "notey" as well, with Cliff and Phil creating this really solid slab of a concrete foundation underneath the structure of the riffs. That was clear to me on the live album and on *Powerage*, especially as I went back to the other bass player, Mark Evans; those earlier records had notier, bluesier bass playing. These were just really cool songs that you could

ABOVE: *Powerage* World Tour, Paradise Theatre, Boston, Massachusetts, August 21, 1978.

OPPOSITE (FROM TOP): "Sin City," used as the B-side on the UK version of "Rock 'n' Roll Damnation," has a great riff and an undertow of bass.

"Rock 'n' Roll Damnation" b/w "Kicked in the Teeth," as good as any punk rock. Holland, 1978.

The definition of rock 'n' roll, "Rock 'n' Roll Damnation" is the one that gets the party started. Here it's b/w "Kicked in the Teeth" on its South African pressing, 1978.

put in your car and in your cassette player. It was just great driving music, but it wasn't a record you could listen to with your girlfriend, which made it this male bonding, "dudes in a van" kind of favorite record.

POPOFF: Paul, how do you position *Powerage* in the AC/DC catalog? I mean, many a studied AC/DC fan consider it their favorite.
KEHAYAS: It's an elusive record, a cult favorite. Everybody likes the underdog. Everybody wants to champion *The Who Sell Out*, even though it was a failure, instead of *Tommy*. And *Powerage* follows up an incredibly strong record, *Let There Be Rock*. I suppose they had their sights set on breaking in the US, because, let's face it, the masterminds behind this were the Albert people, along with George Young and Harry Vanda, who were sort of the production/songwriting nexus that was just operating this tentacle of operations. And they were making an inroad into the North American market, which they'd certainly already done in Europe. But now there was this decided push that they were gonna get more professional with the outreach.

I believe the strength of *Powerage* lies in the fact that it's finally got the sensitivity of the players with each other. Now they changed bassists at this point. Cliff Williams is the new boy, and he used to play with Home in the UK, sort of a prog band on CBS. So Cliff Williams is the new boy and there's a different sound to the rhythm section. Plus, the production makes it sound more crowded and there's a lot more low end too. As well, it's the first record where I find they've got a danceable thing going on. And I think that broadened their appeal.

There's also a hunger—we know how Angus Young is. He's completely driven. I mean, the fact that he is the last man standing . . . if you can believe his energy level in 1978, when he was young man, you knew this band was going to rule the world—you just did. I think that *Let There Be Rock* is the stronger record, but this one has the groove.

POPOFF: And what are a couple of the highlights on the record for you?

ELLEFSON: Well, first, "Sin City" has a great riff, and again, this undertow of bass [*laughs*]. "Kicked in the Teeth" is kind of a style they didn't carry through with *Highway to Hell*. But I love "Riff Raff," with its rowdy chaotic kind of guitar playing. And it's funny, being in Megadeth, of course meeting Dave Mustaine just a few years later, there was this quality about him that's very bluesy, like Angus, very kind of primal like these early AC/DC riffs, very kind of rock 'n' roll in a weird way—he's like Diamond Head meets AC/DC [*laughs*], which is part of what attracted me to him. There was this frantic, frenetic, rowdy energy to his playing.

To me, "Riff Raff" was that song with AC/DC. Because while it's got kind of this twelve-bar blues structure around it with the bass and the chord changes, to have this riff over top of it was a style of rock 'n' roll that I hadn't really heard too much of. Zeppelin didn't really do it, Black Sabbath didn't do it, and Kiss wasn't really doing it. And to kick off the live record with that, those were the first notes I'd heard of AC/DC, was "Riff Raff." And so whereas the earlier AC/DC records, as I would find out, were still kind of primitive in their blues structure, *Powerage* was not a blues record. It was heading toward a refined, almost heavy metal sound. At least hard rock—it was a hard rock record.

KEHAYAS: "Riff Raff," from that guitar intro right through, I mean, it's the embodiment of rock guitar, the ultimate showcase. I could never understand why people would only talk about them in the context of mainstream rock. "Riff Raff" and, say, "Kicked in the Teeth" were as good as any punk rock that ever came out. But "Riff Raff" is the definition of plugging your finger into a socket. I just relate viscerally to that song. That's the one that makes me want to jump around the house and smash windows. On the UK mix, the guitars are just relentless. Seeing that live was amazing, and I was probably the youngest one there. But, yeah, to see that live was insane. It's funny, it doesn't close the record, but it should've, I think.

POPOFF: We've talked about the rhythm section, guitars, production even, but what does Bon Scott bring to the table?
KEHAYAS: The lyric writing is superlative. Bon Scott really was poetic—he's the lovable rogue. You cannot hate this man, even if he's picking your pocket. While he's doing it, he's smiling. And you're saying, you know what, take my money. And he'll sing about it. And that's the thing I love about him. His lyric writing is amazing. The line everybody always cites is in "Down Payment Blues": *I know I ain't doing much/Doing nothing means a lot to me*. And there's *Gimme a bullet to bite on/And I'll make believe . . . it's you*. It just sounds as if the man is in a relationship that is giving him insane amounts of grief. But it's handled in that sort of street poetry kind of way.

But "Rock 'n' Roll Damnation" is definitely the one that gets the party started. I mean, it is the definition of rock 'n' roll. It's got the most classic rock 'n' roll beat going on. And when the maracas hit, and when the chorus hits, you know that this is a monster. How couldn't you? This is in the grand tradition of great opening songs like "Care of Cell 44" and "I Saw Her Standing There," and begins an amazing record.

But back to lyrics, "Down Payment Blues" is like a later version of what "The Jack" was earlier. You know, now we're actually dealing with Bon's life experience as opposed to being toilet rock. The pickpocket has some tales to tell. The lovable rogue now has some tales to tell, and some wise sage advice from this stage of his life. I never find his lyrics banal. I never find him corny, even when he's doing the "Shazbot nanu nanu" at the end of *Highway to Hell*. I never found that corny. I thought he was always being funny. I always loved the man. I'm sure that the reality is probably less than—it always is.

ELLEFSON: To me, well, first of all Bon had tattoos, and that was absolutely frightening and scary. Like he was a tough, fighting, street brawler kind of guy. He had this crazed look in his eye, like you wouldn't want to get too close to him. He was friendly, but he was not a guy that a guy like me, a little Lutheran kid on the farm, would go and hang out with. He was dangerous. That was part of the enthralling charm of who Bon was. He had his shirt off and he had tattoos [*laughs*]. I mean, he was everything disrespectful about what I learned about growing up to be a man. To me, the only people at that point in my life who had tattoos were sailors and the military, who were worldly, rough around the edges, had been to foreign shores, and Bon represented all of that. Yet, here he was a lead singer of a rock band.

KEHAYAS: It was always implied that Bon was older, more experienced. He always came out as not the older uncle, but the older brother. The one who sat you down and got you drunk, fed you your first few beers. He went through stuff telling you how things were going to be for you because he had just gone through them. But he wasn't going to scare you off—that's the vibe. And it played off how young Angus was, and the other guys weren't too far behind. I mean look at the back cover. Remember this is the day of punk rock, and it has that sort of vibe going on, but it also has a sort of superhero weirdness to it. Angus is the cover star. Effectively they've chosen him to be the mascot of the group, which they'd suggested as far back as the international and US *High Voltage*.

Day on the Green festival at Oakland Coliseum, September 2, 1978.

POPOFF: Dave, are you as much a fan of "Rock 'n' Roll Damnation" as Paul is?

ELLEFSON: I loved it; I thought it was a great song. I liked heavy, and I should say I still do—that's just my nature. I love heavy, but I also like melodic. To me, the trick is to make the two work. Because, just to be super, super heavy without the melody, you're only writing half the song. And to me, AC/DC struck this really cool chord where there were melodic hooks, but it was heavier than the Cheap Tricks of the world. By *Powerage*, or even *Let There Be Rock*, they had this kick-in-the-teeth rowdy aggression to their sound, no pun intended.

POPOFF: Although, with the likes of "Gone Shootin'," "Down Payment Blues," and "What's Next to the Moon," there are some pretty laid-back, almost southern-rocking vibes to the record, no?

KEHAYAS: I would agree, because the beats are slower too. Sure, I can hear that. But then again, let's face it, Lynyrd Skynyrd were ripping off all their riffs from Free, who are not exactly southern rock. But it's filtered through that Australian rock ethic. I believe that ethic is still with them quite a bit on *Powerage*, but I have a feeling that they're globalizing; they're trying to make a record that appeals to Americans. This is a bridge record between the old AC/DC and the new, but embracing a different aesthetic. I think they've seen the world, or a bit of it, and I believe what they're trying to do is make something a bit more powerful and lasting.

Let's face it, the next record, that's the one that should've broke them and sold the millions of copies *Back in Black* sold. It should've been *Highway to Hell*. But you could tell they were inching toward

ABOVE: "Rock 'n' Roll Damnation" stereo/mono promo single, United States, 1978.

OPPOSITE: Rehearsing for a TV appearance on *The Midnight Special* with bassist Cliff Williams (right), Hollywood, California, September 1978.

that record. "Up to My Neck in You" certainly sounds to me like it should've been on the next album. It's a precursor to the stuff on *Highway to Hell*. "Gone Shootin'" . . . everybody says it's about somebody Bon knew who had a problem with heroin. I tend to think that's somebody speculating. But "Gone Shootin'" has one of the greatest riffs that nobody ever talks about— Malcolm's riff on that is exemplary. But now that you bring it up, yeah, it does have a slow and southern drawl to it, and I like that.

POPOFF: I guess there's a continuum between the blues and southern rock and then . . . heavy metal? There's a straight line there.
ELLEFSON: Sure, well, "Down Payment Blues" is a good example. Because I was not—I am not—a huge fan of the blues. I know there's a lot of people that would say, "Oh, the blues is the basis of rock 'n' roll," and it is to a large degree. But AC/DC kind of morphed their way out of the blues, played more aggressive, the amplifiers got hotter, it got more distorted, and so they moved on from Zeppelin and the early origins. My age group, as we were getting guitars and amps, on the radio I was hearing Sweet, Bachman-Turner Overdrive, Styx, Kiss, Aerosmith. Music had developed.

But still, in AC/DC, there was something very kind of primitive thing about them. And I think the fact that they were from Australia, it was this land far away that nobody knew much about. And their music was raw, sort of undeveloped, and I think you could hear the fun and rowdiness in it.

Yet, you know, they had songs like "Down Payment Blues," and as I heard it, I'm going, "Okay, like, this is the kind of blues I can get my head around" [*laughs*]. Because it wasn't just your typical twelve-bar jam stuff. AC/DC had gone beyond being a blues band. I probably wouldn't really come to know true heavy metal until I discovered Judas Priest and Iron Maiden and Motörhead just a year or two later, but AC/DC was definitely bridging the gap, taking music in that direction.

But also within their own trajectory, you know, *Let There Be Rock* was really rough and raw. And one of the things I like about *Powerage* is [that] you could tell the band had gotten better at making records. Which I liked. That was one of the things that made it difficult to listen to a lot of early Zeppelin and some of these things that I didn't grow up on that I had to go back and do my homework on. Even early Kiss records. The production just wasn't that good. And by the middle of the AC/DC's catalog, people learned how to make records sound better. The guitars are better, they play better. That to me was probably the biggest transition from *Let There Be Rock* over to *Powerage*.

POPOFF: Paul, in the spirit of us paying heed to the differences in track listings between various territories, originally "Rock 'n' Roll Damnation" wasn't an option, but there was this song "Cold Hearted Man," which is on all European versions, and on none of the US or Australian versions.

KEHAYAS: Yes, Albert is in Australia, Atlantic is worldwide, so Atlantic is rushing the record that has been done in a period of about two months, and they rush a bunch of mixes over, and "Rock 'n' Roll Damnation" is not on this record. "Cold Hearted Man" is on the UK album, and it doesn't get released outside of the UK and Europe until the *Backtracks* box set. It's a phenomenally great song and should have been issued as a single. It's funny, because Atlantic heard it and thought, this isn't a hit. They wanted another thing. So they churned out "Rock 'n' Roll Damnation."

POPOFF: And what are some of the differences we get with this UK mix of the album?

KEHAYAS: It's rawer, it's way more punk. It has its link to the previous records. It sounds like *Let There Be Rock*. The guitars are louder, they're shriller, I believe. There's lots of low end, but it sounds like a demo that is

Chicago's Aragon Ballroom, September 22, 1978.

just slightly polished. There's no real reverb anywhere. It's just very in-your-face. And then Atlantic pushes for a remix for the American market. That becomes the mix that we know.

But, yeah, just looking at my notes, I'll tell you some of what's different. "Gimme a Bullet" has a cymbal crash where Angus's part comes in during the intro, and there's no backing vocals on it. On "Down Payment Blues," guitars pan hard right and hard left, no effect on Bon's voice. "Gone Shootin'" fades later, and again, hard right and left panning. "Riff Raff" has more vocal ad-libs that are missing on the final mix. And on "What's Next to the Moon," there's no solo, no backing and double-tracked vocals, and different chorus lines toward the end, and it's a little longer. "Up to My Neck in You" has different vocal ad-libs, and no lead guitar at the end. "Kicked in the Teeth" has a different intro. It begins with the band, and a different reading of the first line—he doesn't draw it out as long. But overall I think the mixes sound incredibly punk. Which is why I think it worked so well in the climate of 1978, in the summer.

POPOFF: Dave, your fond memories of this album come from the fact that you saw them on what was essentially the tour for the live album.
ELLEFSON: Yes, well, right before *Highway to Hell* came out, supporting Cheap Trick just before *Dream Police* came out—Sioux Falls, South Dakota. I was right in front of Angus's Marshall 4×12 cabinet, which ripped my frickin' head off and I was deaf for about a week after. So yeah, front row, screaming my head off, like a real fan. I mean, I was a Kiss fan, but this was a brand-new band, they were *my* band; they had not hit yet. I loved to be that guy who discovers bands before everybody else in town did and I think that's what made *Powerage* so special—they were still an underground act.

But there was also this: coming out of the Kiss generation, everything was larger than life, a comic book, which appealed to me as an eleven-, twelve-, thirteen-year-old. It was a fantasyland, you know, superstardom, certainly unattainable. Well, by the time I was fifteen, sixteen years old, I'd been in bands now for a few years, because I started playing bass when I was eleven, and got into bands by age twelve, and I'd been gigging around the area. So I kinda started to learn the reality of being a musician in a rock band, and how rock bands play and perform and book gigs; I started to become at least semiprofessional at a pretty young age. And what AC/DC did for me was, these were like regular guys in jeans and T-shirts, with Marshall and Ampeg amps, which those were the altars we all bowed to in hard rock and heavy metal. And so all of a sudden, this was a band that in a lot of ways made stardom look attainable to me.

But I mean, again, I literally stood directly in front of Angus's Marshall 4×12, which was fifteen, twenty feet back from the front of the stage. So I heard everything he played. There were no phasers, no flangers, no tech, no fancy theatrics. What he played, you heard. And that whole concept would later transcend into my own musical journey as I landed in California and we started what became thrash metal.

POPOFF: Anything you'd like to add, Paul?

KEHAYAS: Well, it's funny, my brother, who came to visit me not too long ago, he's a big prog head. He's the guy that goes to Cruise to the Edge and all that stuff. And he looks up and sees the AC/DC box, and he goes, "You don't still listen to this, do you?!" And I go, "Yeah, of course I do. They verify that I'm alive." I still think of myself as perpetually sixteen. They're the lifeblood of rock 'n' roll. They're the least pretentious rock 'n' roll group in existence. There's absolutely no pretense with AC/DC.

MAIN: Bon Scott and Cliff Williams, somewhere in Germany, October 1978.

INSET: Cliff Williams came to AC/DC after his previous outfit, Home, split up. He joined in time to tour *Let There Be Rock*.

HIGHWAY TO HELL

with **JAY JAY FRENCH** and **BRAD TOLINSKI**

All songs composed by Angus Young, Malcolm Young, and Bon Scott

Personnel: Bon Scott—lead vocals; Angus Young—guitar; Malcolm Young—guitar; Cliff Williams—bass; Phil Rudd—drums

Released July 27, 1979

Recorded at Albert Studios, Sydney; Criteria Studios, Miami; and Roundhouse Studios, London

Produced by Robert John Lange

As if to burnish their outsider status, our under-tall heroes from down under took 1979, a notoriously moribund year, by the horns and created what is arguably their masterpiece. Making the party further joyous was the fact that *Highway to Hell* was a summer album the dusty, smoky world over, the heat from the happy sun helping songs like "Highway to Hell," "Get It Hot," and "Shot Down in Flames" fry our minds and burn hotter than hell.

But back to 1979. This was a year that the industry fretted over, a year when most music was deemed bad, a year of complaining, a year that was supposed to be saved by *In Through*

the Out Door, *The Wall*, and *The Long Run* by
a past-due-date Eagles. But putting numbers
aside, numbers that were wilted by the death
of disco and the fizzle of the new wave, in
the world of AC/DC fans, all the beloved
headbanging bands were either self-destructing
or going poppy. Aerosmith was in the tank,
as was Ted Nugent. Kiss was making disco
too late with "I Was Made for Loving You," a
travesty on a dull album called *Dynasty*, while
Blue Öyster Cult pooched it with *Mirrors*
and Angel went *Sinful*. Deep Purple and
Montrose were no more, Uriah Heep was in
the wilderness, Black Sabbath had shed Ozzy,
and (for those who care) the mighty Derringer
became Rick Derringer, and, oh yeah, Starz
broke up too.

The only beacons of very electric light were
Motörhead (but that was a UK thing), Van
Halen was still on a tear (but even they were
looking a little anticlimactic with Van Halen *II*),
and the subject of our salacious study, AC/DC, who did nothing but
continue their stomp to the top, thanks be to the gods of heavy metal.

Highway to Hell found the band most definitely improved, although it
takes some digging to figure out why, exactly. The easy answer is a new
producer, Mutt Lange, who at this point was nowhere near the production
legend he would become. Fortunately, AC/DC get him at the best he will
ever be. Mutt hasn't done much at this point, so mixed in with this lot, he's
more of an equal, maybe even second in command to Malcolm.

But Mutt is also a man of ideas and discipline, and the marriage would
pay huge dividends. Fact is, *Highway to Hell* sounds completely professional,
with flawless but not idiosyncratic or obtrusive production values. What's
more, the band's songs are somehow made more assertive and world-
beating—and this is perhaps an area where Mutt deserves more credit. To
my mind, the good ol' boy charm of *Powerage* is matched, but with increased
energy and an increased sense of winning versus self-deprecation. All of side
two, the less heavy side (oddly, outside of the heaviest song, "Shot Down
in Flames"), Bon is beating his chest. But flip back to side one, possibly

ABOVE: Who can deny
such a magic record,
especially given the
horrible fate that it would
be the band's last by
the beloved Bon Scott?

OPPOSITE: International
cover art, 1979.

the greatest half-record in AC/DC history, and not only is Bon beating his chest, but the AC/DC fan is catapulted into heavy metal heaven.

Quick story on that front, one that has cemented this viewpoint since the very second it happened back in the summer of '79. Me and my buddies had a rating system of songs, three categories—lousy, so-so, and good—and then demarcations within that: lousy, lousy good, average good, and really good (for things like "Riff Raff"). Well, when I called my buddy Forrest Toop on the phone to give him the quick summary, I just had to start with side two, which went average good, so-so, lousy good, so-so, and finally, for the ballad, "Night Prowler," lousy. Letting his despondence simmer, I then told him about side one, which went average good, really good, really good, really good, really good. To put it in perspective, in our minds (these ratings never failed, believe me), AC/DC so far had only a handful of songs heavy enough to be called really good, and here were four of them in a row.

Of course, by the time we graduated high school, we realized that music—outside of math rock—isn't math, and now I love every damn song on the album. Because who can deny such a magic record, especially given the horrible fate that it would be the last AC/DC record croaked by our beloved Bon Scott? To be sure, *Back in Black* may have sold infinitely more copies, but when push comes to shove, the love always comes right back to *Highway to Hell*, where the love belongs, set timeless and infinite through an unfortunate death in the family.

POPOFF: Could you provide a little background here? Where is AC/DC in their career during the *Highway to Hell* era?
FRENCH: The way I look at AC/DC is more than just as a musical act because, you know, I'm a manager, right? Okay, so as a manager, AC/DC kind of started when the disco thing was happening, so rock was quote unquote "dead" at the time. And AC/DC was slowly creeping into the subconscious, or the unconscious of American youth, or radio. We were inundated with disco, disco, disco, '76 onward. And what I was marveling at was AC/DC's slow build on every album, going from 50,000 units to 100,000 units to 200,000 units.

Highway to Hell, I believe, was their first gold in the states, in late '79, platinum in the spring of 1980, even before *Back in Black* comes out. And our band, Twisted Sister, played a lot of AC/DC. However, we didn't play songs from this record. But I marveled at how well they could execute three chords and make it fascinating. You know, Bon Scott had this nasal, raspy, nasty snarl that was so authentic and so legitimate. And Mendoza, our bass player, was in the Dictators, and he toured with AC/DC. He toured with Bon and he used to tell us how great this band was.

They were slowly making their way as headliners. And that couldn't happen today—no one has the tolerance for that. AC/DC built it up in the super-authentic way. It wasn't just the fact that they were a great band and that Bon Scott was a great frontman or that the guitar tones were so perfect. Because they just seemed perfect—there was nothing to criticize about this band. But as they were climbing the ladder, I saw, as a kind a musician/manager, this progression, thinking, "Boy, this is the most perfect progression you could ask for." And then *Highway to Hell*—bang, bang—gets them to gold and then very quickly platinum.

And I guess I always looked at that as being the perfect setup. They could weather the storm. *Back in Black* did, whatever, eight or nine million fairly quickly, and then *For Those About to Rock* did about half, and then all of a sudden they crashed—*Flick of the Switch* and those eighties albums were like 400,000, 500,000. But their foundation was laid so strongly, they survived more or less on ticket sales alone.

POPOFF: Likely aiding in this success is the ushering in of Mutt Lange as producer, right?
TOLINSKI: Yes, but also as background, to see what happened for *Highway to Hell*, it's instructive to understand why these records happened. The first five records, AC/DC was out there. Atlantic Records didn't really have any strong belief in them. They just thought they were sort of this little club band. And I don't think they really believed that they would amount to much. But then they started building this following. Huge in Australia, England, and then in America they started building—against all odds and with very little radio support—a huge following.

So Atlantic steps in and says, "Look, guys, now we sort of believe, and we want to take it to the next level." And so for *Highway to Hell*, they fired their former producers, George Young and Harry Vanda. And said, "Look, you've got to bring in somebody that's going to help polish you guys up and get you ready for radio." And the band itself was reluctant to do that, but you know, Malcolm and Angus, for as much as they don't want to admit it, they do have their ambitions. They sort of went along, I guess, if nothing else, to see what would happen.

Australian cover art, 1979.

(continued on page 92)

MAIN: World Series of Rock with Ted Nugent, Journey, Thin Lizzy, and the Scorpions, Municipal Stadium, Cleveland, Ohio, July 28, 1979.

INSET: World Series of Rock, Municipal Stadium, Cleveland, Ohio, July 28, 1979.

If You Want Blood World Tour, Madison Square Garden, August 4, 1979.

(continued from page 89)

Initially they hire the legendary Eddie Kramer to come in and produce them, and they don't get along at all. I mean, the experiment is a disaster. Kramer is sort of a dick to them, straight off. He asks Angus of Bon, "Can that guy actually sing?" [*laughs*] Subsequently, Angus felt that Eddie thought that he was a bit of a gimmick. That he was just some window dressing, instead of the great guitar god that he was.

So anyway, Angus basically called Jerry Greenberg at Atlantic and said, "Look, we're not interested in this guy. Find somebody else." And they come across Mutt Lange—possibly through Jerry or their manager, Michael Browning, or maybe Doug Thaler—who was, you know, Mutt had some success. He wasn't the name that he became later on. He'd done the Boomtown Rats and some pub rock.

POPOFF: Clover, The Motors, I think every City Boy album.

TOLINSKI: Yes, City Boy and Graham Parker, and I guess when he spoke to the band, he sort of talked their language, and he said, "Look, I see what you guys are doing. I understand it. I don't necessarily want to fuck it up, but I do see ways that I can make it better." And the band accepted it. They accepted the idea that they could be a better band, a tighter band. And what Mutt eventually did in the beginning was he helped Bon out with his singing. He added the sort of layers to their choruses. And you can hear that he did try to focus Angus's guitar playing. I mean, on the first five records, when Angus lets loose with his solos, they're great, but they're sort of just high energy and all over the place. And Mutt does say, "Look, you know, I want this to be a little bit sharper, a little bit tighter."

It's sort of funny, because in some interviews, Angus said he was almost looking for that anyway. Like when he would solo with his brother, with George and Harry, he would always say, like, "Hey, you know, maybe I could go back and sort of fix that, maybe work out something for these sections." And George would always be like, "No, you know, forget about the bum notes. It's cooking, it's cool." George was always looking for the energy and the element of surprise; that was his thing.

And Mutt wanted to get a little bit of structure and Angus responded to that. He didn't necessarily rail against that. Because he felt that maybe his playing could've been a little tighter. But I think later on he was quoted as saying, you know, it usually worked, but just as often, they would go back to the first take for Mutt. You know, there's a sort of myth that Mutt was a real fascist in the studio. But Angus and Malcolm had been around the block. They would say, "Look Mutt, we've done it enough; that's the way it's going to be." So there was a real sort of democracy in the studio, as opposed to how Mutt was with Def Leppard later.

POPOFF: That's interesting. Maybe he didn't have as much power yet. Maybe he wasn't looked upon as the boss as much.

TOLINSKI: Yes, absolutely, and you know, I've chatted with Angus and Malcolm and these guys on a few different occasions, and the truth is, these guys are never going to be puppets. Angus and Malcolm have their vision and I think in a way they are very much like Keith Richards and Mick Jagger. I mean, they'll take advice, but at the end of the day, they're the bosses of their own music. They have their vision. But for that moment, for that initial moment, there was a real excitement that is palpable. And that higher level of discipline on *Highway to Hell*, that sort of lifts them from being this great little high-energy pub rock band into something worthier of the arenas. And that little bit of spit and polish on the choruses, like you hear on "Highway to Hell," makes it just a little bit better for radio too.

FRENCH: The production on *Highway to Hell* wasn't *Back in Black* yet, just the in-between steps. You could tell it was moving in this heavier direction. It filled the speaker more, coming out of the radio. It was more impactful, but it wasn't as dense. The production reached its density on *Back in Black*. But the sound of the album was a progression from where Vanda and Young was. But, you know what? It was a much greater leap from *Highway to Hell* to

Back in Black than the albums were before to *Highway to Hell*. When I heard *Back in Black*, I said, "Wow, there's a different production technique going on." And *Highway to Hell* was the perfect prelude to it. Again, in the history of AC/DC, it was a perfectly placed bridge album.

POPOFF: The title track is one of the band's biggest anthems ever. What is the magic of that song?

FRENCH: With "Highway to Hell," AC/DC started laying down a template of how they liked to build suspense through a song. If you think about it, with "You Shook Me" and "For Those About to Rock," there's a further progression, which I believe probably reflects a Mutt Lange influence. Which is how you gradually layer tracks into a song. You don't just start off at ten. "Whole Lotta Rosie" starts out at ten. "Girls Got Rhythm" on this album starts out at ten. Then again, they started that slow build thing with "Live Wire" and "T.N.T." too.

But "Highway to Hell" is dramatic. Also, this is during the time when you actually listened to side one and side two. You were drawn into a record and you needed a reason to be drawn in and "Highway to Hell" draws you in. "Shot Down in Flames" is great, but it doesn't have that. The art of starting an album dramatically is over. Nobody cares—we live in a track-laden world. But in those days it mattered, and that song is the perfect entrée to how the album builds up. It's beautiful.

TOLINSKI: Yeah, that's an AC/DC trick, isn't it? They do that quite a bit. Listen, the thing about AC/DC . . . it's always a little tricky, like they're always cagey about it, about who actually writes the lyrics to these songs. Sometimes Angus or Mal will say, "Oh, you know, well, Bon contributed that." But I have a feeling that Angus and Mal were always more involved with the songwriting than anybody thinks. Because there wasn't quite as much of a hiccup when you had a change between Bon and Brian, as one would think.

And I sort of think that if Angus and Malcolm weren't in rock 'n' roll, they would be really great copywriters. Because they were great at these slogans and catchphrases. But their product is rock 'n' roll. They come up with these great little titles that you think somebody had to have done before, but nobody has. Double entendres and whatever.

But, oh my God, if there ever was a better title for a rock 'n' roll movie than *Highway to Hell*, you've gotta tell me. But evoking the word "Hell," for them it really has nothing to do with Satan. It just has to do with life on the road. But at the time, radio programmers, politicians, all sorts of people were getting into the act there and were sensitive to any sort of satanic references. But like anything else AC/DC ever did, it was ridiculous, because whether it was sex or it was the devil, it was all done tongue in cheek. So, yeah, of course this had nothing to do with Hell. It's about being on the road with a rock 'n' roll band, and there's no better slice of heaven than that.

You know, something that doesn't get pointed out very often is that, obviously, AC/DC are so associated with heavy metal or hard rock, but there's a real undercurrent of R & B and gospel to AC/DC that nobody ever really talks about. "Get It Hot" is very R & B, very gospel-influenced. Like, I would love to hear some black girls in the background. Same thing for "If You Want Blood (You Got It)"; it's got this Humble Pie influence that you just want to hear when the chorus kicks in. And you can imagine on the chorus of "Highway to Hell" that sort of chorus of black girls kicking in instead of the band—that would've been very exciting. And I think they lose that a bit on *Back in Black* and as the band moves on. They become a little bit heavier and a little more hard rock. But *Highway to Hell* was actually a little more thumpy and has this super-cool, you know, R & B influence.

But back to the idea of building suspense, I know this is a weird idea, but I'm just going to lay this on you. To me, Mutt Lange's production style, the interesting thing about him is that it almost reminds me of techno music, in that Mutt makes everything so tight and pristine. AC/DC fell right into that really easily because the rhythm section tends to be very repetitive. It sets up the groove and it keeps it there and it gets your head bobbing.

And I think Mutt tightened up the screws on that even further. To me, in a weird way, AC/DC was like a group of drummers, because Mal's rhythm guitar is so percussive in nature and so tight. And Bon Scott actually was a drummer. In fact, Bon wanted to initially be the drummer in AC/DC and Angus was like, "No, we already got one of those. You're much better off doing this other thing, you know?" So you have this super-rhythmic, super-tight, very controlled rhythm section, a controlled band.

Which is like in techno music where they're setting up this groove, and suddenly the next element sort of kicks in. In techno music, it's usually the bass that makes a difference; it drops in and pulls out, creating this super drama. And that becomes one of AC/DC's big dramatic tricks. You hear that on songs like "Thunderstruck," which has the delayed bass after the

ABOVE: For AC/DC, evoking the word "Hell" really had nothing to do with Satan—it was about life on the road. "Highway to Hell" b/w "If You Want Blood (You've Got It)," Japan 1979.

TOP: With "Highway to Hell," AC/DC started a template for building suspense through a song. French jukebox promo single, 1979.

initially long setup, and in "Let's Get It Up," just to name two I can think of. On this album "Touch Too Much" does that and it's super effective; they probably do it better than any other rock band. But it's because they've set up the groove, and the groove is so strong before the bass even kicks in. And when the bass arrives, it just takes you up to the promised land.

FRENCH: That's an interesting point, but back to the earlier point about the titles—look at them. A lot of times people write songs based on titles. Bachman-Turner Overdrive is a perfect example. They come up with an idea and they go, "Let's write a song based upon 'taking care of business,'" you know, famous phrases. Well, look at "Highway to Hell"—*I'm on the highway to hell*—it's become such a great phrase. "Girls Got Rhythm," "Walk All Over You," "Touch Too Much," "Shot Down in Flames" . . . tell me if these are not incredibly charismatic titles. Titles that you don't forget. And they wrote great songs about them. That's part of the beauty of some songs. You remember these titles because they represent to you a time, a place, a feeling, or a cliché that you've used at some point in your life to describe an event.

POPOFF: And what did the character played by Bon Scott—if indeed he was playing a character—bring to the situation?

FRENCH: Well, although Bon wrote songs about sex and even snarled about sex and their songs were all full of innuendo, you didn't necessarily see their posters on the wall, thinking that they were sex objects, in the way that you would Mötley Crüe or Van Halen. AC/DC was kind of like schoolboy sex, if you get my drift. It was nod, nod, wink, wink, nasty school talk. But nothing so obvious as ripping clothes off groupies in the dressing room. Angus was never . . . the schoolboy uniform kind of precludes him from being a particularly sexy sex object. And Bon Scott, this is pre-MTV days, so how much did we see him either? We didn't see them very much before MTV came out. It was very limited exposure. As well, Bon Scott had not developed the frontman legend that could've happened had he stayed alive. Having said that, who knows if he would've been the right singer for *Back in Black*? Who knows if those songs would've been written for *Back in Black*? We'll never know the answer to that question.

TOLINSKI: Bon Scott knows how to sell a song like nobody's business. Outside of Bob Dylan, Bon did more with less than any rock singer I can think of. He's like a 1940s character actor who's always cast as the thug or the low life. Bon took that character and he sells it. I mean, he has no range, but he is so expressive on songs like "Dirty Deeds Done Dirt Cheap" or

"Highway to Hell." You absolutely buy everything that is coming out of his sort of lusty lip-smacking grin, you know? So on *Highway to Hell*, Mutt and the band tighten up the music, and at the same time Bon becomes a better singer, because Mutt is helping him, teaching him how to sing and how to project better. And suddenly all these great elements that were already there just get that much more potent.

POPOFF: Jay Jay, I just wanted to get this in, because one reason I wanted you involved in this, you have always told me, as did Dee Snider many times as well, that Twisted Sister were designed as sort of a synthesis between Judas Priest and AC/DC.

FRENCH: That is absolutely true. First Dee came in and heavied up the band, but when Mendoza came in around December '78, it kind of solidified it. Because Mendoza loved AC/DC and Priest, I would say that that's where we started changing our song list, and we added a ton of AC/DC and a ton of Priest and the fans loved it—loved it! And when Dee started writing and did "Shoot 'em Down"—that was a direct homage to AC/DC. I mean, it's pure— all it is is an AC/DC song written by Twisted Sister. So Priest and AC/DC absolutely had a dramatic effect on this band. I can tell you this. I'm an R & B guitar player, right? So I love that aspect of AC/DC. But I love the twin guitar tone of Judas Priest. We matched the guitar tones of Priest—because they were using particular Marshall amplifiers ganged all together—with the style, sexiness, and R & B of AC/DC. And that's the connection between Twisted Sister and AC/DC.

POPOFF: There are a number of pretty heavy songs on the record, but "Beating Around the Bush" deserves special mention.

TOLINSKI: Sure, I mean, "Beating Around the Bush" is fantastic. It's a bit of a rip of Fleetwood Mac "Oh Well," and I know many people have pointed that out. But what I also think is really interesting is, Angus and AC/DC, in general, were a huge influence on Van Halen. AC/DC is, without doubt, one of Eddie's favorite bands. In fact I tried to get those two together one time for an interview, but I just could never work it out. Eddie was really, really disappointed because he just loves Angus. But "Beating Around the Bush," for as much as it's taken from Fleetwood Mac's "Oh Well," I think it's also really the predecessor to those hopped-up eighties songs like "Hot for Teacher" that became really popular among all the hair metal bands.

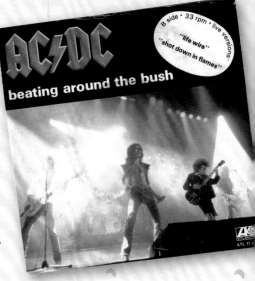

POPOFF: And Jay Jay, what's a favorite of yours on this record?

FRENCH: God, when I think of "Girls Got Rhythm," I get chills. It is an unbelievably electric track. Just from a visceral response, it's just got an incredibly great riff. It's not exactly your typical AC/DC riff, but it drives like crazy. The intro to "Walk All Over You" obviously slows the record down before the song gets going. It's unbelievably dramatic, again, when you look at how the record is constructed, how the songs are constructed and then woven through the course of the record. The pacing takes you up and it takes you down and it takes you up and it takes you down again. "Highway to Hell" sets the table, "Girls Got Rhythm" just kind of roars, and both "Walk All Over You" and "Touch Too Much" are so dramatic.

TOLINSKI: I agree, and I think "Touch Too Much" is really awesome, and a great guitar song, a great example of how Angus and Malcolm can be totally locked in, in terms of the rhythm playing. But what's really great about it, I think—and maybe this is where you start seeing the Lange influence—is that the first solo is cool. I mean, it's Angus doing sort of his Chuck Berry/Keith Richards chordal, double stop, rock 'n' roll guitar solo. But what's really good is that when they come back at the end, he ditches that and he does his piercing sort of single notes for the climax. And that really drives the song. At the end, Angus is much more of a stylist like B. B. King. It's not so much that he writes memorable solos like Jimmy Page—it's just his voice, his vibrato. The thing that creates excitement is literally his touch, which adds this extra drama to anything. Like with B. B., you can't really hum many of his guitar solos—it's just sort of the blues boxy thing. But the sound of the note itself just brings drama and excitement to anything he does. And Angus is the same way.

FRENCH: He's like a manic bluesman; he has that kind of manic vibrato. He has a blues foundation, but he goes for it. I mean, it's pentatonic scales— that's what he does. There's no Yngwie in there. There's not even any Glenn Tipton in there; he's not going for any of that. He's using a really basic pentatonic blues scale, but just done with the right feel. The feel is the key and the feel is immaculate. Whether he's on rhythm or on lead. But bottom line, AC/DC use the same three chords, but they do it in a very sly manner. They've always been smart about it. And I can tell you as a guitar player, Angus and Malcolm have found the perfect tone.

Predecessor to those hopped-up eighties songs like "Hot for Teacher." "Beating Around the Bush" b/w "Live Wire" and "Shot Down in Flames," Holland, 1980.

Typical AC/DC riff, but it drives like crazy. "Girls Got Rhythm" EP, with "If You Want Blood (You've Got It)," "Hell Ain't a Bad Place to Be," and "Rock 'N' Roll Damnation," United States, 1979.

POPOFF: Brad, we may as well end this with a look at the last song on the album, "Night Prowler." What are the particular charms of this quiet and yet disturbing closer?

TOLINSKI: The thing I liked about "Night Prowler" was that when Angus was asked about that a little bit later, he was like, "Oh, you know, people just make a big deal out of it. That song was simply like a romantic song about a man sneaking into his lover's room." But Bon is the very soul of perversion on that song [*laughs*]. Anybody who can imagine this is somehow Bon crooning a romantic song about a man sneaking into his lover's room has got quite an imagination.

Like I said, it's hard to know who wrote these lyrics because the band's not been clear about it. But I love lines in "Night Prowler" like *A rat runs down the alley/And a chill runs down your spine*. That's a great line [*laughs*]. And I think you see the difference between this record and *For Those About to Rock* is that "Night Prowler" is essentially a slow song, but it maintains its tension and a real momentum. And you lose a bit of that later, as the band goes down and the formula sort of runs out.

But also, I have to point out that the song is great if you want to really hear the powerful majesty of Malcolm's incredible rhythm guitar. On "Night Prowler," he's killing it. But, you know, AC/DC were huge Stones fans, and it's not far-flung to think that they thought they were doing their version of Mick's "Midnight Rambler." But I think they also knew that they were getting into dangerous territory, so it ends with, of all things, Bon going "Shazbut nanu nanu" [*laughs*], which is from a popular TV sitcom *Mork & Mindy*. Now, what *that* has to do with "Night Prowler," I have no freaking idea [*laughs*].

Jaap Edenhall, Amsterdam, November 12, 1979.

BACK IN BLACK

with DAVE ELLEFSON and PAUL KEHAYAS

All songs composed by
Angus Young, Malcolm Young,
and Brian Johnson

Personnel: Brian Johnson—
lead vocals; Angus Young—lead
guitar; Malcolm Young—rhythm
guitar, backing vocals; Cliff
Williams—bass, backing vocals;
Phil Rudd—drums

Released July 25, 1980

Recorded at Compass Point
Studios, Nassau, Bahamas

Produced by Robert John
"Mutt" Lange

It still seems improbable, surreal, that *Back in Black* is the second biggest selling album of all time, after *Thriller*, and just ahead of *The Dark Side of the Moon*, the soundtrack for *The Bodyguard* (never in a million years would I . . .), *Bat Out of Hell*, and *Their Greatest Hits* from the Eagles, mortal enemies of any self-respecting AC/DC fan.

And I suppose that's the magic of this record—that in some strange way AC/DC still feels like a band for the metalheads. I mean, sure, "You Shook Me All Night Long" halfway panders, but there's nothing particularly compromising about "Back in

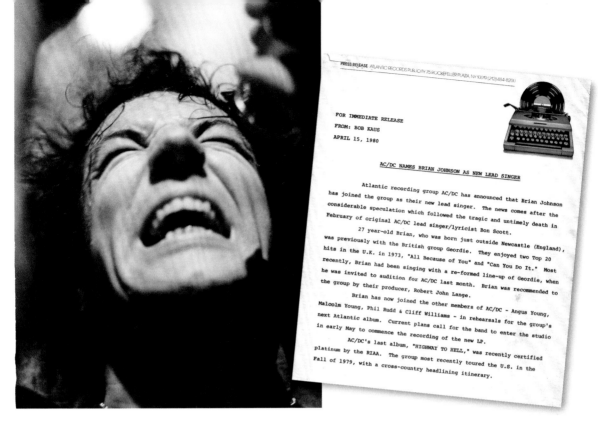

FOR IMMEDIATE RELEASE
FROM: BOB KAUS
APRIL 15, 1980

AC/DC NAMES BRIAN JOHNSON AS NEW LEAD SINGER

Atlantic recording group AC/DC has announced that Brian Johnson has joined the group as their new lead singer. The news comes after the considerable speculation which followed the tragic and untimely death in February of original AC/DC lead singer/lyricist Bon Scott.

27 year-old Brian, who was born just outside Newcastle (England), was previously with the British group Geordie. They enjoyed two Top 20 hits in the U.K. in 1973, "All Because of You" and "Can You Do It." Most recently, Brian had been singing with a re-formed line-up of Geordie, when he was invited to audition for AC/DC last month. Brian was recommended to the group by their producer, Robert John Lange.

Brian has now joined the other members of AC/DC - Angus Young, Malcolm Young, Phil Rudd & Cliff Williams - in rehearsals for the group's next Atlantic album. Current plans call for the band to enter the studio in early May to commence the recording of the new LP.

AC/DC's last album, "HIGHWAY TO HELL," was recently certified platinum by the RIAA. The group most recently toured the U.S. in the Fall of 1979, with a cross-country headlining itinerary.

Black," and certainly "Hells Bells" is a flat-out heavy metal rocker as dark as the sober wrapping around it. But the fascinating part is, dig further, and for as much a part of the pop culture fabric that this record supposedly is, most passersby wouldn't know a heck of a lot about it past those three songs.

And that's what makes *Back in Black* more for the music fan purists than anything else in the catalog, and quite deep into it. But again, the cover's all black, there are no pictures of the band, the songs aren't even in order on the back, and then, more materially, this new guy singing is arguably less accessible than the old guy. I'm serious about that—sure, any gathering of AC/DC scholars might point to Brian Johnson's added melodic range, and his propensity to use it, over and above Bon Scott's, but it's still a paint stripper of a voice and what he's saying contains mostly menace.

So all of these things, even these arguably inconsequential visual cues, work in concert to create a record that again, which somehow feels more cult than its massive numbers—26 million certified around the world, and estimates beyond certification upward to 50 million—would suggest.

Further acceptance by me an' the buds, who of course were all in turmoil over the forced necessity of the band getting a new singer, came readily from the fact that the record is pretty much uniformly heavy, supported most convincingly by the aforementioned "Hells Bells," "Given the Dog a Bone" (with its corkscrew riff), the brooding "Let Me Put My Love into

MAIN: This new guy singing is arguably less accessible than the old guy. Sure, there's more melodic range, but it's still a paint stripper of a voice.

INSET: Atlantic press release announcing the hiring of Brian Johnson.

OPPOSITE: More for the music fan purists than anything else in the catalog—the cover's all black, there are no photos of the band, and the songs aren't even listed in order.

You," and finally "Have a Drink on Me," all joyous cymbal crashes and headbanged groove.

Which, well, brings up a point. Apropos of nothing, me and my sullen bed-headed buddies were in grade eleven, grade twelve, when *Back in Black* rolled down our rural highways like a hearse. And I gotta tell ya, this record had an insane ability to make teenagers chuck down drinks. At bush parties, around the car, in the car, strolling down the middle of the street, in culverts, down the riverbank, at tense house parties . . . but I suspect this was the case all over the world. To reiterate, there was just something about the stone-faced look of the damn record. The negative space shroud that is *Back in Black*'s wrapper underscored a backstory of death due to drink, of fatalism, of cold, even of suicide in a sense, that made booze seem like necessary medicine for those just learning to get hammered. Drinking took on an elevated purpose—it was now a ritual conducted in funereal respect to Bon.

Before we move on, I gotta say I'll forever be bitter about how Mutt Lange wrecked a perfectly good band called Def Leppard, and then by proxy countless more guitar-charged acts, which, ill advised, would seek that horrible, doomed-to-be-dated sound throughout the eighties. But, man, *Back in Black* sounds plush and rich and analog, oddly, compared to the all-business knob job applied to *Highway to Hell*.

Which is why—one more personal reminiscence, if you'll indulge me—*Back in Black* was our go-to stereo test record when we needed to raise the stakes, o'er at the local hi-fi and record shop I worked at after school. Sure, we couldn't drop needle on "Hells Bells" for old folks, but the recently graduated lunch-bucket brigade suddenly making those big union bucks up the hill? It was routine to have them drop five, seven grand—I even remember one guy spending a cool twenty thousand on whatever it was . . . Yamaha 3020 receiver, Bose 901s, Klipschorns, JBL L300s with the glass tops. And what made it so easy (play it in your head now, please) was having "Hells Bells" unfurl before our ears, shaking the place from the basement up—bell, guitars, drums, bass, and finally the voice of that swarthy biker-type guy whispering in your ear that you only live once.

And so therein lies yet another source or signifier of this record's magic, one additional sullen, stupid-shouldered deep dimensional source of cool, which, again, somehow makes this record feel, incongruously, like a dark, intimate, hard rock experience, almost a bedroom album, and not a massive braying, loud party crashed by the whole world. *Back in Black*'s hooks sunk in deep and meaningful, but one supposes, the meaning is personal to every one of those 50 million people who partook of the experience.

POPOFF: New era for AC/DC, but first we must close the chapter on the old—what are your memories about the death of Bon Scott?
ELLEFSON: There were two guys who died when I was growing up that just absolutely shook my life to the core, and those were Sid Vicious and Bon Scott. I was still in Minnesota, didn't move to California until 1983. In 1980, I was probably fifteen, going on sixteen, and so that was a huge moment of my musical growth, my musical journey, and the bands and artists and musicians that I listened to in those two years would eventually shape the rest of my life. I was in high school, and I remember it was cold, kind of a cold, dark lonely season, even for Minnesota.

And I remember hearing it, and there just being this feeling of loneliness. As a fan, I felt this grief, like, "Oh my God, my favorite band." Because at this point they hadn't become a huge band. They weren't everybody's band yet. They were still my band, and I'd just seen them play in Sioux Falls with Cheap Trick, and I was just totally and completely enthralled with all things AC/DC. I mean, they probably were at that moment, my absolute favorite band. So, when Bon died, it was definitely . . . it was the shot heard around the world.

Now that seems familiar . . . Brian Johnson gives his Geordie bassist a hoist on the French picture sleeve of "Electric Lady" b/w "Geordie Stomp," 1973.

POPOFF: Paul, how did you and your buddies react to the new guy?
KEHAYAS: Well, we accepted him a lot better than hearing that Jon Anderson and Rick Wakeman were being replaced by the Buggles, let's put it that way. I had no idea who he was. It would take me years before I would hear Geordie. It happened so quickly, because Bon dies in February and this album is out by the summer. But as soon as anyone heard it . . . I went with my friend down to Records on Wheels, we picked it up, and then we went home and listened to it. And as soon as the bell came on, okay, this is interesting. And then the first riff of "Hells Bells" comes on, and then Angus, and then we get into the groove, and as soon as Brian starts singing,

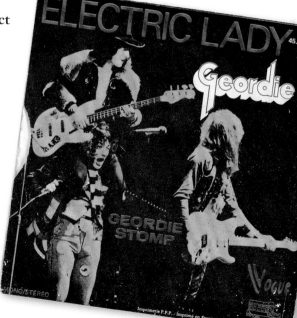

(continued on page 108)

Toledo Motor Speedway Jam II with ZZ Top, Humble Pie, and Sammy Hagar, Toledo, Ohio, August 17, 1980. This would mark the last time AC/DC raised the curtain as an opening act until "SARSstock" in Toronto in July 2003.

TOLEDO SPEEDWAY JAM
II TOLEDO OHIO

FM 104
Chicago Productions
Belkin Productions
ANNOUNCE

ZZ TOP

AC/DC

SAMMY HAGAR

HUMBLE PIE

Special Guest
To Be Announced!

plus
800 KEGS of BEER!
WILL BE SOLD
DRINKING AGE 18 IN OHIO - BRING I.D.

...ay, AUGUST 17 - 11:30
...tes open at 9 a.m.

...$12.50 advance $14.50 day of show

TICKETS DON'T GET IN!
...VERTISED OUTLETS ONLY!

AUGUST 17

TOLEDO SPEEDWAY JAM TWO
TOLEDO OHIO 81710G.A.
DATE/EVENT CODE

Z Z TOP

11:30A SUN AUG 17 1980
GATES OPEN 9:00AM
NO CANS/BOTTLES/FIREWKS
NO REFUNDS/RAIN OR SHINE

TOLEDO SPEEDWAY JAM 2
GEN
$12.50
08/16

(continued from page 105)

you're sold. But you were sold pretty much with the first riff. It comes on, and you're like, oh, this is amazing. When Brian comes in, he doesn't sound out of context—it works. And then as soon as the chorus hits, you're lying down, you're rolling over dead—you've been won.

ELLEFSON: Oh, "Hells Bells" was great. That was the needle-drop song, just like "Riff Raff" on the live album, "Rock 'n' Roll Damnation" on *Powerage*, and "Highway to Hell" on the previous record. AC/DC were masters of really hooking you with a killer song right out the gate. And "Hells Bells" has this kind of theater production, almost similar to what Pink Floyd would come up with, with the bell at the beginning [*laughs*]. And then the riff comes in, followed by this smooth bass. It was almost orchestral the way it came in. And this is back in the day and age when the bigger your speakers were, the better your stereo sounded. So you're just getting your stereo warmed up, and all of a sudden you've got this subwoofer-level bass coming out with this killer guitar riff laying over it.

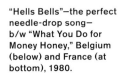

"Hells Bells"—the perfect needle-drop song—b/w "What You Do for Money Honey," Belgium (below) and France (at bottom), 1980.

But then the biggest thing was, what does this new singer sound like? Because I had just kind of gotten to know Bon Scott. And there were things about Bon that were very rough around the edges that in a lot of ways, you know, probably would've kept them from really big mainstream success, just because of the sort of rowdy nature of his voice. And now suddenly Brian Johnson was acceptable. It was funny—I didn't listen to Brian the same way I heard Bon. Bon had this authority as sort of the barroom brawler, like we're gonna kick some ass and get in a fight tonight. And suddenly Brian Johnson was singing these songs that maybe your girlfriend would listen to because it was Brian singing them. Brian had a seductive nature to how he sang those lyrics.

POPOFF: Paul, how about a little more on the personality of Brian?

KEHAYAS: He's part of the gang. He wasn't the aloof older brother who came and dropped in and wrote songs about his life and informed the boys about how things could be. Bon Scott was, as I said earlier, the older brother, getting you drunk with a few beers, telling you stories about what he's just been up to. Brian is the co-conspirator, right? He's one of you. He's shielding his eyes with a cap—it was always rumored that it was because of baldness—but it made him look guilty, as well as blue collar, that sort of workmanlike, roll up your sleeves, we're gonna rock. But he was not a rock star—he was one of you.

POPOFF: And one of them too, right? One of the band.
KEHAYAS: Yes, one of them, exactly; so now they were a pack. It was the Supremes as opposed to Diana Ross and the Supremes. It was always implied that the star was the singer, along with the lead guitarist. Now the lead guitarist was the only star. It made it easy for that transition to happen, for Angus to become the guitar hero and pretty much the focal point of the group—that transition, as underscored by the album covers, was now complete.

Angus takes a cuppa while on tour for *Back in Black*, October 1980.

POPOFF: We've got Mutt Lange back recording for the band, but there are some other interesting circumstances when it comes to recording.
KEHAYAS: Yes, well, first off, *Back in Black* is everything that you wanted this album to be but were afraid it wouldn't. And it was a natural follow-up. I have the feeling that, because they had no time to grieve, the band operated as a band. This was recorded in—of all places—Compass Point Studios in the Bahamas. Terry Manning worked there. But at that point, Chris Blackwell operated it, so you can imagine a bunch of guys in shorts creating this. And from what I understand of the recording, this nonsense about Bon Scott singing *Back in Black* stuff, I've never heard one that hasn't been debunked.

From what I understand, the riff to "Back in Black," Angus had been toying around with that for years, and a couple other riffs may have been there, but I don't think it was cohesive and in song form yet. And certainly the lyrics were not worked on until Brian got there. He was writing in the studio while they were recording. But this record was done rather quickly. I think this was their therapy; this is something you want to do for a fallen brother. And you have something to prove. Your record company is also hoping that the record would do something for you. It must've been a very strange situation, but it's the one time that they pulled something out of their ass and it happened to be gold.

MAIN: Le Bourget, Paris, November 29, 1980.

POPOFF: Let's dig in a little further and look at the songs. Walk me through the album, maybe with an eye of how it is sequenced or how it hangs together. Because that's one thing about it—there's a uniformity, which perhaps comes from the simple arrangements.

ELLEFSON: Yeah, well, one of the things about this record, I'll just say it—it was a perfect ten. Perfect songs, perfect performances, perfect the way it was recorded, the flow of the record, the way that the song list lays out from "Hells Bells" all the way to "Rock and Roll Ain't Noise Pollution." The album is absolutely perfect on every level. It starts dark and haunting with "Hells Bells" and then the key changes with "Shoot to Thrill," which I think is in the key of A. And that's a big thing, that I now know—songs changing key change your mood or change your optimism level. So we transition from "Hells Bells" into this happy, upbeat, more traditional AC/DC kind of song.

"What Do You Do for Money Honey" is sort of Bon Scott lyrically, because it's talking about chicks and it's sex and it's kind of nasty and dirty and forbidden. And "Given the Dog a Bone" is another classic rocker, like something you would hear on *Powerage*. "Let Me Put My Love into You" is like, "I should turn the stereo down. My parents

shouldn't hear this song." And then you flip the vinyl over, and you're into "Back in Black," and suddenly here's the anthem, the upbeat anthem.

"Have a Drink on Me" is a classic drinking song; even if we were all too young to drink, we would all raise a glass at the party. "Shake a Leg," that reminded me of "The Rocker," just kind of rowdy and obviously there's the visual connection with Angus. And then "Rock and Roll Ain't Noise Pollution" was kind of this "screw you" authority song. And it starts off with Brian with a sort of drag of the cigarette, okay, [*sucking sound*]; it had everything that was dirty and wrong about rock 'n' roll that we all loved it, because it just sounded so right.

POPOFF: Then there's the elephant in the room: "You Shook Me All Night Long." One for the girls?
ELLEFSON: It is, yeah [*laughs*]. And it's funny, because that's pretty much the least provocative song. There's some pretty flat-out almost pornographic kind of lyrics on this record. And it's also odd that the two kind of real

INSET: Perfect songs, perfect performances, perfect flow all the way to "Rock and Roll Ain't Noise Pollution." Australian single b/w "Hells Bells," 1980.

money-shot songs on the record, they're track one and track two on side two. Traditionally, or at least in this day and age, those songs would kick off side one.

KEHAYAS: I agree. It's ironic that it's the first song that got women into the band, and it's also, statistically, one of the top stripper songs of all time. But it's a gateway to a larger audience, and it's got a fantastic solo in it and it's totally deserving as a single. I mean, it's got one of the band's greatest hooks and the drums are huge. And, let's face it, it's an allegory in the great tradition of car songs, you know, car as ode to woman and woman as ode to car. It works on so many different levels. And the way it ends is fantastic too, ending on the fifth, you know? It sounds like it should go right back to the G, but it ends on the D. It was a brilliant way to end the song. And it would also be great for DJs because it would set up their next track. It was a great thing to hear on radio. I was always a champion of that song.

POPOFF: And the title track is of course the other big track. "Hells Bells," "You Shook Me All Night Long," and "Back in Black" are massive, super-famous songs, but they're actual all pretty much equal in stature, correct?

KEYAHAS: Sure. And "Back in Black"—I still don't know how to play it right. I still do not play it right. It's too monumental, you know? I mean, I'm always afraid of screwing it up. It is a colossal work of brilliance from the beginning of the pick scratching and the two clicks on the high-hat, and then they're right in. It is the definition of riff rock. There is no fat on this record. There's no fat on that song. They're not known for middle eights, this band, but the bridges are fantastic, the transition from the chorus into the vamp where it gets all jazzy all of a sudden. That shuffle section is brilliant, as is the way it transitions back to the beat. Again, rock-solid drumming, rock-solid performance, bass doing exactly what it needs to do. Deceptively simple, but this thing shuffles, and you can still dance to it. I defy anybody who hears this on the radio, who doesn't want to crank the stereo. It's just is one of those moments.

I have to say that this all becomes flesh and blood when I go to see them, Maple Leaf Gardens, July 28, 1980. Nine thousand people. We see this thing, which is the bell. And as I found out later on, that's the actual bell on the record. They were trying to record a church bell, but of course had technical difficulties involving some birds getting in the way, and they actually went to where they were making this bell for the road, and they recorded it. It's tuned to A, right? So they struck it and they dropped it into the track. This is the same bell. It was a ton—that's how much it weighed, and later on this would become the standard way of opening the concerts.

But to see this come to flesh, to have this happen in front of me, and to have it unfold as this machine plays . . . I think I had Angus's sweat raining down on me every time he shook his head. I remember walking out of the Gardens and going down the stairs and I felt the back of my head, and my hair was stuck together. I've never had that experience. I was telling my buddy, "Look at this!"

But it was fantastic. It was me and my friend, both at thirteen, and a whole bunch of guys who looked like Lemmy—bikers and us. But half-filled, right? Because that place held almost eighteen thousand people. The record had only come out three days earlier and obviously hadn't blown up yet. But I mean, it translated well. If you look at the set list, they do quite a few things, about four or five songs, from that record. But really, honestly, I don't think anyone in that audience left wondering what happened to Bon, which is sad, obviously. But that's where it starts. It starts off like the album, like, this is a moment of reflection, and then now we're going to continue with a legacy that is brand new.

POPOFF: *Back in Black* worked well live also because there was something accessible about the album. And yet I can't put my finger on what it is.

ELLEFSON: No, but you're right it is. See, we were playing in bands, and mostly we'd play a lot of cover tunes to get gigs. So suddenly, here's AC/DC with an album that actually has songs that you could play, and you could actually get hired [*laughs*]. You could play these songs, and legitimately, you just didn't have to play .38 Special and Eddie Money and Skynyrd and all the kind of typical AOR songs in order to get gigs. Suddenly, we could play these songs, and we could play the high school dances and not have superintendents and principals looking at us sideways getting ready to throw us off the stage for our set list choice. Which was probably one of the greater benefits of *Back in Black*. It became kind of this teenage prom dance record that you could still get away with. And that was clever; I thought that was cool.

OPPOSITE (FROM TOP): "You Shook Me All Night Long" would prove a gateway to a larger audience. Here, it's backed by "Have a Drink on Me" on the Italian release, 1980.

"What Do You Do for Money Honey"—here the B-side of the Aussie "You Shook Me All Night Long"—is lyrically a little bit of Bon Scott—nasty, dirty, and forbidden.

"You Shook Me All Night Long" US promo single, 1980.

"You Shook Me All Night Long" b/w "Have a Drink on Me," Germany, 1980.

And I mean, you couldn't go to any kind of high school teenage party and not hear this record. And regardless that it became popular, it was still a great kickass hard rock record and AC/DC were still cool. They hadn't risen into the stratosphere of being untouchable yet. And there was something kind of cool that everybody is starting to discover something that I had already discovered. And part of me, there was a sort of pride of ownership [*laughs*], that "See, I told you. I knew these guys were great. I've been telling you about them for two years now."

POPOFF: Dave, you saw the band on this tour as well. How did that go?
ELLEFSON: When I went to see *Back in Black*, it was at the Met Center near Minneapolis, September 11, 1980, and Blackfoot was opening and Rickey Medlocke was killer. And AC/DC comes out, big arena headliner, and suddenly, you know, just a couple years earlier, I was front row, down in the front, I could almost touch AC/DC. And they could see me and I could see them. Now, I'm sitting several sections back, I'm kind of up in the nosebleeds, and suddenly my little favorite pet band has become everybody's band and they're this big global sensation.

Part of me was happy because they were successful; I knew they would be around now for a while, to make records. But at the same time, you know, *Back in Black* was the end of the magic for me because I didn't find *For Those About to Rock* to be a record that connected with me. All of a sudden, my girlfriend had a new boyfriend, and they're going to go see AC/DC together [*laughs*]. It was like, fuck you, you know? All of a sudden they became a band that the same people who listened to Supertramp *Breakfast in America*, now they like AC/DC.

But I never turned my back on AC/DC. Later we would do shows with them, and they still held this great moment in my life. But even as we did shows with them later in 2001, the songs that really resonated with me were the songs that resonated with me back in these days I talk about as a teenager. "Bad Boy Boogie," all those songs. The songs that I wanted to go out and watch them play in the stadiums as an adult were the same ones that had that emotional impact on me as a teenager.

POPOFF: Back to the record itself, the album cover was the opposite of that party vibe we all loved in the songs, totally incongruous with the music inside, right?
ELLEFSON: For sure. It did have a somber tone about it—it's dark, it's black, the singer just died. And then needle drop it and the first thing you

hear is this haunting bell. It was an intriguing era for the band. In a lot of ways, they took something tragic and wove this really clever kind of narrative that would lead you into this next record. It was very well done, because it was almost like this seamless transition out of darkness into these really spirited party songs. And, yeah, I guess in hindsight as adults, you look back on it and realize how cleverly it was done.

It didn't happen like David Lee Roth to Sammy Hagar with *5150*. It was pretty much a clearly defined change of style with Van Halen. But with AC/DC, I remember people talking about it. Many of my peers would reference, "Well, we can change our singer. I mean, AC/DC, and Van Halen did it." And quite honestly, they're the only two bands that ever did it successfully [*laughs*]. And the fact that Bon had died, it wasn't like they fired him. Essentially AC/DC got a hall pass, kind of like they got the credit card handed to them going, "Hey, we're your fans, we'll stand by you no matter what you do now. Because we still love you as fans."

KEHAYAS: This is in honor of a fallen brother. They wanted it to be totally black, but as a concession to the record company, it's embossed and the band logo is outlined, right? Interesting to note, when they put this out on CD, they made the logo completely white or, in some cases, at least bordered in white, and the album title in white. And it filled the square more, meaning it was larger in proportion to the black space. The original intention got lost during the initial CD creation.

But then again, I don't know, that original cover was also really cool to the heads, and I was probably lumped in with all those cats. What would you have wanted? A record that looks like an Oingo Boingo cover? I didn't want color, I wanted stark. I think of that as a winter album, even though it came out in the summer, probably because it reached its saturation point during the winter of '80–'81. But this album cover doesn't embarrass the band, nor do I think it puts a cloak down on them. The point is [that] you forget what the album cover looks like as soon as you put the needle down, even if it starts with a funeral bell. It's kind of dancing at a gravesite. So, yeah, it's got death written into it, but it transcends the death into a wake. And I think that's the whole point of it—*Back in Black* is a wake.

Radio flyer announcing the February 27, 1981, gig at Myer Music Bowl, Sydney.

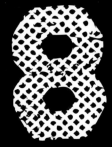
FOR THOSE ABOUT TO ROCK WE SALUTE YOU

with **PHIL CARSON, JAY JAY FRENCH,** and **BRAD TOLINSKI**

All songs composed by
Angus Young, Malcolm Young,
and Brian Johnson

Personnel: Brian Johnson—lead
vocals; Angus Young—lead guitar;
Malcolm Young—rhythm guitar,
backing vocals; Cliff Williams—
bass, backing vocals; Phil
Rudd—drums

Released November 23, 1981

Recorded on Mobile One at
H.I.S. Studio, Paris, and Family
Studio, Paris

Produced by Robert John
"Mutt" Lange

FOR THOSE ABOUT TO ROCK

Iron Maiden, Angel Witch, Quartz, Tygers of Pan Tang, Riot, four middle-finger records from the fiery Van Halen, *Ace of Spades*, *Fire of Unknown Origin*, *Heaven and Hell*, and even *Mob Rules* (but then not particularly, ahem, *British Steel*) . . . AC/DC suddenly had a lot of competition for the eyeballs and eardrums of excitable and surly male teens in 1981. And by a massed measure of nonplussed unanimity, *For Those About to Rock* didn't cut mustard, the attuned and knowledgeable fan sensing the reality that AC/DC had yawed sideways, yawned from exhaustion, and turned in a yawner.

Relative yawner that is. For when the rest of the weakly competitive eighties albums shuffled in, *For Those About to Rock* would rise somewhat in stature, sort of a son of *Back in Black* that was viewed more positively than negatively. It's a reassessment that could only happen because *Back in Black* continued to steamroll through the decade, almost irrationally becoming more and more important in rock history (the insanity surrounding *Appetite*

OPPOSITE: A record that basks in a light so blinding eventually glows with a golden tan itself—a metallic bronze even.

BELOW: *For Those About to Rock* could have been seen as incredible manna from heaven. But the base suddenly turned demanding.

for Destruction a generation later being an apt comparative). The idea I'm proposing is that a record that basks in a light so blinding eventually glows with a golden tan itself, a metallic bronze even.

To be sure, the performances and production all over *For Those About to Rock* are in line with those of *Back in Black*, AC/DC evolving over a second Brian-era record into a slightly laid-back band of patient strummers. This plush and reclined vibe is underscored by Mutt Lange's production, which, if anything, is even more pillowy and analog than that of *Back in Black*, which though it had been a move in that direction, now looked like the riotous violence of a different band altogether.

The production of *For Those . . .* is one thing hard-assed fans complained about, but I think it's a proxy fight for the tempos, rather, and the songwriting, both of which droop. Point being, I would have been fine with these fat drums and wallowing and wide-open spaces with songs screaming to be heard. Instead, AC/DC were seen by me and many as settling on second-guessed and self-aware concepts and lyrics—and then mapping out passive soundtracks on which to drape their much ados about nothing.

I mean, you have to give fans credit. On paper, and with some level of scientific detachments, *For Those About to Rock* was kinda more of the same, which could be seen as incredible manna from heaven. But the base suddenly turned demanding, knocking the band down a notch. Of course, amid this, one could be excused for not noticing, given that the band continued their relentless rise in the press and in ticket sales for years to come. But again, the qualifier would have to be that the tour for the current record—along with the tours for the subsequent records of 1983, 1985, and 1988—were in essence multiple victory laps for what the band had so boldly achieved on *Back in Black*.

POPOFF: Let's begin with a general assessment of *For Those About to Rock*. How does this second record of the Brian Johnson era compare with its predecessor, *Back in Black*?

TOLINSKI: Well, I was thinking about this, how to talk about these records. And, you know, one way to look at *Highway to Hell*, *Back in Black*, and *For Those About to Rock*, they are sort of the Mutt Lange trilogy. And the way I was thinking about it is that booze and cocaine are actually an excellent idea until they aren't. AC/DC was sort of like this greasy, drinking barroom band, and what Mutt did—metaphorically—was add a line of cocaine that straightens them out a little bit while keeping things fun. Mutt Lange comes in and adds that extra polish and extra bit of sharpness. They did that for three records, and you sort of hear the arc. You know, on *Highway to Hell* they'd had a couple of shots and the coke is just starting to kick in, and there's a lot of energy. They're a little sharper than they were in the past. *Back in Black*, the coke has really sort of kicked in, and then *For Those About to Rock*, they're drunk, they're high, and losing a little steam and becoming a bit boring—they're repeating their stories and are a little obnoxious [*laughs*].

FRENCH: I thought to myself at the time, how the hell are you going to succeed *Back in Black*? Like, how in the world is that going to happen? So here's my thinking. If *Highway to Hell* was the equivalent of *Revolver*, and *Back in Black* was the equivalent of *Sgt. Pepper*, then *For Those About to Rock* was the equivalent of *Magical Mystery Tour*. Which is, how do you follow *Sgt. Pepper*?

For Those About to Rock was predictably overproduced and it wasn't anywhere as authentic. The song itself, "For Those About to Rock," is a great song. I'm not saying it isn't a great song—it *is* a great song. But the record just felt like it was forced. And it didn't have the same visceral impact. If you think about the tracks that were played constantly in bars and clubs, there were only two tracks, "For Those About to Rock" and "Evil Walks." And that really does say something. Because it's based upon kids going up to the DJ booth; in the old days, that's what they did. They go to the DJ booth to get these songs played.

On *Back in Black* almost every single song was requested. But on *For Those About to Rock*, they were not. And here's something interesting: Twisted Sister played "You Shook Me." That was a no-brainer. You kind of had to do it. But we also played "Evil Walks." We did not play "For Those About to Rock." We thought that "Evil Walks" was just more sinister and darker-sounding, and so we concentrated on playing it and enjoyed playing the song.

But it did not go over anywhere near as well as "Whole Lotta Rosie" and all the other AC/DC songs we would play. It just didn't have the same impact. It's kind of like, they lost their R & B mojo, to a degree, right? And the record, of course, sold very well, but it wasn't *Thriller*. It was *Bad*. Look, who has a *Thriller* and who has a *Back in Black*? Who has a *Sgt. Pepper*? Only the greatest bands in the world. So I don't take away anything. *Stay Hungry* was our *Sgt. Pepper*, and look what happened to us. It's really

hard. Look at *Guns N' Roses*. They have *Appetite for Destruction*. They started *out* with *Sgt. Pepper* [*laughs*] and have been doing nothing but *Let It Be*'s ever since.

POPOFF: Indeed, the title track was a big deal on this album, and I remember as a teenager it sure turned some heads. It's the most atmospheric and open architecture thing they'd done to this point, right?

TOLINSKI: Sure, well, I think the first three songs are all pretty killer. But I agree, "For Those About to Rock" is really quite different and super-theatrical, almost like an Alice Cooper song for them, with that stop/start thing. And then "Put the Finger on You" is also different for AC/DC. It's almost like one of those Mike Chapman/Nicky Chinn pop songs. It just felt like the most successful, most poppy version of AC/DC that I'd ever heard to that point. It really sounds like one of these British glam pop songs.

POPOFF: Well, now that you bring that up, how would you describe that technique that drives that song?

TOLINSKI: That sort of plucking sound? That's an interesting sort of rhythmic effect that ends up becoming part of Angus's signature sound, and you also hear it at the beginning of "For Those About to Rock." It's a new technique that Angus is using, where, instead of using the pick, he's sort of plucking the strings with his fingers. And it's something that Eddie Van Halen picked up on and started doing after all of this as well.

But I also want to go back—because I am a guitar nerd—and talk about Malcolm on the title track. Malcolm Young is one of rock's greatest virtuosos, in a very strange way that doesn't get talked about much. On that song you're sort of drawn in by Angus's finger-plucking rhythm. But really, if you listen to the opening chords, when Malcolm comes in, you hear, right away, underneath the finger plucking. He's totally in the groove, but he's doing something a little bit different every time. You think he's doing the same thing, but he keeps moving around the beat just a little bit, in different ways. And it totally adds to the rhythm of this thing and totally pulls you in. Angus is a fantastic, exciting guitar player, but Malcolm is the heart and soul in the sound of AC/DC. And Angus will tell you that any chance that he gets.

POPOFF: It's a real slow burn of a song, isn't it?

FRENCH: It's über-dramatic, but I have to tell you, when I heard that track for the first time, and it finally kicked in, it didn't kick in enough for me. I thought it was dramatic, but it didn't close the deal. Not the same way that "Back in Black" closed the deal. Not the same way that "Highway to Hell" closed the deal. It seemed to get me to ninety percent, and then it became cliché. I don't know how else to put it. Maybe I'm too cynical. I just thought it was too much of an obvious track and not real—that's how it hit me. It doesn't mean that over time I haven't learned to enjoy it and like it more. But I just felt it wasn't a record that needed to be made, and it just wasn't quite there. And then as a whole, the album was overproduced. There's a whole thing about the richer you get, the heavier the production, the less records you sell. The more money you spend, the less you make back. It's an inverse proportion.

POPOFF: What does Brian Johnson bring to the party?

TOLINSKI: To bring up Van Halen again, Bon Scott was, to some degree, like David Lee Roth—not the most technique but genuine personality. You know, you could really feel the person, and he was this force of nature. And Brian is sort of like Sammy Hagar. He's a more proficient singer, he's popular, a little more radio-friendly, but you don't quite believe the jokes as much. And you certainly don't believe in the character quite as much either. And I think that, again, it worked on *Back in Black*, but the successor sort of suffers a bit because the joke and the excitement are wearing thin.

FRENCH: First of all, Brian's a great singer. And I really wish I knew how much Brian wrote, because there's a lot of controversy in regard to giving credit to Brian. But Brian is also a salt-of-the-earth guy and I think that shines through. I'll give you an example. Brian has always been a wonderful friend to Twisted Sister. We were playing in Newcastle in 1983, and he sent a couple of guys who work for him to pick us up at the hotel. We spent the day at his house. And he ordered food in for us, and then we went to see him jam with a little blues band. It was so freaking cute, Martin. He was playing with a blues band, in a corner bar, in Newcastle, in between AC/DC tours. And we went with him to this bar, and there were all these dudes who looked like they were ninety-nine years old. And there's Brian at a local pub singing songs.

And then he came on stage with us at a rhythm and blues festival in England about seven years ago. And he did "Whole Lotta Rosie" with us, which I have on video. He was so great and so nice. At the end of the show, he came off stage and we were standing back by the trailer, and my bass player said, "Would you call my girlfriend? Because she's such a big fan of yours." And he gets on the phone, "Hello, lady, it's Brian."

And she basically like doesn't believe it's Brian. And she's saying, "Fuck you, you drunk, fucking idiot. I don't know who you are. I don't need my boyfriend telling some guy to tell you he's you. Fuck you." So Brian looks up and he has this puzzled look on his face. He hands back the phone, "I don't think she believes me, laddie." At one point, ten other people see him doing this on the phone, and there's a line in front of Brian. Of people who wanted him to call friends and say, "This is Brian Johnson from AC/DC." And you know what? He did. He did it for everybody. And he took me out to lunch the next day with my daughter. He's a wonderful guy. But what does he bring? Amazing voice. A perfect foil for Angus. Not sexy, kind of like a longshoreman sings heavy metal. You know, but not threatening.

But it's really something how that all even happens, this awesome and life-changing direction that eventually broke into Brian Johnson and *Back in Black*. I mean, you couldn't have made a more perfect album. They were up against the wall. How do you replace someone like Bon Scott, who was so iconic and great? Not only replace him, but almost evaporate everything that came before.

But those things, Martin, happened not in a vacuum. They happened because of confluences of circumstance. And the confluence of circumstances that led AC/DC to *Back in Black*, after this progression that leads you through *Highway to Hell*, could never have been created by man deliberately. It's kind of like the Beatles didn't have Kennedy assassinated, but getting over his assassination was one of the foundations of the Beatles' success. We were looking for a reason to be happy. You know, they didn't have him killed, but they were the beneficiary of an extraordinary confluence of events. And AC/DC was a beneficiary of the same confluence of events. The fact that disco was finally dissolving, rock radio was finally waking up, nobody could have predicted it. They were the perfect band at the perfect place at the perfect time with the perfect music.

CARSON: Brian had a great rock 'n' roll sensibility, and a great tongue-in-cheek sense of humor. He's also a terrific performer, and that's what he brought to the band. Great singer, great songwriting ability, and he really made it happen with *Back in Black*. But they were all good; they worked their buns off the whole time. They were very focused on what they were trying to do. They put all their energies and all their money into it, and they made very, very little money in the early days. They cared about making the records work. They cared about their fans. That's what they did.

POPOFF: And it seems that they had found the perfect producer to match their ambitions. Yet I think we can all agree that it's not working as well. Although to these ears, the production on *For Those About to Rock* is quite similar to that of *Back in Black*.
CARSON: Mutt is a great producer, and the fact is, *For Those About to Rock* took rather a long time to make. And it was an expensive record, and it didn't achieve what it should've done. But I certainly don't blame Mutt for that.
TOLINSKI: You sort of hear Mutt's influence in a different way on this record. Take "Night of the Long Knives." I think music is changing at this point, you know? And they're trying to move with that a little bit. It's a little less heavy metal. You start getting into sort of that poppier, hair metal area. And I just don't know whether the band is totally feeling it. I mean, "Night of the Long Knives"—Mötley Crüe pretty much outright stole the opening riff for "Dr. Feelgood." But I think the chorus goes on a bit too long.

POPOFF: We should also talk about "Let's Get It Up," which I'd say is the second biggest song on the record.
TOLINSKI: Yes, "Let's Get It Up" is interesting. It's probably one of the slinkier and genuinely sexier songs that they've ever done. The experiment of AC/DC and Mutt Lange with Atlantic Records was to try to make the band a bit more radio-ready. But AC/DC is a funny band. I mean, Angus and Malcolm are very strong-willed guys. I've interviewed them many times, but I've never talked to either one about these particular songs. But it sounds a little bit on this record that they're giving it a shot, but it's half-hearted. I do love the riff in "Let's Get It Up." As I say, it's genuinely sexy as opposed to dirty [*laughs*]. You hear how Van Halen was influenced by AC/DC on this song. And you hear the seeds of Mutt Lange's work with Def Leppard. The sing-along choruses are big, but it starts feeling too clean and a bit pedestrian for AC/DC.

OPPOSITE: *For Those About to Rock* tour, Brendan Byrne Arena, East Rutherford, New Jersey, December 6, 1981.

The morning after the band's December 10, 1981, performance at Maple Leaf Gardens, the caption in the *Toronto Star* read, "A mighty roar from AC/DC's Angus Young, and 14,000 fans are in heavy metal heaven."

And I feel the same way about "Night of the Long Knives." They found a great chorus and they just sort of drove it into the ground. It starts out cool, but ultimately ends up being bit boring. And by the way, I think "Spellbound" might be one of the worst songs that they've ever done. This is where I just feel the drugs have kicked in, the coke is making everybody crazy. And I'm speaking about cocaine metaphorically. It's just a less good version of "Hells Bells." It's a little too slow, you know, where in "Hells Bells" the tempo is used to create tension. "Spellbound" sounds like they've run out of gas and they're playing behind the beat a bit too slowly.

POPOFF: *For Those About to Rock* **has sold less than a quarter the number of copies as** *Back in Black*. **Phil, you signed the band and you were there to see this miscalculation of having Atlantic issue** *Dirty Deeds Done Dirt Cheap* **in the US in the interim between** *Back in Black* **and** *For Those About to Rock*. **What went down there?**

CARSON: Yes, well, it was many years later, wasn't it? They decided to release *Dirty Deeds* in America, at totally the wrong time, because, in fact, they followed a Brian Johnson vocal with a Bon Scott vocal, which I think really had a negative impact on the development of the group. They had a huge hit with *Back in Black* and then record company greed manifested itself, and they found that they had an album that they had forgotten about

Probably one of the slinkier songs that AC/DC's ever done. "Let's Get It Up" b/w "Back in Black," Japan, 1982.

in the vaults and decided to put it out. Much against the band's wishes and my wishes. And I remember telling them at the time that if they did that they would create a new sales plateau for AC/DC, which would be far less than the what they had achieved with *Back in Black*. And of course, I was right.

POPOFF: And do you think it directly affected the sales of *For Those About to Rock*?

CARSON: Yeah, of course it did. It was madness to put that record out when they did. Absolutely a stroke of crass stupidity to put it out. The band didn't want it out, I didn't want it out, but the guys at Atlantic in New York—you know, Doug Morris in particular—I told him, this is a bad mistake to do this. And Doug's response was, "Well, you know, we've already made our numbers for this year. It's gonna affect our bonuses." And it will affect our bonuses, but it will also affect the career of the group. But, you know, they went ahead anyway.

I think we'd sold something like five million of *Back in Black*. I mean, it really just started to be the album it eventually became. And I remember Jack saying, "You know, we sold five million of *Back in Black*. The worst thing that can happen is we'll sell two million." And I said, "I think you're absolutely right. It will sell two million, but that will mean that's as far as the next album will possibly get." And no album after *Dirty Deeds* sold two million

in its initial phase. Obviously, some of them have gone on to achieve greater numbers than that because of the length of time, but it was a stupid mistake.

POPOFF: But also, as we've been alluding to, perhaps the follow-up just wasn't up to snuff.

TOLINSKI: Yeah, I almost wonder if the some of the songs or ideas might have been leftovers from *Back in Black*. Because that can happen sometimes. Some of them just feel a little like less-good versions of those other songs. I wish I could be a bit more positive, but like I said before, it's the best they could do. You know, it's returning to a formula. It's them trying to duplicate the success of *Back in Black* and it's just not working. They're probably exhausted and they're probably tired of working with each other. And the reason it wasn't as successful was that it just wasn't as good, and that's the truth.

FRENCH: I remember the CFO of Atlantic Records, Sheldon Vogel, told me an interesting statistic about AC/DC. One day when *Stay Hungry* had one-day record sales of 118,000 copies, he said to me, "Congratulations, you came in at number two to Prince," in the entire one-day sale of all records that day, in America, right?

And I'm thinking, "Wow." And I said, "Well, can you give me some perspective as to what that means? And he said, "Well, I can tell you that the biggest selling artist we've had is AC/DC." And I said, "Well, what are their records?" He said, in one eighteen-month stretch, from *Back in Black* through *For Those About to Rock*, including *Dirty Deeds* being re-released, they sold a million records a month for eighteen months straight.

Now, that is a statistic, Martin, that is kind of mind-blowing. This is why they released *Dirty Deeds* again, because they needed a bridge record between, I guess, *Back in Black* and *For Those About to Rock*, and they were under a lot of pressure to keep the numbers up. But I can't even begin to grasp what one million records a month for eighteen months straight is. That's crazy. Even though Quiet Riot's given the credit for bringing metal to America and being the first metal album to go multiplatinum so far, I don't think you can discount *Back in Black* and what it did to the entire music scene. It just upended everything.

But with the follow-up, I thought the gas had run out of the engine. I thought it was overproduced, too thick, too dense, too much. It was Mutt Lange throwing the kitchen sink in. And it didn't live up to the expectations, in the same way that *Bad* did not live up to Michael Jackson's expectations. You need to understand that the amount of pressure on a band in this position is enormous. The record didn't—it couldn't—do what it was supposed to accomplish. It was supposed to begin with *Back in Black* and take the band to another level. It was almost an impossible expectation.

TOLINSKI: As I say, I think the record's as good as it could be. You know, in movies, you have your blockbuster, and the directors and actors are then obligated to do the sequel. And the sequels are just never as good. Everybody's trying too hard, where they're trying to replicate the formula. And somehow it just never captures the excitement of the original. *For Those About to Rock* suffers from that. And there are probably a bunch of different reasons for it. It's the third record with Mutt, they're all probably getting a little tired of each other, and Mutt is probably becoming more confident and he's trying to push them into a more poppy area. And I'm not sure what the band actually thought about that.

Also, they tried recording this record at a different studio. And I guess they couldn't get a good sound out of the studio. So they recorded a lot of these tracks and then were completely frustrated with them and ended up scrapping the whole thing, going to different studio and re-recording them. But I think also, they were touring their asses off. It's always difficult for a band when they're in the throes of their huge success, to be able to sit down and buckle down and write a great follow-up. And I think *For Those About to Rock* is a good record, but I don't think it's a great record. I don't think it has anywhere near the excitement level that *Highway to Hell* had, that sound of discovery and newness. And I don't think the songs are as good as *Back in Black*. You know, the worst thing you can possibly say about a record is that when you're listening to a song on it, you're thinking of another song that they did that was somehow better [*laughs*].

POPOFF: Jay Jay, any closing thoughts?

FRENCH: Just that all the great bands go through these massive periods of sturm und drang. *For Those About to Rock* was the end of the monster sales for AC/DC, and then you saw a precipitous drop for several years. Not that it battered them in terms of their ticket sales. Because I will tell you this about AC/DC: they are the only band except McCartney left on this earth that I will stand up for, for the entire show. The last time I saw them, I stood for the entire two-and-a-half hours, and my girlfriend was like, "You're like a little kid." And I go, "Yeah, because if I don't have that, I have nothing left." And that is what AC/DC can still do for me.

All songs composed by
Angus Young, Malcolm Young,
and Brian Johnson

Personnel: Brian Johnson—
lead vocals; Angus Young—lead
guitar; Malcolm Young—rhythm
guitar, backing vocals; Cliff
Williams—bass, backing vocals;
Phil Rudd—drums

Released August 15, 1983

Recorded at Compass Point
Studios, Nassau, Bahamas

Produced by AC/DC

FLICK OF THE SWITCH

with MARK CICCHINI and MICHAEL HANNON

Maybe it's just me an' my buddy Tim Henderson (we started a little mag together called *Brave Words & Bloody Knuckles* that ran in print for fourteen years and now lives on as bravewords.com), but we support the metalhead code that *Flick of the Switch* is the best AC/DC album, or at least the heaviest. Or certainly—certainly—the best of the Brians. Let's go with heaviest of all and best after *Highway to Hell* for now.

And let's also chuck in that it's analogous to Black Sabbath's *Born Again*, the red-headed stepchild of that doomy catalog, but the one all members of our metal army love without apology. To my mind, similarly analogous, it might be viewed as the band's first record of the eighties, the one that acknowledges the feisty competition coming from the hotshot New Wave of British Heavy Metal, not to mention Ozzy and even a reinvigorated Kiss.

Stark and white like *Lick It Up*, *Flick of the Switch* is even less adorned with respect to the record's famously dry and midrange-fatiguing production values. The band had recorded once again at Compass Point in the Bahamas, but they ditched Mutt and did it themselves, Tony Platt presiding as engineer. As one would be crazy to attempt it, I'll not defend the production, although it's not one of a distracting badness either. The record, in fact, seethes with electricity and distortion as Malcolm intended, but it's not particularly hefty. Then again, *Back in Black* and *For Those About to Rock* were both hefty, but neither was particularly powerful.

Here, there's an increased and welcomed level of power ("Rising Power," as it were), but more than that, the record kicks ass start to finish—band on a mission, most pointedly, a mission to reclaim their hard-core fans rather than expand the base, to bring it in, to make the party fit the room but then blow the roof off for the added square footage required to get wasted.

ABOVE: Angus in Michigan. *Flick* kicks ass start to finish—the band was on a mission to reclaim their hardcore fans rather than expand the base.

OPPOSITE: *Flick* seethes with electricity—just as Malcolm intended.

Therein lies the metal majesty of *Flick of the Switch*—this furtive messaging to the lapsing, angry, bed-headed punter in a jean jacket—that AC/DC remember a time when it was them against the world, them and the fans who knew them before the gold and platinum. Almost a foregone conclusion, the record very famously did not sell, but there's no taking away that AC/DC reclaimed the scrappy junkyard dog turf last defended as home—love it or leave it—way back on *Let There Be Rock*. Like that incendiary riot of guitars, this was a record of defiance, and for all the grousing about its relative commercial flop, rest assured that the mainline delivery of a record like *Flick of the Switch* to the partying faithful produced considerable goodwill as the band made their way through a decade sometimes unforgiving to their legacy.

POPOFF: The main storyline around *Flick of the Switch* is how raw it is. Why do you think they went for that more abrasive sound?

HANNON: It had gotten too polished. As a kid, I loved AC/DC. I started on eight-track tape with them. While *Back in Black* was great, I did not find myself playing *For Those About to Rock* very much. And I was an AC/DC freak. I bought *Dirty Deeds* as an import way before it was reissued. And *For Those About to Rock* just didn't jump out at me. It sounded too controlled, I

Limo driver Patty Hipp takes Simon, Angus, and Brian to the Denver airport on October 25, 1983.

guess. Back then, as a kid, I just knew it didn't work. Like Malcolm always says, over and over we would play the same songs and cut and paste pieces together. And that's not what AC/DC is. They're just a groove and a pocket. That's what makes them so good.

And they were done with it. He said it took way too long to do that album, and you'd do parts of a song over and over and over again and forget what song you were even doing. So with *Flick of the Switch*, they just went for capturing the lightning in the bottle.

And I have no problem with the sound. The drums don't sound as gated. They sound just like a real snare drum. It's not like the mid-eighties sound. On *For Those About to Rock*, everything is like compressed and small and tiny. It doesn't sound loud no matter how you loud you play it. Whereas if you play *Flick of the Switch* loud, it's a live band playing in front of you. I got the same thing out of *Fly on the Wall*—only *Fly on the Wall* is even dirtier. It sounds like it was done in an even quicker rush and with a few more drinks.

POPOFF: **What did Tony Platt bring to the table?**
HANNON: What people don't know, Tony Platt kind of coproduced it with Malcolm and Angus, even though it says produced by AC/DC. Tony Platt was the engineer on *Back in Black* and he mixed *Highway to Hell* so he knew how to get their sounds. Basically, the producer is the guy who helps with arrangements on songs and the engineer gets the sounds. But what you're hearing, the only change is the quickness and the live feel, which is what Angus and Malcolm were all about. Which they learned from Vanda and Young and all those classics like *Let There Be Rock* and *High Voltage* and *Powerage*. And I guess Vanda and Young had something to do with this, because they are the special thanks on it.
CICCHINI: *Back in Black* and *Flick of the Switch* were both recorded in the same studio, Compass Point. But what's the missing ingredient? Mr. Mutt Lange. And because of that rawness you mentioned, which comes from the band producing with just Tony, not only is *Flick of the Switch* one of my favorite albums, but to me, it's Brian Johnson's *Let There Be Rock*. Meaning that *Let There Be Rock* didn't have the production that *Highway to Hell* and *Back in Black* had, but it had the songs and those songs overcame the rougher production. And if you look at all the Brian Johnson records, this one stands out as having the least production values, maybe tied with *Fly on the Wall*. And then a couple albums later, they produce their most

polished sound. But I don't think if Mutt would've been at the controls it would've been better.

POPOFF: Okay, so talk about these songs. Which ones are highlights for you?

CICCHINI: I love every song on that record. I love the vibe of the record. *Flick of the Switch*, to my ears, is the end of an era. It's the last of the consistently well-written AC/DC albums. The very first record after *Flick of the Switch* was the first one with filler, in my opinion. But like I said, it captures that early AC/DC rough sound. They've progressed as a band, and the particulars of a song like "Bedlam in Belgium"—that is the spirit of AC/DC. Now I think everybody would agree that the true nature of AC/DC is the spirit of Bon. And I think they channeled it really, really well, not just on "Bedlam in Belgium" but even "Rising Power" and especially "Brainshake." You can almost hear Bon singing those songs, you know?

POPOFF: Now that you bring it up, what is the story with "Bedlam in Belgium?"

CICCHINI: That, I believe, happened in October of 1977. AC/DC was playing in Belgium, obviously, at a festival, and the opening band didn't show up, and they then had to be the ones to find out that the power was all fucked up. So normally, if the first band would've went on, they would've found bugs in the system. Well, the first band doesn't show up, then before AC/DC goes on, they're like, "Oh, we're having power problems." So AC/DC's supposed to go on at 9, they ended up going on at 10:45 or something.

And in that long break, a bunch of the punters, as they say in England, were running around the festival grounds. And some of them were standing out front and I guess were openly urinating. And some of the locals called the police, going, "Hey, there's a bunch of longhairs pissing all over the place, and basically running through my shrubs."

And, next thing you know, the cops come and they start looking for the organizer. And it wasn't very well organized. And they're like, "Hey, you can't be playing like this after eleven o'clock. We've got a curfew." And AC/DC were literally like two or three songs into their set. The cops started giving the road crew a hard time, and then some fists were thrown, and then finally a gun was pulled on Bon. That didn't go over too well, and Bon basically told the cops to go fuck themselves. Some more punches were thrown, they started playing again, and about thirty seconds later, they physically turned the power off, and there was a great big fight—that was the bedlam in Belgium.

I think that's probably my favorite song on the record, because even before I knew anything about the story, the first time I listened to it, Brian's emotion in that really channels Bon. Every time I hear it, I can almost hear Bon singing it. Even though, obviously, the rest of the guys told Brian what happened and he came up with a great set of lyrics about what was a true story.

POPOFF: What else does Brian bring to the band, versus Bon?
HANNON: There's a lot more grit, I think, by far, with Brian Johnson. And it's a whole different kind of voice. He's brings more of a screaming metal sound. Whereas Bon had more of a sense of humor and a sly, almost sarcastic, tone to his voice. Brian Johnson's got a grit that's tough to sing. I was amazed that Axl Rose could do it. Try singing "Back in Black"—that's way up there, man. What a great singer.

POPOFF: And what about his personality?
HANNON: He's from Newcastle. He's a Geordie. Right on the Scottish border. Boy, you can't understand those fuckers at all when they get drunk. But they're great people up there. But I think with the hat and the whole shielded eyes kind of thing, he just looked like a regular guy. He really fit in with them perfectly. He just looked like a regular blue-collar guy who just came from the factory.
CICCHINI: I think Bon was more of a poet, and I don't think he gets enough accolades for his work in that period. Whereas Brian really was what AC/DC is and still remains: a working-class pub band that just happened to get really, really big [*laughs*]. I mean, let's go have a beer, play some pool, shoot some darts, have a great time—that is Brian. Although I don't know him. I've never met him, but from everything I've read, down in Florida, you go to the bar, he'll hang out after the race. He's that kind of guy.

POPOFF: Michael, as a bassist yourself, what does Cliff Williams bring to the party?
HANNON: He's a much better bass player than he gets credit for. Because a lot of times, sure, he's just playing with Phil, but if you listen really closely,

New guy Simon Wright
with Brian Johnson.

he's doing a lot of great little runs there, and ending phrases and starting them, and yet he plays exactly what you need. AC/DC was the first band that I can remember playing, where the eighth notes were prominent on the bass. You didn't hear it as often with other bands.

In Deep Purple, Roger Glover would use eighth notes. He would do that on a couple of songs, "Smoke on the Water" and stuff, but if you listen to "Maybe I'm a Leo," it's jazzy and bluesy. He's never really pounding it. Whereas AC/DC, they were the first band I can remember doing eighth notes a lot of the time. Cliff was pounding away. If you listen to Phil Rudd going with that, Phil Rudd's bass sound is *boom, snare, boom, snare, boom, snare,* and the eighth notes go along with that so well. It creates such a strong groove pocket; the guitarists just had all the room in the world to do whatever they needed.

And then, of course, what Malcolm and Angus do is over top, Malcolm has a big Gretsch, with a hollow body, which has a deeper sound. And Angus always plays an SG, which is a thinner, higher sound. So the two guitars separate. If they both played the same guitar, you wouldn't hear the separation. And that's what really fills up the spectrum above Phil and Cliff, and makes the sound so big and strong.

POPOFF: What do you know about Cliff and his choice of bass? What does he use?

HANNON: His main thing is the StingRay by Music Man and other Music Mans, but there was this time where he got one of those crappy square basses with no headstock, a Steinberger. But most of the time I've seen him, definitely in the old days, he used a Fender. It was either an old Fender Jazz or P Bass.

POPOFF: Okay, back to the record, specifically, and the songs, what are some other high points on *Flick of the Switch*?

HANNON: I think "Guns for Hire" is the best song on the album. And they must've thought so too, because they made a video, a single, and they opened their tour with it. I had a weird concept in my head, ever since this record came out, and I heard it working at a Peaches Records and Tapes. I think somebody at the record company screwed up and put side one as side two, and side two as side one. I still think "Guns for Hire" should've been the first song on that album. Because it starts sort of dramatically and gradually, right?

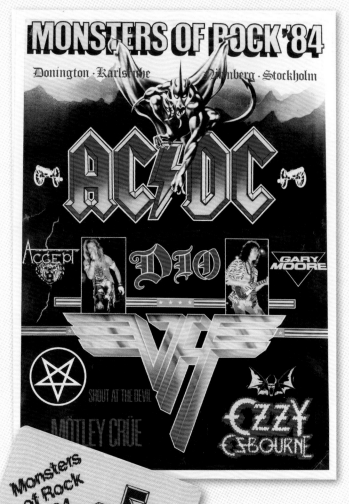

Monsters of Rock
tour, August and
September 1984.

"Highway to Hell" starts with that bare riff and drums, no bass, and *Back in Black*, you've got the bell, and then the best song on *For Those About to Rock* starts off the album. This album's first song, "Rising Power," is just a middle-of-the-road song by them. But "Guns for Hire," the first one on side two, starts with that very cool scraping guitar, which picks up in intensity, and then Phil comes in with those big snare drum whacks. *That's* the first song of the album, or it should've been, if you ask me. That's how you start an album. When Angus starts that scratching across the strings, you just feel it in your bones. And live, it blew the shit out of anything on *For Those About to Rock*. Nothing on that record can touch that song.

And like I say, more proof was that "Guns for Hire" was a video and a single off that album as well. They did three videos, which I love too. Because they were just in a circle in an airplane hanger and had the cameras going around them and the monitors facing them playing real loud. But you very rarely saw them on MTV at the time. Because they were a dirty rock band with T-shirts and there were no special effects.

And, you know, even though Phil Rudd played on the album, Simon Wright is in the videos, because he became the drummer after the album was finished. I guess the drummer from Procol Harum, Barrie Wilson, played drums on three tracks that were never released. These have not even surfaced on YouTube, but you can read in a bunch of books about them. But like I say, to this day I think that's side one—I think somebody screwed up with the label.

CICCHINI: Okay, this is why I love what you do, Martin. I never thought of that! I'm going to be thinking about that for the rest of the night. That makes perfect sense! Because when I first put it on . . . let's face it, remember the magic the first time you heard "Riff Raff" and all those great AC/DC tunes with those classic buildups? I remember when I put the needle down on "Rising Power," I was like, "Okay, this is fine, but this isn't an opening song." But then when I got to the chorus, it's like, okay, I was fine with it—I get it. Maybe it's strong enough. But sure, the first time that I heard "Rising Power," it was slow. I was expecting something grandiose, because the two albums before had grandiose openings. This started like we were in the middle of side two. Damn, that's been in plain sight for the last thirty-some years and I just noticed it because you said it [*laughs*].

POPOFF: Hey, that wasn't my idea. Thank Michael for that one. But, okay, what are some other interesting wrinkles about this record?
CICCHINI: Okay, here's one. Let's talk about the timeline. In '83, I was a big heavy metal fan, with Maiden, Priest, and Saxon, all that glorious stuff. Don't get me wrong, I'm a Christian, I'm a Catholic, but I'm not one of those in-your-face types. Well, the in-your-face types were telling people that you shouldn't listen to bands like AC/DC. What was it? Kiss was the Knights in Satan's Service, and AC/DC was After Christ Devil Comes. There were all these stupid acronyms they were coming up with.

Well, it's funny, because, what does Brian do at the beginning of "Landslide?" The very first thing is, *This is for all you bad boys/This is a story of the Satan rock 'n' roll/I want you to put your hand in your pocket/Take ten dollars out and send it to me.* He's goofing on the religious protesters. I always thought that was cool. Because it was like, yeah, in your face. And the rest of the song, too, where he talks about the preacher. He's basically saying just leave the boy alone, man. He's going to bowl you over like a landslide. You don't need to pick on him. These religious folks . . . it was the Peters Brothers, from Minneapolis. I've got a book of theirs and it was all against rock. They said that *Flick of the Switch* is evil because flick is a street word for having sex, like AC/DC are telling young kids to have a flick. That never made sense to me. But if you Google them, you'll see some of their anti-AC/DC stuff. It was really strong around 1983.

POPOFF: And what do you make of this strange album cover?
HANNON: It's pretty generic, but, let's face it, *Back in Black, For Those About to Rock, Flick of the Switch,* and *Fly on the Wall*—none of them are great album covers. It's just a color, right? That's AC/DC. And then you put something,

(continued on page 146)

Palais Omnisport de Paris-Bercy,
Paris, September 15, 1984.

(continued from page 143)

anything, on it, a cannon or a bell or whatever. But I always thought the *Flick of the Switch* cover was kind of making it look like a bootleg record. And even the sort of pencil-looking writing on the back for the song titles—it's just like somebody handwrote it. It's like they're going, "Look, we're back to basics; we're producing it ourselves. We don't need Mutt Lange because we've been doing this for ten years and we know where we're doing."

CICCHINI: To this day I like that cover, but you see, it always reminded me of the *Draw the Line* album cover, and I love that one too. It was basic, but it was cool. I do remember thinking that it didn't jump out enough at me, although I was just an excited eighteen-year-old in 1983 and just happy that I had brand-new AC/DC music. But I sure do remember being horrified when the next record came out. When I saw the *Fly on the Wall* album cover, I almost pissed myself. I couldn't believe it was the same band. It was that much of a contrast.

POPOFF: So we can all agree that *Flick of the Switch* is a good album, if more so for the diehards, right? But we have to ask, why didn't it sell?

CICCHINI: What was coming out? Mötley Crüe and Twisted Sister. And you had two other strikes against it: *Back in Black* and *For Those About to Rock*. If you were a radio listener, those were beat to death. You had AC/DC all the time on the radio. I really believe that played into it. Plus, as I said earlier, Mutt Lange was missing. The AC/DC that you were hearing now didn't sound like the *Back in Black* AC/DC, and I'm just talking about casual radio listeners. I don't think it excited them. It didn't capture the imagination, maybe all the way from the album cover down, the way that Mötley Crüe or Twisted Sister did, or even for that matter, the polished sounds of Journey and REO and Foreigner.

Where did "Nervous Shakedown" fit on FM radio? Put "Nervous Shakedown" against "Looks That Kill" or whatever the Journey song or REO song had been on radio. Whereas "You Shook Me All Night Long" could compete, and to a lesser extent, "For Those About to Rock." *Flick of the Switch*, including any of those three singles, was a little too raw. But I was crazy about it. I remember when I bought it, I thought, hell yeah, it was just another great record in a row of them. From that album back, they don't have a bad song—I like every single song. There's not one I would skip.

HANNON: I worked in a record stores when *Flick of the Switch* came out, and I remember it sold really well right away, because it was AC/DC. But it didn't get any airplay at all here in Columbus, Ohio, which was an AC/DC stronghold. AC/DC broke here. You would hear "Live Wire" and all those deep album cuts all the time, man. They were as big as you can be. That's back when radio stations could play what they wanted and they did. But they didn't play but one song off of *Flick of the Switch*.

The album went gold right away, but it took eight, nine years to go platinum. But for the deep fans, they're burnt out on *For Those About to Rock* and *Back in Black*, and they go back and revisit it and realize that it's a great record. Who needs to hear "You Shook Me All Night Long" again? You don't. *Back in Black* is like Van Halen *I* or *Paranoid*, some of those albums you've heard so many times you don't need to ever again.

CICCHINI: Ultimately, even with *Flick of the Switch*, although no one bought it, the magic of AC/DC is in it. It's just like McDonald's or Nestlé Crunch bars, anything that just makes you feel good. Any time you went and saw them live, they proved it. As you know, I'm a huge Kiss fan, and the thing about Kiss lately is, oh, it's a tribute band. Geez, man, with AC/DC there's not even an Aussie-born guy in the band anymore. And I think if you ask nine out of ten people, they wouldn't know that. In other words, AC/DC just finished a successful tour with a singer from another band, Axl Rose, and people didn't care. They just went anyway because they knew they were going to get their money's worth. It's like Disney World or any other iconic business. I think that's what AC/DC represents to the world: getting your money's worth.

MAIN: Poster for the canceled show at Stadio Roman Valero, Madrid, September 14, 1984.

INSETS: Ticket stubs from the fall and winter 1983 US leg of the *Flick of the Switch* World Tour.

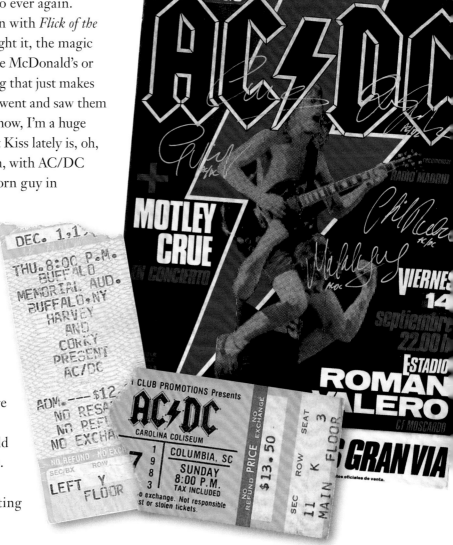

FLY ON THE WALL

with MICHAEL HANNON and SIMON WRIGHT

All songs composed by
Angus Young, Malcolm Young,
and Brian Johnson

Personnel: Brian Johnson—
lead vocals; Angus Young—lead
guitar; Malcolm Young—rhythm
guitar, backing vocals; Cliff
Williams—bass, backing vocals;
Simon Wright—drums, percussion

Released June 28, 1985

Recorded at Mountain Studios,
Montreux, Switzerland

Produced by Angus Young and
Malcolm Young

After accepting with open arms—for whatever reason—
Flick of the Switch, I found myself standoffish about
another brown AC/DC album. I dunno . . . part of the problem is
that kiddie and cartoony album cover. I really think this is part of
what turned fans off Twisted Sister around this time as well. But I
also think *Fly on the Wall* gets off to a dopey and distracted start,
with the title track, but not all of it, just the opening 1:13.

Then we are somewhat off to the races, although a second
flaw shows itself, and that is the desperate straits of Brian's vocals,
which are rough and cawed and clawed and frantic and then not
given a fighting chance when pushed back in the mix. So I found

myself always uneasy listening to this raft of itchy, scratchy songs, rooting for a return to vim and vigor of a band I was now feeling a little sorry for, like they'd been politely set aside.

Set aside for what? The New Wave of British Heavy Metal had fizzled, and in its place, metal went wholesale to the sunny climes of California. There was a nascent thrash movement, with initial offerings from Metallica, Megadeth, and Slayer. But more Scorpions, Judas Priest, and Ozzy were flying high again, Def Leppard was stratospheric, and Los Angeles was becoming the locus of a next metal movement with the likes of Quiet Riot, W.A.S.P., Ratt, and Mötley Crüe. Among this new-look glam, sure, it could be accepted that AC/DC were also-rans, but why weren't they blasting along on the top line in concert with the other seventies bands suddenly doing well? Truth be told, one supposes, in 1985, Scorpions, Priest, and Ozzy were also suddenly past due date, as was Kiss, who was losing steam after its second wave. More pointedly, AC/DC was missing the boat big time with 1983's *Flick of the Switch*, a bold record but a box office bust.

Whatever comparisons one cares to make, AC/DC in 1985 were not exceling, even if concerts were still well-attended. *Fly on the Wall*, despite an admirable seething electricity to the production and mix, seemed to comprise a bank of songs that found the band searching for the next sly permutation on themes used multiple times previously. Sex, violence, rocking, a pervasive sense of menace . . . it was all here again almost like a concept record, and often within the same song, line to line, verse to verse,

ABOVE: New York City, June 1985. Despite its seething electricity, *Fly on the Wall* seemed like a bank of songs that found the band searching for the next sly permutation on familiar themes.

OPPOSITE: *Flo* on the Wall?

underscoring the muddle that is *Fly on the Wall*, graphically exposing the empty threat that AC/DC represented in the late eighties.

POPOFF: First off, Simon, a big change in the AC/DC camp is that they have a new drummer and that drummer is you. But going way back, what was your first introduction to AC/DC? What album was your entry point?
WRIGHT: Oh, it wasn't an album. I was sitting in my parents' living room, and we were watching TV. And this new show like *Sight and Sound in Concert* came on. It was called *Rock Goes to College*, and you had your TV and it would sync up to the radio and you could turn your TV volume down and listen to the radio. It was quite innovative back then. And the band that was scheduled to be on was Nazareth, and they canceled, and then all of a sudden this band came on, AC/DC, playing at a college. And I remember me and my father were sitting there going, "What the fuck is this?!" It was unbelievable, the energy, the power, the riffs, the whole vibe of the thing. Two or three days later, I went out and bought *Let There Be Rock*.

POPOFF: And why do you think millions of people love AC/DC?
WRIGHT: Well, number one, that guitar sound is just amazing. I mean, talk about raw; it just had this crunch to it. And there's the guitar interplay and stuff. And the songs, they're based on simple riffs, but they're hooky and catchy and yet not corny, you know? And their tongue-in-cheek lyrics have always gotten me. I mean, there's nothing bad about them—the drums are solid, the bass guitar is pumping, and the guitars sound great, and there's those great lyrics.

POPOFF: Flash forward to *Flick of the Switch*, when you became their drummer. Why do you think you got the job?
WRIGHT: I don't know [*laughs*]. I mean, I'm not the tallest guy in the world—that might've helped [*laughs*]. But like Brian, I come from a working-class kind of background in Manchester, and I like to get on with things and do the job right. And I think they might've seen that. They auditioned a lot of drummers. I'm just thankful I got that break.

POPOFF: I hear they tried like three hundred people.
WRIGHT: The only thing I know is that I did hear that they had been rehearsing people in New York before they started rehearsing in London. And, yes, I heard something like three hundred–odd drummers that they

were looking at, which is just mind-boggling. I don't really know why they chose me, but I'm glad they did.

POPOFF: What was the audition process like?
WRIGHT: The drum tech was there, Dickie Jones, lovely Welshman. He's funny, very down-to-earth, great guy, been with them for such a long time. He was there and he asked me to play along with these three songs. There was a drum kit with the PA and monitors and I played along to "Black Dog," Led Zeppelin; "Tush," ZZ Top; and "Shoot to Thrill," AC/DC. And I kind of knew them as I had played them all before at some point or another. I got through it and he seemed to like it, and they called me back.

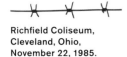

Richfield Coliseum, Cleveland, Ohio, November 22, 1985.

POPOFF: Michael, where does this album fit within the AC/DC canon for you?

HANNON: This is my favorite era. I'm one of the few people who love this era. I equate this era of AC/DC—*Flick of the Switch* and *Fly on the Wall*—as the same thing Motörhead was doing with *Orgasmatron* and *Rock 'n' Roll*: making very dirty, live rock albums. It sounds live in the studio, warts and all. Even Angus gets that really frantic, abrasive sound. They sound like a band in a room together, which was magnified on *Fly on the Wall*. Man, that's their *Orgasmatron* right there. That's the *Let There Be Rock* of the Brian Johnson era, if you ask me.

WRIGHT: We all played together. We all put the backing tracks down, pretty much raw, not too many overdubs. We would go for the take, the right feel, and it ended up being what it was. And Montreux was such a surreal place to record—beautiful place, obviously, as most people know, Lake Geneva. And then the folklore behind "Smoke on the Water," the Deep Purple song, just incredible. And there were some good pubs around that we would frequent, when we finished at the end of the day, so that was good [*laughs*].

POPOFF: How would a place like that affect the sound of the record?

HANNON: It's basically a big room. It's an old casino. You would get nothing but loud room sounds. If you listen to the drums, they're big, man. The one thing that is kind of back in the mix is the bass guitar. It's more of a presence than actually hearing it. Sometimes you can't tell exactly where the bass comes in, if you listen to stuff like "Send for the Man" or even "Playing with Girls." There's just a presence there. *Shout at the Devil* by Mötley Crüe was like that, where you can't really hear what the bass is doing, but you know it's there. The guitars are really sticking through, though, and what you get is that midrange, white boy metal.

POPOFF: People complain that Brian is also set back in the mix, and to boot, he sounds kind of scratchy and desperate, like he's fighting with the guys to be heard.

HANNON: I'd agree with that. But it works. Not to go back to *Orgasmatron* again, but it's kind of like that. It's live, but it is back there, as is the bass. Maybe it's not that the vocals and the bass are back so much—it's just that the guitars are up so much. It's a weird album. Angus and Malcolm produced it, but it was taken back to Australia to mix, by the way, to the Vanda and Young studio. And you could tell that was the attitude and

OPPOSITE (FROM TOP): "Danger" was one of just two singles off the album. Here it is b/w "Hell or High Water" on the New Zealand single, 1985. "Shake Your Foundations" appeared on the *Maximum Overdrive* soundtrack, helping prolong the life of the album. Japanese picture sleeve b/w "Send for the Man," 1985.

opinion on this new album. We'll take this to our friends who took care of us on *Let There Be Rock* and *Powerage*. Because, remember, there were three albums in a row that they were away.

WRIGHT: Mal and Angus were just really getting on with the songs and writing the songs, I guess trying to make business as usual, although there were a couple of things that were changing within the whole structure of the organization. There were different road crew and they weren't using Mutt Lange. They were just doing it themselves. There was a time where they sort of didn't have a manager, but a road manager and an accountant, who is the guy I dealt with. But it was pretty relaxed, a "get your head down and start working" kind of atmosphere.

Mal would have some tapes, and he'd play them. We'd start playing and they'd change a little bit and Angus would have an idea. Angus would also come in with a couple of songs, say, that he had on tape. And we would start off with that riff and just slowly, gradually build the song up. And some songs came in complete, although more so with the *Blow Up Your Video* album.

POPOFF: I understand both Mal and Angus would sometimes play drums on their demos?

WRIGHT: Yes, Mal did a little bit and so did Angus. And other songs would have drum machines. And then sometimes it would just be the riff, one of them just hacking away on a riff. And we would just say, "Oh, okay, that's what it is, we'll start working from there." Build it up and start actually playing it. But, yes, Angus likes to play the drums and there were a few tapes that were full of drums [*laughs*].

POPOFF: What did you see between those two guys when they would be playing rhythm guitar parts?

WRIGHT: Well, a technical word I've learned is *latency*. I'm not sure that's the right word, but they kind of don't play exactly together. They're a little bit off and it creates, from what I can tell, this kind of wall of brutal guitar. I'm not sure who is late on it, or ahead, but yeah, they're able to create this incredible wall of noise.

POPOFF: And what are some of the highlights on the album?

HANNON: Well, "First Blood" is a great one for the lead alone, when Angus goes into that frantic and dirty twenty-fourth note stuff on the solo—that just kills me—and then he does it again "Playing with Girls." And there's finger-picking as well. It gives a song a nice flavor and feel and some added texture. A lot of those country cats do that a lot. But "Hell or High Water" and "Sink the Pink" both start with that technique. I think "Sink the Pink" is great; I think the title track's fantastic, as is "Back in Business." I really like "Send for the Man," even though it's just one groove over and over. It's just got a big groove and pocket. I really love it because it's just big and mean. I just love this album.

POPOFF: It's funny—no one I know particularly likes "Danger," and yet it was picked as the first single.
HANNON: I know, that's the most sedate song of that album. They only floated two singles off that album, "Danger" and "Shake Your Foundations," but it's funny, "Sink the Pink" was probably the song that got the most traction. But "Shake Your Foundations" and "Sink the Pink" both went to the *Maximum Overdrive* movie, and they were on that soundtrack as well. That came out right after and helped prolong the life of the album.

POPOFF: *Fly on the Wall* had a lot going against it though as well, right?
HANNON: Yes, beginning with the album cover. I think that it hurt this album a lot. It's crappy-looking and makes them look like a teenage pop band, doesn't it? The cartoon eyeball. It's like, does that say "*Flo* on the Wall"? No, it's "Fly on the Wall"—good God.

POPOFF: I always thought it looked kind of country and western or at least southern rock.
HANNON: Yeah, with the wooden fence. And I don't know if they were searching for a mascot—like Iron Maiden with Eddie— with this little fly. Plus, they must have really believed in the fly because it was featured in that concept film. They had five songs off the album on it and had all those hipsters playing while they were playing a seedy little bar called the Crystal Room, which doesn't exist. They had New York in the background, and there was this fly flying around.

And it's interesting, by the way, the concept of being a fly the wall, and the band being so secretive and closed shop, right? Because part of the

Was AC/DC searching for a mascot—like Iron Maiden with Eddie—with their little fly?

storyline was this guy with the flash camera, always peeking around the corner and trying to take pictures of them doing stuff. But yeah, all the songs are played in a club and there's barely anybody there. It's an art crowd, a disco guy, like a bunch of phonies, and by the end of these five songs, they're finally grasping AC/DC and getting into the music. But the videos were done so horribly, in that mid-eighties way, with people who don't even look like AC/DC fans, wearing the red spandex jumpsuits and all that weird shit. And it really turned a lot of people off.

They did play that a few times on like *Headbanger's Ball* or whatever it was called then. But it turned me off on the album a lot.

Plus, they're lip-syncing the songs, with all this noise and sound effects in between, which interrupts the flow of the songs and hearing the lyrics. Not that these lyrics are profound or anything—you just want ass-kicking rock 'n' roll. And the ass-kicking rock 'n' roll is separated by everyone who's talking and supporting this so-called plot this thing had.

So you have the video and that goofy album cover. You know, people buy what you sell. If that album cover were black with fearsome teeth on it—like Airbourne's *Black Dog Barking*, to keep it Australian—if that was the cover, and they would've done black and white videos of them just jamming like *Flick of the Switch*, then it would've sold twice as many. It's how you present it, and what they presented here just looked goofy.

POPOFF: Then there was Richard Ramirez, that serial killer in California who left an AC/DC hat at one of his murder scenes.
HANNON: That album and the tour did okay, and then he lost an AC/DC hat at one of the killings. So all the religious whack jobs, of course, were calling AC/DC devil worshipers and all that horseshit they like to come up with. Like AC/DC, "Antichrist Devil Child"—all that kind of garbage they would come up with.

POPOFF: And he was called the Night Stalker, which was then tied to "Night Prowler," off *Highway to Hell*.
HANNON: Yes, and no matter how much Malcolm says that it's about sneaking in to see your girlfriend, that's bullshit. Bon is singing, *And you don't feel the steel/Till it's hanging out your back*. So Malcolm was just trying to kind of

shift it away. I had just moved to L.A. at the time, and you had all the religious whackos in all the papers talking about AC/DC promoting devil worship and all this garbage. They're about as blue-collar and regular a band as you can come up with. It made no sense. There were bands like Venom that actually did put upside-down crosses in their records and said, "Hey, we're devil worshipers." But AC/DC were easy targets because they were a huge band.

POPOFF: They were getting all this grief from the religious right, but on the other side, metal fans had found a new flavor of hard rock, namely Mötley Crüe, Ratt, Quiet Riot–type stuff. I suppose you had to admire how the band didn't succumb to the times and turn all hair metal.
HANNON: Oh, for sure, they were going so against the grain of what metal was at the time. Everything was so polished and keyboard-saturated, compressed when it came to the drums, and everybody had those pointy guitars. Everything was fluorescent green and orange and pink and polka dots and stripes and spandex and I hated that. You had Bon Jovi and all that kind of crap, and believe it or not, yes, it was called metal at the time.

And with *Fly on the Wall*, they said, "Look, do it again, but let's make it rougher, because metal is getting really wimpy. And we don't want to sell out and be like all the spandex bands." Remember, when *Fly on the Wall* came out, Angus had the longest hair he ever had, and they were really nasty-looking. But also, you know, I think a lot of people didn't like both *Flick of the Switch* and *Fly on the Wall* as much, because people equate something good with how many sales it made, and both of these records only got to platinum.

Fly on the Wall World Tour, Festhalle, Frankfurt, January 31, 1986.

POPOFF: Simple music from the least pretentious band in the world.
WRIGHT: Yes, you could say that. Angus and Malcolm are pretty much working-class kind of people. And I think Brian came from the same kind of ethic and background, and that probably made things a lot easier for them to immediately have something to grasp hold of it and get along with. And they definitely learned a lot from George and Harry as well. Because they were pretty much kids when they started and George was their mentor, I guess. He put them right, and like you say the whole thing with the band

seems to be about simplicity. There's never even anything over-the-top about their album covers, and nothing over the top about their music, this incredible music. It's just straightforward. It's basically who they are. Hit you in the nuts and leave by the back door, kind of thing.

I'm happy with *Fly on the Wall*. I must admit, at the time I did notice that there wasn't a "Back in Black" on there, or a "Shoot to Thrill" or anything, but then I was basically just the drummer. I wasn't involved in any of the songwriting. And I thought Brian did a good job. No doubt they were going for a rougher-edged album. And Brian was singing his ass off. He was singing along when we were doing the takes, helping us along doing what's called a guide vocal. It just helps you out, in terms of where you are in the song. And it gives you a feel, if you need to pick it up a bit, from a drummer's standpoint. I much prefer if the singer is there to help out with that. Don't forget, Brian brought life back to the band. I'm not sure if they knew what they were going to do after Bon passed away, and it was good that Brian was there to continue it on. But they're both brilliant and both brought so much to the band.

I play in a band called Dio Disciples, and what's amazing is, on so many occasions, like the other week, there was this guy at one of my shows. He came back after we played, and he was the head of this online AC/DC club that got has like 670,000 members, and he wanted me to sign *Fly on the Wall*.

And as I'm signing it, he says, "This is the best AC/DC album there's ever been." And I said, "Really? Why?" And he said, "Because it's so raw and it's so honest." And, you know, he wasn't saying it to pacify me because I was standing in front of him—he was saying it wholeheartedly. And it seems to be happening a lot more. I think things get easier for people to digest as they age. Like, it's a certain time and a place in the career of a band, and they start to see things in a different light and appreciate things more—or less, you know? [*laughs*]

POPOFF: You say it was hard to notice a decline when it came to playing live, right?
WRIGHT: It was a weird phenomenon. The record sales weren't as strong as *Back in Black* or *For Those About to Rock*. I was aware of that, but the shows were still huge; that didn't change. They didn't get smaller. If anything, they got bigger. The live show was really what it was about. That might've had something to do with, you know, bands have these enormous albums that sell, and there's always a kind of grace period afterward.

But who knows? You're right—it may have been the musical climate. It could've been everybody buying the next Warrant album or something. There were so many bands through the eighties that it maybe just flooded the market. I'm not sure. An AC/DC album is great anyway, whichever way you look at it. Doesn't matter which one. But you think, in the beginning, AC/DC were more like an underground band, coming up from nowhere, knocking down doors when they first started. And now, there's so many hits on the radio that it's not quite as underground, and you're not perceived as the same kind of band. People stop spreading the word because everybody knows about them now.

POPOFF: So no real concern about their career that you ever detected?
WRIGHT: No, we never broached that. There never seemed to be a problem with, "Oh, our career is going down the crapper." It was just business as usual the entire time. We'd tour, we'd take three or four months off, maybe get back together, and Malcolm and Angus would start banging out songs—business as usual.

LEFT: The label included a make-your-own Gibson SG in vinyl editions of *Who Made Who.*

BELOW: Some believed the 1986 odds 'n' sods collection *Who Made Who* gave *Fly on the Wall*'s follow-up, *Blow Up Your Video*, a boost.

BLOW UP YOUR VIDEO

with **MARK CICCHINI, MARK STRIGL,** and **SIMON WRIGHT**

All songs composed by Angus Young and Malcolm Young

Personnel: Brian Johnson—lead vocals; Angus Young—lead guitar; Malcolm Young—rhythm guitar, backing vocals; Cliff Williams—bass, backing vocals; Simon Wright—drums, percussion

Released January 18, 1988

Recorded at Miraval Studio, Le Val, Provence, France

Produced by Harry Vanda and George Young

BLOW UP YOUR VIDEO

I suppose if we apply some crude math to the commercial results of AC/DC's tenth international album—with no tenth album pizzazz—then dragging back producers Harry Vanda and George Young seemed good for about half a million records. Both *Flick of the Switch* and *Fly on the Wall* sold to all the diehards immediately, achieving gold quickly, though neither saw platinum status until 2001. *Blow Up Your Video*, on the other hand, quickly hit platinum . . . but it's never gone double, and one might argue, for good reason.

Indeed, one might have thought that with 1990's *The Razors Edge* being such a massive return to awesome numbers for the

Aussies, it's near predecessor might have been dragged forward by the momentum, but not so. Fact is, few look at *Blow Up Your Video* as much of a critical success, some even ascribing its decent numbers to the slingshot effect of the odds 'n' sods *Who Made Who* (1986), whose title track is pretty much the band's most beloved anthem since anything from *Back in Black*.

George's threats to little brother Malcolm to pull out of the project unless the latter cleaned up his act with the boozing fell on deaf ears, and against all odds, the band was productive penning an extra five songs, three of them being finished properly and eventually each released as singles. Writing sessions in England shifted to recording in France, and whether it's the incongruity of both of those climes for this band, the results are uninspired, from the riffs through to the lyrics. As for the production, there's no question the record was slicker and more headphone-sympathetic than the two self-produced noisefests previous. But their sort of soft and second-guessed play for what Mutt did—call it three-quarters *Highway to Hell* and a quarter *For Those About to Rock*—couldn't save the fact that this was a band scratching their heads, wondering how to make their usual party record, but for a party they had to throw on the Sunset Strip, unfamiliar with the venue.

As for drilling down into the off-putting songs, I can appreciate that "This Means War" was fast and note-dense, but even like the slow ones and the numbing numbers in between, it's the notes I couldn't and didn't warm to. Highlights would be "Heatseeker," with its Scottish jig melodies in the verse and widdly riff come chorus time, and "Kissin' Dynamite," the most heavy metal song on the album, blessed with an ornery ripsnorter of a riff that would have formed a gang and terrorized the locals on *Flick of the Switch*.

OPPOSITE: Few look at *Blow Up Your Video* as much of a critical success.

BELOW: Some ascribe *Blow*'s decent numbers to the slingshot effect of the odds 'n' sods *Who Made Who* (1986). Here the band tours *Blow Up . . .* at Madison Square Garden, New York City, August 30, 1988.

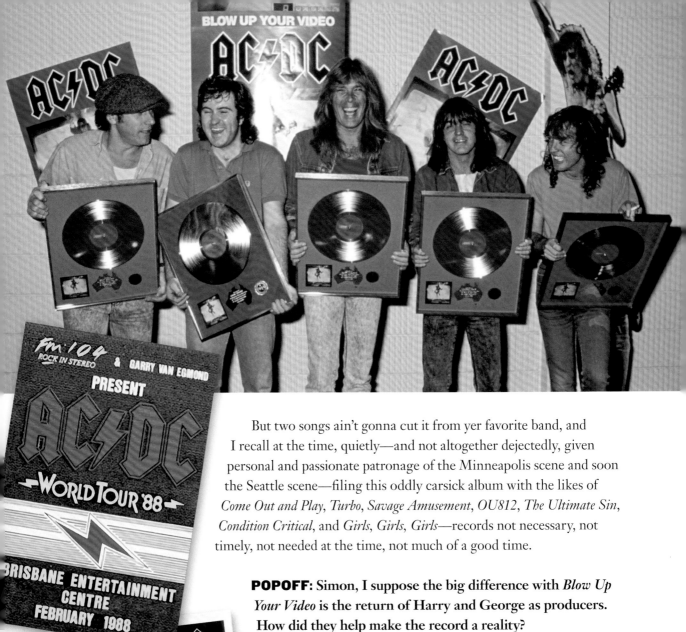

But two songs ain't gonna cut it from yer favorite band, and I recall at the time, quietly—and not altogether dejectedly, given personal and passionate patronage of the Minneapolis scene and soon the Seattle scene—filing this oddly carsick album with the likes of *Come Out and Play*, *Turbo*, *Savage Amusement*, *OU812*, *The Ultimate Sin*, *Condition Critical*, and *Girls, Girls, Girls*—records not necessary, not timely, not needed at the time, not much of a good time.

POPOFF: Simon, I suppose the big difference with *Blow Up Your Video* is the return of Harry and George as producers. How did they help make the record a reality?

WRIGHT: Oh, they brought so much. They're a great team, very musical and a big help. George is good with guitar parts and getting the sounds. And Harry was really good at getting the sounds as well. They would be moving around Angus's cabinet and stuff, getting the best sound, move it around again to get a different kind of lead sound. But the thing I do remember about George and Harry was that it was more

MAIN: *Blow Up Your Video* quickly hit platinum, but it's never gone double. The band collects their discs in February 1988.

LEFT: Forest National, Brussels, March 16, 1988.

productive than it had ever been. There wasn't much downtime. There was a set plan for the day that we would try to achieve with regard to getting songs down and stuff. It was a great time. I have the greatest respect for those two gentlemen and what they've done in the past. They're a couple of classy guys.

CICCHINI: I think they got George and Harry again because they were trying to recapture that magic. It's like someone along the line went, "You know what? Let's go back to being AC/DC, but let's try to make it radio-friendly." And I think it worked. I liked the results from *Blow Up Your Video*, but I think they accomplished the radio-friendly element more on the next one, and I didn't like the next one. To this day, I have a hard time getting through "Moneytalks" and some of that stuff.

POPOFF: Was there an older-brother dynamic going on, with George there?
WRIGHT: Yes, it's something that is just there. He's definitely the older brother. The dynamic doesn't change. You get the feeling he is the older brother who keeps the train on the tracks.

POPOFF: Mark, your thoughts in general about the album?
STRIGL: I thought it was a very strong record, and I also thought *Fly on the Wall* was a very strong record. Maybe it's because of the age I was at the time, seeing AC/DC for the first time on the *Fly on the Wall* tour, which is one of my top-five concerts of all time for sure. I think *Blow Up Your Video* is the last great AC/DC record. There was a chaos and out-of-control sound that I believe the band started to lose after that point. Even though I consider *The Razors Edge* a great record, and it has, in my opinion, probably a handful of songs that are better than what is on *Blow Up Your Video*, this one as a complete album is more powerful to me. You had them bringing back Harry and their brother George. Those two had worked on a couple tunes on *Who Made Who*, but this was the first record with them since *Powerage*. And I feel that old excitement from the Bon era on this record, and Brian's voice is still great. You look at songs like "Kissin' Dynamite" and "Two's Up," there's a sense of chaos that I feel they lost after that. And also, an interesting thing, this is the last record where they gave Brian Johnson a songwriting credit.

Exiting the rocket, Brendan Byrne Arena, East Rutherford, New Jersey, May 20, 1988.

POPOFF: Kind of odd that the album was recorded in France, in a chateau. Simon, any memories of that?

WRIGHT: Oh, it was great, very old world, because some of it was crumbling. Great atmosphere there. It was a great, long barn-like room with lots of wood around, and it gave it a great sound, especially for the drum kit. Weren't many pubs around that I remember [*laughs*], but that didn't stop us. But, you know, it was a great atmosphere. I do remember one strange thing. I got put in a bedroom, and it was up in this kind of tower, and the window was open, and there were all these bits of weeds and leaves on the windowsill. So I brush that away; don't want to get it in the room. And I went back down, and I guess Brian was talking to the lady there, and he was asking her, "Why all the leaves on the windowsill?" "Well," she's saying, "monsieur, that stops the scorpions." I'm like, "Oh shit" [*laughs*]. So I run back upstairs and I'm trying to get them back on the windowsill. Yeah, it keeps the scorpions out of the room or something. I think, actually, Brad Pitt and Angelina Jolie bought that place. It's a winery as well; they've got these huge old barrels there, huge place. Fantastic.

POPOFF: And how long did this record take versus *Fly on the Wall*?

WRIGHT: How long was I there? Maybe two weeks, two and a half weeks. It wasn't constant drum takes every day. They would go back and do vocals and stuff, break it up a little bit. All the songs were written before we got in the studio. And this time, actually, there were more of the demos that were done by Mal with his drum machine, versus Angus. A lot of it was already figured out before we actually started rehearsing, which is good—we were able to get down to it and get on with it.

POPOFF: Of course, all the songs are credited to Malcolm, Angus, and Brian anyway.

WRIGHT: Yes, they would share pretty much everything, and there was never a problem with it. You'd sit and watch ideas go back and forth with each other. Mal would say, "Change this. Hey, that doesn't work; we'll try that. We need something there." Their heads are in the same place when it comes to that. Mal would start up with a riff, and Angus would come up with a bridge or a chorus, and they would throw that around or vice versa. It was like healthy competition. Because it was a given that it would be Young, Young, and Johnson—it was going to end up like that at the end of the day anyway.

(continued on page 168)

Madison Square
Garden, New York City,
August 30, 1988.

Simon Wright would depart
AC/DC to join Dio in November
1989—a year after the conclusion
of the *Blow Up Your Video*
World Tour.

(continued from page 164)

But I admired their work ethic. It was constantly about the band, but in kind of a relaxed way too. It's hard to explain. They knew their stuff so well, and coming along, being a stranger, not being involved with them before, they were very focused with regards to both the songs and the business and how to deal with all of that. I kept my ears and my eyes open and learned quite a lot from them.

POPOFF: Mark, you mentioned "Two's Up" and "Kissin' Dynamite." Why do those stand out on the record for you?

STRIGL: "Two's Up, especially, has a very simple sound, although I suppose they all do. I mean, they could play an A chord over and over again, and because of the energy and the attitude, it would sound great. If another band played those songs, they just wouldn't be as good, but because of the AC/DC combination, including their third brother George, now back in the fold, it sounds great. Another song I like is "Go Zone," which has that fingerpicking thing that Angus does on so many songs, including on *For Those About to Rock*. But he does this insanely, insanely fast yet melodic version of the finger plucking, right before the guitar break, the guitar lead, on that song. One of the things that made *Back in Black* so great was the melody in Angus's guitar solos—you felt every note that he played. And his solo on "Go Zone" stands up there with the greatest in my opinion. After the breakdown with the plucking of the strings, he goes right into this crazy, melodic, awesome, classic, perfect Angus solo.

CICCHINI: I agree on "Go Zone," love that one, but not on "Two's Up." In my opinion, "Two's Up" was right there battling with "Ruff Stuff" as their worst song ever. There's ten minutes of my life I'll never get back. But I think "Ruff Stuff" could be the worst AC/DC song ever. It's just bad all the way around. Otherwise, pretty solid effort. A lot of sex songs, tough guy songs. "That's the Way I Wanna Rock 'n' Roll," always loved that one—great AC/DC vibe and a cool little intro. But I like that there are these extra non-album tracks, B-sides, if you want to call them that. Actually, two of them were just straight up unreleased. "Let It Loose" is an unreleased straight-up rocker, sounds like AC/DC.

POPOFF: But that never got recorded properly. That's just a rehearsal thing, right?

CICCHINI: Correct. I've got a ton of AC/DC bootlegs and the quality on that one is always really rough. But yes, written during those sessions, and a real "If You Want Blood" vibe, which is maybe why they didn't work on it more. "All Right Tonight" is also from the same sessions, but it's a mid-tempo throwaway. And then there's "Snake Eye," which was actually finished and used on the "Heatseeker" single. Solid tune—I think it should've been on the record. "Borrowed Time," another solid song, is the B-side on the "That's the Way I Wanna Rock 'n' Roll" single. "Down on the Borderline" was added to the "Moneytalks" single in 1990, and actually all three of them are in the *Backtracks* box set. So, to clarify, there were five songs, three of which were used, two of which were never properly recorded.

But back to the album itself, "Heatseeker," to me, is everything an AC/DC song should be. I love everything up to "Kissin' Dynamite," where now we have some problems. I just think it's a throwaway, really—weak chorus, weak song construction. I love "Nick of Time," which has this cool buildup; the beginning's got this little high-hat/guitar duel over a really high bass note.

Angus dons the trademark devil horns on the 1988 tour.

POPOFF: And a very melodic chorus for them, right?

CICCHINI: Yes, and it's a cool song. And next up is "Some Sin for Nuthin'," which I just think is ruined by a weak chorus. It's like they're trying to write a Mötley Crüe song; it just sounds like something that would be on *Dr. Feelgood*. Just ain't my thing. And then "This Means War"—cool! It's like a nod to "Beating Around the Bush." It really has that sort of boogie vibe.

POPOFF: Where did AC/DC fit in the music climate of 1988?

STRIGL: I remember the singles, "Heatseeker" and "That's the Way I Wanna Rock 'n' Roll," got significant play in the New York and Philadelphia area. I lived in Trenton at the time, which is kind of halfway between New York City and Philadelphia, so we would get the Philly radio stations and the New York FM stations. Those two songs were quite heavily played, but

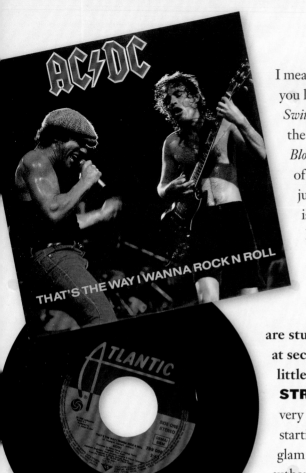

I mean, "Who Made Who" probably more so. And when you look back on *Fly on the Wall* or especially *Flick of the Switch*, those albums received very little radio airplay in the Northeast. Starting with *Who Made Who*, rolling into *Blow Up Your Video*, there was definitely kind of a reprise of them on rock radio. But I thought Brian's vocals were just great on "Heatseeker." I think, in general, that this is one of the last records where they're still top-notch. He's still on fire on this record.

POPOFF: But you see Warrant, Whitesnake, Bon Jovi, Poison, Guns N' Roses, and everybody going multiplatinum, and AC/DC are stuck at platinum and having three records in a row at second tier. Is there something about them being a little yesterday's news?

STRIGL: Well, I never felt that. I felt like they were still very cool, and in some ways, even cooler than what was starting to happen on MTV with the third-generation L.A. glam bands. To me, that stuff was not as nearly as real or authentic as what AC/DC was doing on *Blow Up Your Video*. But I suppose if you were fifteen in 1988, hey, AC/DC is your older brother's band or your uncle's band. I could definitely see that hurting them. A lot of these bands go through this period, and you've seen it with Kiss, where they're not the cool guys anymore. And I suppose that was starting to happen with AC/DC around this time.

CICCHINI: When I was growing up, Led Zeppelin was Led Zeppelin, you know what I mean? In '75, I was ten, but my older brothers and sisters had the records. When I was ten, I started getting into Kiss for obvious reasons. If you were ten in 1985, well, cool, you liked *Back in Black* if you had older brothers and sisters, but you liked Mötley Crüe and you liked Twisted Sister. The nod to the past was cool, and the music was the kind of music you liked, but it wasn't yours. I think that's how the MTV generation looked at it— they wanted something that was theirs, and I don't think AC/DC was theirs.

POPOFF: You raise a good point. AC/DC weren't an MTV band, nor did they try in a big way to play ball. Their videos weren't much to look at, nor did they glam up their look.

Singles "Heatseeker" and "That's the Way I Wanna Rock 'n' Roll" got significant airplay. German picture sleeve pressing, b/w "Kissin' Dynamite," 1988.

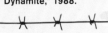

CICCHINI: For sure, and I tell you what. Look at a band that was very similar in tone and everything to AC/DC—Krokus. They didn't have AC/DC's success, but look what happened when they tried to doll them up for MTV. The results were horrible. And to this fan, they ruined the band. I can't get into "Midnight Maniac"—I like "Headhunter" [*laughs*]. Actually, what saved AC/DC in some ways were those singles that weren't album tracks, "Who Made Who" in the lead-up time to this album, and in 1993, "Big Gun," both of which got a lot of airplay. AC/DC hooked up with two successful movies, and those movies helped generate business for the single. Guns N' Roses did the same thing with "You Could Be Mine," and I believe Aerosmith did this as well. It was corporate now. It wasn't five little guys on stage making a big noise.

POPOFF: Simon, what do you remember about recording those *Who Made Who* **songs?**
WRIGHT: We went to Nassau in the Bahamas, which was, "Wow, great!" and there was a great studio there. But it was a little strange because there were TV monitors put up, and for some of the tracks, we would actually play along to that part of the movie, just so we could get a feel of it. Plus, there were a couple of blues things that we did where we just played. It was short and sweet, and it got done, but again, a great time. Stephen King came out said hello and stuff. The song "Who Made Who" turned out really well and I was really happy with the drum sound. It really didn't take a long time to fiddle with. We just got it and went for it. But yeah, good groove, simple riff, great chorus. I believe I used my white Sonor kit, and the snare . . . it was definitely a light drum and it had a really good kind of crack to it.

POPOFF: Do you remember any discussion about how they came up with that strange title, *Blow Up Your Video***?**
WRIGHT: I think that was Angus's idea. Angus comes up with a lot of the ideas. There was no real debate about that. I think what they were just trying to say there was, "Hey, turn off your TV and come to a show."

POPOFF: Mark, would you say with that title that there's an element of the band resisting change?
CICCHINI: Yes, that's a lyric from "That's the Way I Wanna Rock 'n' Roll." This was them expressing frustration, because now they're having to be with the MTV bands. And let's face it, they had the Angus shtick, but they

couldn't compete with the Vince Neils or anyone who was on the cover of *Metal Edge* [*laughs*]. Sure, they put AC/DC on the cover of *Metal Edge*, but it was a small picture. They had a big one of the clown from Poison. That's what they were selling. They weren't selling music. They were selling this shit to teenage girls. It wasn't guys who bought that.

STRIGL: AC/DC started long before music videos and probably didn't need music videos. I always thought it was kind of a middle finger to the MTV music video generation.

POPOFF: The band ends the album in a blaze of glory with "This Means War." I don't know if it's the heaviest song on the album, but it's the fastest.

STRIGL: Yes, and that's a perfect album closer, because it ends the record like an ice pick in the forehead. It's this fast, up-tempo, angry type of closer. I don't know if you would call that a boogie-woogie groove, but it ends the album with a bang, even though it recalls, for me, an older song like "The Rocker." It's got that tempo, that fast, driving, AC/DC train running -off-the-rails type of vibe where you think somebody's gonna get hurt [*laughs*]. It's also another example of how unorthodox in structure some of their songs can be. Even going way back to "Let There Be Rock," there's no real chorus in that song. It's verse/solo, verse/solo, right? But it's got attitude and a sense of chaos, as does this song. There was a danger there that made it so intriguing. You could just feel it in your heart. Sure, AC/DC had great songs, but it was the attitude and the drive behind them. They would take these simple songs and shove them down your throat and that's what makes them so great.

POPOFF: Once the album was out, we had the strange situation where the nephew, Stevie Young, was brought in for tour dates. What happened there?

WRIGHT: Malcolm was having a lot of problems with his son at home, and he started drinking a lot. And he just needed to step away. That's when Stevie Young came in, thank God. There had been a show in France we did, and it was in a field, and it was a stage setup, and Malcolm had had a few, and yeah, you can't blame the guy. He had so many problems at home and stuff, and he didn't really need to be on tour, but he had these commitments to tour. It just got to him. And we all felt so, so bad for him. We really did all feel bad for him.

But yeah, we finished up, and it was not one of the greatest shows that we've ever played, but there were stairs going down, and at the bottom, after we finished, Malcolm and Angus were getting into it and fists were flying and this kind of thing [*laughs*]. I couldn't analyze, really, exactly what caused it, but I don't think Malcolm was blaming his brother for all his problems, but probably his brother was, you know, in the right place the right time. It was awful. It was really awful, seeing someone so strong and so confident in all things, suddenly get so upset and out of control. But he went home and he got better, and his son got better. We carried on with Stevie, as history has shown us, and we just kept going. And thankfully Malcolm came back.

Madison Square Garden, New York City, August 30, 1988.

POPOFF: **What kind of guy was Stevie?**
WRIGHT: He's cool. He's a lot like Malcolm in a way. He definitely has that kind of fire. Gets his head down and gets on with the job. It was a massive thing for him too, being in the band. Of course, he's family himself, and his band Starfighters opened up for the band years and years ago. But yeah, he did a great job, and as history would have it, twenty-five years later, Stevie would step in again.

THE RAZORS EDGE

with **MIKE FRASER** and **JOEL O'KEEFFE**

All songs composed by Angus Young and Malcolm Young

Personnel: Brian Johnson—lead vocals; Angus Young—lead guitar; Malcolm Young—rhythm guitar, backing vocals; Cliff Williams—bass, backing vocals; Chris Slade—drums, percussion

Released September 24, 1990

Recorded at Windmill Road Studios, Dublin, and Little Mountain Studios, Vancouver, Canada

Produced by Bruce Fairbairn

After a couple records that felt, frankly, phoned-in, AC/DC wind up in the place where every tired band goes to recharge their batteries: Vancouver.

Now, the band first tried to make the record in Ireland, of all places, before their bounce to what is called "supernatural" British Columbia, a destination that would revive the careers of Aerosmith, Bon Jovi, and Mötley Crüe, and catapult the Cult further onward and upward beyond the success they had had with their previous couple of albums.

And the music on *The Razors Edge* sounds like a band trying harder than they had in a decade, working with the craft and purpose and mission last transmitted to their millions of fans via a little something called *Back in Black*.

Annoying lack of an apostrophe in the title notwithstanding, *The Razors Edge* is full of action and energy and swagger. Sure, there's the open architecture of "Thunderstruck," the beguiling charm of "Moneytalks," the nervous energy of "Fire Your Guns," and a really heavy hit in "Are You Ready." But the back half of the album is loads of noggin-nodding fun as well, even when it's slow, as with "Got You By the Balls," and bluesy, with closer "If You Dare" finding the band commandeering light and shade like Led Zeppelin.

And the marketplace would respond, when really, given shifting music trends, one wouldn't expect it. I mean, with hard rock and heavy metal being huge from sort of 1983 through to about 1989, bigger than it had ever been, AC/DC had fallen back in the pack with three consecutive critically dismissed albums that reached only single-platinum status. So it was even more of a surprise that in 1990, with thrash and hair metal still doing well, but all forms of heavy metal about to tank (mostly displaced by five years of grunge), AC/DC would bounce back onto the world stage, powered by their big bald and brand-new drummer, with a record that would go an astounding five times platinum.

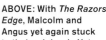

ABOVE: With *The Razors Edge*, Malcolm and Angus yet again stuck to their rulebook. Yet somehow the band created a tight and disciplined record that included what would be their last huge hit.

OPPOSITE: Annoying lack of an apostrophe aside, *The Razors Edge* is full of energy and swagger.

Truth is, *The Razors Edge* is a record worthy of those numbers. The geometry and calculus of how Malcolm and Angus configured their riffs, how they worked yet again right at the middle of their rulebook . . . that hadn't changed perceptibly against the previous three to four albums. But somehow, whether it was the sea-to-sky mountain air outside Little Mountain Studios or an uneasy look around at the competition, AC/DC responded vigorously, creating a tight and disciplined record of shiny diamonds, one of which would be their last huge hit and, quite possibly, the band's most endearing and culturally invasive classic of all time.

POPOFF: There's a sense of a reset for the band with *The Razors Edge*. How do you view this record versus *Blow Up Your Video*?

O'KEEFFE: Straight off the bat, it was the first thing I bought when I was a kid, on cassette tape. But the production is on a whole different level. It's really defined, but it's also just a great rock 'n' roll album from start to finish. It's still big and bombastic, in a way, but it's not like *Blow Up Your Video*. *The Razors Edge* is like a razor—it cuts you down the middle.

POPOFF: That's a good way to put it, and I agree that it has to do very much with the production, which was handled by Bruce Fairbairn of Loverboy, Bon Jovi, and Aerosmith fame. How did the association with Bruce happen?

FRASER: Bruce was having a lot of success at the time. He'd done *Slippery When Wet* with Bon Jovi, which was a huge record, plus *New Jersey*. He had done the Aerosmith records, *Permanent Vacation* and *Pump*. AC/DC had been recording that album with their older brother George, and there was a sickness in the family. And I don't remember if it was George or some other member, but anyway, George couldn't finish the record. So management said, "Okay, what other producers would you want to work with?" "Oh, how about let's check out Bruce Fairbairn?" They liked what they saw and they came up to Vancouver to finish the record.

O'KEEFFE: This was the first album they did with an outside producer again, since *For Those About to Rock*. This is them going back outside again, to another producer. And Fairbairn had a lot of good runs at the board at the time, and Mike Fraser, who engineered this and mixed it, he just did our album, *Breakin' Outta Hell*. And at that point, Mike had a lot of good runs on the board as well. And so you've got a real rock 'n' roll Canadian dream

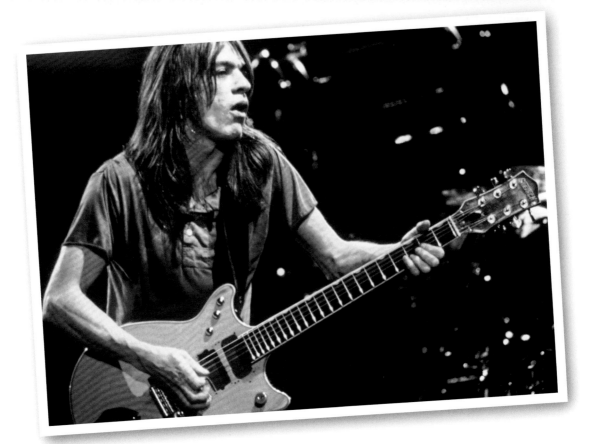

team here. But that's the benefit of an outside producer, and why they got this great album, because he's the one cracking the whip.

POPOFF: Joel, this record was your entry point as a fan. Mike, you started working with the band on this record, but where was your entry point as a fan?

FRASER: I'd first seen them open for Aerosmith. I didn't know who AC/DC was, but they kicked my ass. Aerosmith came out and they were really bad. They were at the height of their sort of drug days, so the show was really bad, but, "Oh, who is this is?" Must have been the *Highway to Hell* tour, because I definitely got to see Bon Scott live, which I didn't really know it or appreciate it. So I guess *Highway to Hell* was the first record I checked out and bought. Then I was a big fan every since.

POPOFF: Where did they slot into your ranking of favorite bands in '79–'80?

FRASER: They shot right to the top, and I went and checked out their old stuff. "Long Way to the Top" has got to be one of my all-time favorite songs. That clip with them on the back of a flatbed truck driving through the middle of Melbourne, rocking away in front of a handful of people,

maybe a hundred people watching. If they only knew back then that they were witnessing the beginning of rock greatness.

POPOFF: And then you would go on to work with, on and off, Brian Johnson for pretty much twenty-three, twenty-four years. What does Brian bring to the band versus Bon?

FRASER: Brian brought sort of a more sophisticated voice. In my opinion, Bon had a gravellier voice. Brian, with his background with Geordie and whatnot, was kind of a crooner, you know? The rock crooner kind of thing. So he brought that sophisticated smoothness. And Brian's got a higher range than Bon ever did, so that added another dimension to the band. When you hear songs like "You Shook Me All Night Long," there's some friggin' high notes there.

POPOFF: *The Razors Edge* would begin a string of records made in Vancouver, with only *Ballbreaker* recorded elsewhere. Although it's the only one at Little Mountain.

FRASER: That's right, well, Little Mountain was one of the premier studios in Vancouver at the time. Warehouse didn't exist at that point. Little Mountain had a nice big recording room, and because it was built in the seventies, it was very dead. It was built as a jingles studio, so there's carpet everywhere and deadening on the wall, and so it was very dead, so you could get a very close drum sound.

And then we had a loading bay, so you could open one of the doors and funnel the sound out there and have separate mics in the loading bay. And so you could have a combination of dry sound and loading bay sound very easily. They liked that because their drum sound is very, very dry and in your face. But with the extra loading bay sound, as a mixer, I could add in more ambient drums, say, in a chorus or something, just to make the drums seem like they're getting bigger. And then by the time we were doing *Stiff Upper Lip* and the other records, Little Mountain doesn't exist as a studio anymore. The Warehouse was the closest thing to the drum room that Little Mountain had.

POPOFF: I've heard stories about how despite there being No Smoking signs everywhere, at the end of an AC/DC session, there were cigarette butts everywhere.

FRASER: Yep, well, when we did *The Razors Edge* they came in and all their crew is loading the gear in, and Bruce is kinda talking to them, and here's this room and here's the kitchen, and sort of giving them the lowdown. And he says, "I only have one rule in my sessions. I don't like any smoking in the control room. But, you know, feel free to smoke anywhere else," and all that. And both Angus and Mal, sort of right at the same time, lit up a cigarette, said, "Yeah, well, we smoke in here too" [*laughs*].

And not being assholes, but that's just who they are. If they're going to spend all the time in the control room, they're smoking. And years later, you know, the smoking laws changed, you can't smoke inside anywhere. But the Warehouse Studio, again, Mal and Ang says, "Nah, we're gonna smoke." So they said, "Oh, we're gonna have to, at the end of the session, charge you a cleaning fee." And they said, "Yep, no problem. We're smoking" [*laughs*]. Because that's their only vice. That's all they do. They smoke and drink tea. A couple of the guys, Brian and Phil and Cliff, you know, they'll have a few beers or a glass of wine, but Mal and Angus, nothing.

POPOFF: And what did Bruce add to the equation?

FRASER: Well, production-wise, Bruce always likes to have hooks and things that the audience goes to. So there's the basic structure of the song, with the bass and drums, but Bruce . . . for instance, in "Thunderstruck," that was his idea to put that intro guitar on, and that became a hook through the whole song. Another one of Bruce's ideas was the background vocals in that one, because that draws the listener in. "Oh, hey, that's interesting, let's continue with this song." It draws you into wanting to listen to more of the song. So Bruce is very good at adding little tidbits on top without overly cluttering the song.

O'KEEFFE: Classic track, yeah, and the pull-offs that Angus plays, if you notice, they go through the whole song. If you put your headphones on, it's being pulled down in the mix and keeps coming back. That song builds and builds. I've read that they spent a bit of time with that one. They didn't have the whole idea of the song, including the chanting part. It's a song that just grew.

FRASER: We were working on "Thunderstruck," and Bruce Fairbairn said, "Hey, we need some sort of an intro or something for the song." And Angus said, "I've got a little something here," and he lit a cigarette and he put it in his mouth, and he started out with that *deedle-deedle-dee* thing. So he started playing it and we recorded it, and we were going along, and he did the intro, and the first verse hits and he's still playing. And first chorus hits and he's still playing. And he played it one take, all the way through the song [*laughs*]. And at the end of the song, the cigarette is still hanging out of his mouth and it's just one long ash, and he's like, "Well, what did you think of that?" But Joel's right. Listen back to that song and you can hear it through the whole song. We just sort of dip it down in parts in the mix, but you can hear it through the whole song. One take.

POPOFF: That became a monster anthem. I mean, it's the reason the album sold through the roof.

FRASER: For sure. It's a heck of a song, and I knew when we recorded that it was going to be a good song. But back then, you didn't have any inclination that it was going to be one of their anthemic songs. I think it's right up there with "Shook Me" and "Back in Black" and "Highway to Hell." It was a huge song for them. Definitely one of my faves from back in the day from the stuff I've worked on.

POPOFF: What are the contours of the rest of the album?

O'KEEFFE: There's a certain sound on this album different from all the others, but anyway, the album starts big with "Thunderstruck." Then you get into "Fire Your Guns," and they kick you right in the balls. My favorite solo would have to be "Fire Your Guns." And then "Moneytalks" was a big single as well as a big sing-along. "The Razors Edge" is darker but then "Mistress for Christmas," I love that song—always play it at Christmas. And later on, "Are You Ready" is a big song that always gets me going— I love that as much as I love "Thunderstruck." You can't top this album at all. "Rock Your Heart Out" is amazing, and if you really listen to the two guitars, that's a good one for interplay. Same as "Shot of Love"—two separate guitars really working well. That's a real AC/DC trait.

POPOFF: So how would you differentiate between Malcolm and Angus when they are both playing rhythm?

O'KEEFFE: Malcolm is more of a machine, where it's like, you get all the power chords from his right hand. Mal will just give you the whole chord and keep it simple. So when you put the two guitars together, it sounds a lot bigger. Sometimes Angus would just pick the notes. He'll just play a few notes of the riff as opposed to the whole power chord, and then you put them together and it sounds really cool.

POPOFF: Is there an element to this interplay that is inspired by the famed Rolling Stones weave, as Keith Richards describes it? The way he and Ron Wood weave the story between each other and their parts?

O'KEEFFE: They're huge Rolling Stones fans, so I would imagine. Being brothers—like myself and Ryan in Airbourne—sitting around playing guitar, they just would've done it naturally as well. Because the younger brother's gonna do what the other one is doing, because he's the big brother. And then you do that, I'm gonna do my thing—they challenge each other. But as the story goes, Malcolm is an amazing lead player; he could play all of Angus's solos and all that stuff. He's a guitar virtuoso. But he says, "I'm gonna hang back and do this."

POPOFF: Along with this interplay, there's a subtle sophistication to the arrangements as well.

FRASER: You're right, the songs may sound very simplistic, but when you really get into it, there's kind of a complicated simplicity, which is really hard to do well. Because there's no hiding behind layers of an orchestra or blocks of vocals or keyboards or anything. It's really bass, drums, and guitars and a vocal on top. It's very simple, but they have to have the arrangements right. The tempo has to be right, the song . . . everything's got to be perfect about the song to kick off. You can't hide behind any of the fairy dust because there isn't any.

POPOFF: And when Angus solos, what do we get?

O'KEEFFE: Each one of Angus's solos—and this is a great album for it— there's always a few moments in each solo, some stars, like stars in the skies,

"Moneytalks" was a big single as well as a big sing-along. AC/DC carried the theme through its promotional materials for the album.

The solo to "Are You Ready" has a classic Angus hook that he can hang his schoolboy hat on.

some hooks, where you remember it. There's a classic moment in "Thunderstruck," there's a classic moment in "Are You Ready." There's a classic piece that makes the solo iconic. It's always steeped in the blues, but if he didn't do that additional memorable hook, it would just be a solo and that would be it. But he always puts something to hang his schoolboy hat on, in the solo.

FRASER: Well, Angus just loves the blues. You know, he'll talk forever about the blues. He has his list of favorite artists who I don't even know who the heck they are. That's his background, and you hear that in a lot of his solos, a lot of the bluesier licks. And he rocks them up a bit more than the slow blues bendy stuff. But that's where he's at and what he loves to do. And in the studio, it's amazing doing solos with him, because we we'll say, "Let's do three or four takes," and he'll whip up three completely different solos and you have to try to decide which one is better. And neither is better or worse than the other one. It's just, this one's a little different, but this one's cool too. It was always a hard decision, which solo to go with, because he was always so amazing. Mal never soloed, though Angus would be quick to tell you that Malcolm can play solos better than he can. But Mal always said, "Angus, that's your job—you do them."

POPOFF: And how strict is this rule the guys have about Malcolm being in the left speaker and Angus in the right?

FRASER: That's always been the thing from day one: Malcolm is always in the left and Angus is always in the right. But it's funny, geez, I forget which record, but I was driving to work one day here in Vancouver, and one of the local stations played their "brand-new single just out today!" I can't remember the song.

Anyway, it comes on and I'm going, "Hey, Angus is in the left speaker. Mal is in the right!" So I phoned the program director in the station as I was driving in, and I said, "Hey, you've got a problem with your station. Your outputs are flipped." "Oh, it's your car." I said, "No, it's not my car. My car has always been right." So I went in there later that day, and back in their control room, they played the record and it was correct: Mal was to the left,

Angus was in the right. So I checked out my car, and no, the speakers were right. So I don't know what happened there.

About a month later, the program director phoned me up and says, "You know what? You were right." Routine maintenance check or whatever, it was something to do with their feed to their transformer—somehow it got flipped left to right [*laughs*].

POPOFF: Funny. Now, one odd thing—and I've heard it was because he was preoccupied with his divorce—but this is the first record where Brian is not in on the song credits. What's going on there?
FRASER: Well, on that record, I believe, you know, he would sit with the lads and . . . I would always be busy running around recording and doing something else so I wasn't privy to a lot of that. I would see him sort of bouncing ideas around with the brothers, but from my understanding, after *Blow Up Your Video*, which Brian was the lyricist on, I think the brothers just wanted to sort of pull everything back into the family. I don't really know what went on there.

POPOFF: It's odd that they've got a Christmas carol on here!
FRASER: Yes, it was. Bruce says, "Hey, we need a couple more songs." And they always have a stockpile of little riffs and little ideas that had never quite developed into songs. And Mal and Ang said, "Okay, give us a day or two." So they went back to their hotel room and worked through all their little riffs and came back to the studio with this thing. And then they talked about lyrics and all that, and they said, "Well, let's do something that maybe they can put out for Christmas." And make it a little bit dirty; they loved their sort of double entendres in their songs.

POPOFF: We've talked about the production being a factor in this record's sound, but they've also got a new drummer in Chris Slade. How did that affect the band's sound?
O'KEEFFE: Chris Slade brings a different intensity and attack, and you can hear it in "Fire Your Guns." In that song he brings a real stadium-style drumming, which is what you get in "Thunderstruck" and "Are You Ready" as well. And it's still simplistic like you would have with Phil, but you don't have Phil's shuffle or groove. It's different, more of an attack. It's more let the hammer down as opposed to sitting back.

With Chris, they definitely went and found themselves again, and they found a whole lot more too. I think having Chris Slade there brought a

new energy to the band, a whole new spark. Because if you look at them at that concert from Donington, every song is a little bit faster. He brought a real energy to that band when they needed at the most. And they just stepped up. Like, "Whole Lotta Rosie" is so fast live—it's just going.

POPOFF: And then why was Chris Slade out of the band again so quickly?
O'KEEFFE: Well, Phil wanted to come back, and so AC/DC were like, "Yeah, we're really sorry, we've got to take him back." And I think Chris Slade wasn't too happy about that. But you know, Phil, he's just got a certain sound. So they wanted to do that again, and that's why with *Ballbreaker* and *Stiff Upper Lip*, they stripped it all back again. I gotta say, I love *Ballbreaker*. When I was a kid and got *The Razors Edge*, *Ballbreaker* was the next one, and I know they spent a lot of time on it, although from what I hear Rick Rubin didn't do a lot.

POPOFF: And Mike, how about your assessment of Chris as a drummer?
FRASER: Well, most of the drums were already done so I didn't work much with Chris. They had worked in a studio in Ireland. They

Chris Slade brought a whole new attack and energy to the band. Wembley Arena, London, April 15–17, 1991.

had pretty much the whole record done and all they wanted us to do was the lead guitars and the vocals. Brian started singing, and he was having trouble hitting some of the notes in the song—it was the wrong key for him. We had to change the key of the song, which we did, and we had to re-record the guitars and the bass to change the key. And Mal liked the sound of the guitars so much better we ended up re-recording all the guitars, and we changed keys on two or three of them along the way.

But by the time we were done with everything . . . I think Bruce said, "Hey, we need a couple more songs, just to sort of round this record out."

So we recorded, I think, just two more songs, one being "Mistress for Christmas." So there were only two that I recorded drums with Chris on.

As far as a drummer, I think Chris is a really good drummer. He's a bit of a departure from Phil. Phil is a real thumper, and to me, one of the heartbeat souls of the band. Chris is really good, but he's a little bit more . . . I want to say straighter than Phil. You know, he played everything really nicely, Chris. And it worked out, but my personal preference is Phil on the drums.

POPOFF: And as we were saying, *The Razors Edge* put the band back on top, selling an astounding five times as many copies in America as *Blow Up Your Video*. Was this the point where they became an institution?
O'KEEFFE: Well, in Australia they were always an institution. Like, I mean, they're the biggest rock 'n' roll band in the world as it is, and back home, that's certainly what it's like. It's like Rolling Stones, AC/DC, Rolling Stones, AC/DC, the two big guns like that, that keep playing rock 'n' roll.

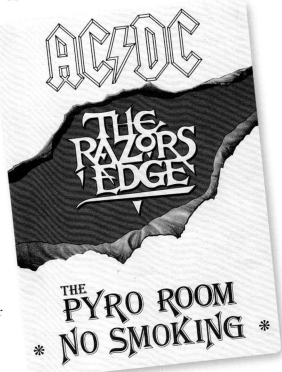

Dressing-room door sign, *The Razors Edge* World Tour.

And even then in the beginning, they were the biggest Australian pub rock 'n' roll band, coming out at the time with the Angels, Billy Thorpe & the Aztecs, Skyhooks. There's a lot of bands that were going around Australia at the time, that had limited success overseas. But Australia, being what it was at the time, it just had so many great bands that could have a huge following in Australia. But it was AC/DC that took it to the world. Rose Tattoo, Cold Chisel, they all went overseas—and Rose Tattoo was really well respected in Germany and certain places—but it was AC/DC that did it.

So AC/DC back home, they're the biggest. When they come out to tour, it's the biggest touring act to come to the country. But yeah, no question, with *The Razors Edge*, they cemented their legacy. It was undeniably a great album. Instead of just trying to spray the jungle with a machine gun, it was basically all sniper bullets hitting the target. Every last song hits the target.

CHAPTER 13

BALLBREAKER

with MIKE FRASER and ROBERT LAWSON

All songs composed by Angus Young and Malcolm Young

Personnel: Brian Johnson—lead vocals; Angus Young—rhythm and lead guitars; Malcolm Young—rhythm guitar, backing vocals; Cliff Williams—bass, backing vocals; Phil Rudd—drums, percussion

Released September 26, 1995

Recorded at the Record Plant, New York City, and Ocean Way Studios, Los Angeles

Produced by Rick Rubin; co-produced by Mike Fraser

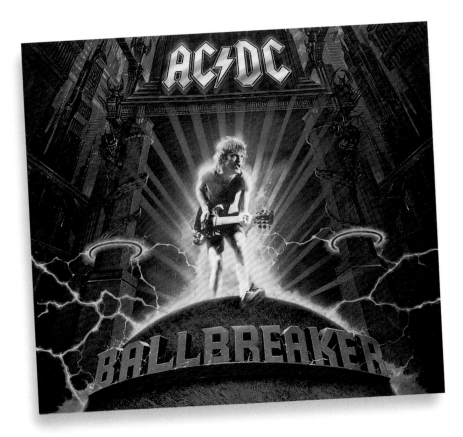

After six records in the seventies and five in the eighties (also six if one includes *The Razors Edge*, 1990), with *Ballbreaker*, AC/DC shift into a phase that one might call semiretirement or, put another way, part-time band status. Fact is, in the past twenty-five years, AC/DC have given the world four studio albums, *Ballbreaker* being the first in this subtle transition away from working (and workingman's) band toward life as gentleman rockers of leisure.

And the album's comfy vibe somewhat reflects that, despite what we know of its assembly in the hustle and bustle of New York and L.A., partly under the auspices of marquee (and little else) producer Rick Rubin and with engineer Mike Fraser, really, saving the day.

But putting that aside—and in fact incongruous to that bicoastal and American drama—*Ballbreaker* sounds warm and even twee, as if it was the work of George and Harry at Albert. There's an element of the expensive, but not of grandeur or heaviness, more like Keith Richards in smoking jacket with a snifter of brandy in his library, admiring an antiquarian volume in gauzy seclusion from the noise pollution of the record industry outside the door and past the guardhouse.

So the effect is of a record that on one hand lacked urgency or purpose—not flung out by the band or begged for by the world—and on the other hand is a news event, like a ZZ Top record, like a Rolling Stones record. It's news, especially after five years away, but it's happening on a plane away from reality, the reality in 1995 being post-grunge hard alternative, industrial, techno, singing/songwriting girls of empowerment, pop punk, Britpop . . . anything but heavy metal or classic rock.

Into this lively gaggle of shiny, happy, well-meaning people, the old men of AC/DC drop the crudely titled *Ballbreaker*. The album instantly sells platinum, achieving double-platinum status six years later, but one conjectures that part of that is due to pent-up demand from this very long wait for a new record. Remember, as well, there was no downloading or streaming yet, and indeed, not even an Internet, really. But the main point is that there was little critical excitement about this often quaint and billowy and pillowy record, and certainly very little cultural impact. Adding insult

OPPOSITE: *Ballbreaker* sounds warm and even twee, as if it was the work of George and Harry at Albert Studios.

BELOW: Fact is, *Ballbreaker* is the first album in AC/DC's subtle transition from workingman's band to life as gentleman rockers of leisure.

to injury, none of these songs have lived on, as one suspects will be the fate with all the material past side one, track one of *The Razors Edge*.

POPOFF: Okay, to kick things off, a general question: What are the distinguishing factors with *Ballbreaker* versus *The Razors Edge*?

LAWSON: It's a bit of an odd record, but it's got a couple of neat things going for it, one being the return of Phil Rudd. To my mind, on all those early classic AC/DC records, Phil Rudd is the driving force; his sound is just incredible. So having him back is really interesting. Second, the idea of them being produced by Rick Rubin is pretty interesting. They kind of auditioned him, by doing the song "Big Gun" for the Arnold Schwarzenegger movie, *Last Action Hero*, and that did pretty well. The video with Arnold Schwarzenegger dressed up in the schoolboy uniform next to Angus is kind of a novelty stunt casting thing, but that's going to get airplay. If you put that image in a video, people are gonna play it just for the odd sight of these two famous guys together. But then the album kind of didn't do so well.

POPOFF: What happened?

LAWSON: Well, it's not that it didn't do well sales-wise—there's no issues there. I just think artistically, the band didn't seem too happy with it. The common complaint is that Rick Rubin was distracted during the recording, because he was doing the Red Hot Chili Peppers record, *One Hot Minute*, at the same time. So there was an initial report that they spent multiple weeks in a New York studio just doing the drums, and nothing salvageable came from that. So they were all pretty disgruntled. And then they moved to L.A., and Rick Rubin spent most of the time with the Chili Peppers, and he was leaving the engineer, Mike Fraser, to finish the album.

POPOFF: Mike, would that be a fairly accurate assessment of the situation?

FRASER: Yes, that's pretty much it. I got the call when they were getting ready to do that record. They wanted to use Rick Rubin because they'd just worked with him on "Big Gun." So we said okay, great, and I met with Rick in L.A., and we got on really great, and I was quite excited to be working with him. And the band wanted to do it in New York, because, I guess, Rick gets distracted a lot when he's home there in L.A.. So they said, "Let's go do it in New York."

I was working on another project at the time. We were setting up to start recording in about a month's time. Well, somehow, I don't know why, somebody moved the dates up. It was still two weeks before we were set to start and I get a phone call. They're now loading into a studio in New York. Rick Rubin and one of his assistants or something scoured studios in New York and decided to record at the Record Plant. Okay, great, that's supposed to be a great studio.

Wembley Arena,
London, June 21, 1996.

I said, "I can't make it 'til I'm finished this project." And they said, "Okay, we'll just get it going with Rick. We're setting up sounds and all that, and then as soon as you get away, come on out." I think about three days later I get a call from Angus saying, "Please, you gotta come out here, we're struggling with trying to get a sound and everything."

The Record Plant, at that time, had a big kind of round really ambient room. And we were trying to get very close, in-your-face drums. So a lot of the problem was we couldn't get a dry enough drum sound. We'd put baffles all around the drums, and then we put baffles and big heavy blankets around them, and had to hang lights so Phil could see. And that still wasn't working, so at one point, Rick even rented a circus tent. We had to cover the whole studio in a circus tent to stop the drum reflections. And we even stapled up burlap sacks on all the walls to try to deaden down the sound—nothin'! And I think we tried for about four or five weeks, and we just couldn't get the drum sound we were looking for. So we pulled up the pegs and moved to L.A., went to Ocean Way, and got the drum sound in about twenty minutes [*laughs*].

POPOFF: What was the state of the songs? Was there writer's block? Arguments on the creative end as well?
FRASER: Not really, you know, they had all the songs written. But another problem, in New York we had the problem with the sound and everything, but now we go to L.A., well now they've already played through all these songs a million times. And everybody is getting kind of bored. So it's a little bit tough going there. And then Rick wasn't really showing up much. He'd show up at seven, eight o'clock at night, and we'd all been there since noon. So there's a few tensions going on with that record. But anyway, we got it done, and I think I

got the co-production credit just because I was there the whole time. But Rick produced the record. The band didn't want to play anything until Rick was in the room in case he wanted to change something on the spot. You know, we could sit there and record all the songs, and then Rick would come in and change things, and the band didn't want to do that.

POPOFF: What would Rick change? What was his main function on the creative end?
FRASER: Rick's the kind of guy . . . he's really good at knowing when something's magic. So when the magic hits, he'll go, "Yes, that's what I want!" But other than that, there weren't too many creative things he would put in. And a band like AC/DC is actually pretty hard to produce. Because they don't really need a producer. They know exactly what they want and how to get it. But what they like out of a producer is for them to be able to pick the gold nuggets and go, "Yes, just the way you played that, that's great, let's do that!" And that's where Rick was good. But then Rick was just too distracted with whatever else he had going on. And the band didn't really like that. Why are you here, you know?

Melbourne Park,
Melbourne, Australia,
November 7–9, 1996.

POPOFF: In what way was your role increased? What did you do in terms of production?
FRASER: Once we sort of got the songs down, I really worked a lot with Brian and coaxed him along, and tried to keep his spirits up. Because, again, after doing the song so many times, it was like, "Oh, yeah, this song again." So again . . . not our energy level, but it was sort of down, you know? We were kinda, not down in the dumps, but at the end there, it was sort of work to try to keep the energy up and keep excited about the songs. Because we lived with them for so long [*laughs*].

POPOFF: I understand that Rick would make Malcolm do takes over and over again.
FRASER: Yep, over and over and over and over, and finally, the band would say, "Well, what are you looking for? Why are we doing it again? Did you like that one?" "Yeah, no, that was a good one. You know, I'm just looking for the right one." "Uh, okay" [*laughs*].

Quite an entrance. The Forum, Inglewood, California, February 21, 1996.

POPOFF: And Robert, what do you think? Was all the work worth it?
LAWSON: It sounds like an AC/DC record, although I think it's a little colder than what we saw in the past with the George Young/Harry Vanda records. Which is a much more organic sound. You know, from what I heard Rick had Malcolm do up to fifty takes sometimes, and for a basic, meat-and-potatoes rock 'n' roll band like AC/DC, they tend to lose steam after a few takes. They tend to capture the fire early on. And you know, I have fond memories of buying this record when it came out, playing it at my first apartment in Toronto, and it didn't grab me. I was a hard-core AC/DC fan and this was the first one that just fell flat for me.

One thing I wonder about, not that guys like Angus and Malcolm need their hands held, but they need a producer that they could really trust, and who really kind of believes in them. And Rubin just showed early on that he wasn't that guy. And if they don't have that support, I don't think they bring their A game. Like, if he doesn't care about them enough in their eyes to try to capture that first take, and then he runs off and spends most of the time with the Chili Peppers, you know, they're being neglected.

The band were really cared for by George Young and Harry Vanda, and George was the older brother, and Bon was Australian and they recorded at Albert . . . there was a real family atmosphere in Australia when they started, and I think that's significant. The band has always been very close-knit. And so for them to trust outsiders . . . it's manifest as well in why they only kind of get so many substitute players. When they have to, it's got to be people they know and trust. They're a real clan.

FRASER: That's right, and they are very private as well. As far as the Young brothers, their whole lives, that I know, when we were doing records is hotel room, studio, hotel room, studio [*laughs*]. Occasionally, maybe we'd go out to eat, but rarely Malcolm or Angus would join us. They're just more comfortable being in their own little environment. So we spent the whole time in the studio. We'd arrive . . . well, us crew guys would arrive ten-thirty, eleven in the morning, and the band would show up at noon, and we'd work quite often until midnight, or one a.m., or something like that. No, they're very dedicated, and they're doing this because they love to do it, not because they need to do it. So that's another cool thing about working with these guys.

But to clarify, this thing with the Chili Peppers, it was sort of more toward the end of the tracking. At Ocean Way, all of a sudden Chili Peppers showed up in the opposite studio, and Rick was bouncing back and forth between the rooms. But he assured the band, "No, no, we're not actually working; they're just working through songs and rehearsing and stuff." So I don't know if they were actually doing the record then. But yeah, he'd bounce back and forth. And that was probably a good thing, because I think he was there more—maybe not in our room, but at least he's in the building [*laughs*]. We could always grab him when there was a question: "Hey Rick, come check this out," and he was there.

POPOFF: Robert, walk me through the record a bit. What are some of the highlights?

LAWSON: Well, "Hard as a Rock" has a pretty nice ringing guitar sound. I don't think there's much more to it. I should mention, it's interesting that they tell Brian that he can't write lyrics anymore for them, and Malcolm and Angus are going to take over, and then this album has terrible lyrics [*laughs*]. It's like they're obsessed with teenage sex. I mean, the cheeky humor that some of the earlier songs had, sure, that would also be primarily about girls and sex, but kind of in a fun way. This is nothing like that.

I think "Hail Caesar" is probably the best song on the album. It sounds like it's written for the road, which is what AC/DC used to do. They used to play a lot of their albums on the road when they first started. Records were written to be performed live. And this one sounds like it could be performed live. And it was part of the set list. It's also got a great solo, and I thought what was also interesting was the brief little spoken word portion in it with Brian talking; he sounds almost like Bon Scott.

FRASER: "Hard as a Rock" turned out to be a great song title, the way it works in the chorus. I quite like the drum sound we ended up getting on that. It had a really good sort of poppy kind of pushy snare thing to it. So yeah, that was a good song. And I agree on "Hail Caesar." Me and Brian like that one a lot. "All hail, Caesar!" We thought, oh, that's gonna be a good one live, because you could have the audience singing along to that one.

LAWSON: Another neat tune on the record that is really different for them is "Burnin' Alive." Just because, although it doesn't go into too many details, it's reportedly inspired by the Branch Davidian cult in Waco, Texas, which, for a band like AC/DC, they don't dip their toe in political waters too often.

POPOFF: And I guess even "The Furor" and "Hail Caesar" have a bit of politics to them. Do you buy that?

LAWSON: Sure. Malcolm commented in a couple of interviews around the time of this record, saying sometimes you have to stand up and be counted. Which I know is a lyric from "For Those About to Rock." But he's saying that sometimes you have to say something. I know they like to kid that they just put out the same record every two years, and it's kind of a cliché with these guys, but it shows that they have a little bit of a consciousness going on.

POPOFF: I remember eyebrows being raised a bit over "The Furor."

FRASER: It makes me laugh because everybody is become so politically correct, you can't even mention Nazi or Führer, without everybody thinking, "Oh, that's offensive." Oh, give me a break [*laughs*]. And "Hail Caesar" is about being a gang. It's not promoting friggin' anything.

POPOFF: Mike, what stands out for you on the album?

FRASER: Well, "Boogie Man" I liked a lot, because Brian was able to get into that sort of range, that type of growl he likes to do. He doesn't necessarily enjoy his screaming and high singing, I guess, because it's a lot of work. But he likes to get that smoky, "Hey, I'm a boogie man" kind of thing. He really enjoyed doing that. So that was kind of fun, to put that on top of one of their sort of groovy songs. It's his old man, evil man voice, kind of thing.

LAWSON: I had a lot of hopes for "Boogie Man" when I first got the record, because I like the old AC/DC, when they'd do little blues things.

And they hadn't been doing that much. Unfortunately, lyrically, which falls on Malcolm and Angus, it's just completely empty. Now, there's an unreleased rehearsal version of this song that you can find on a bootleg called *Nutcrackers*, and on that, Brian is having a lot of fun doing his John Lee Hooker impersonation; it's actually more interesting than the album version. It's obviously not release-quality, but it's nice hearing Brian having some fun, especially during sessions where they're saying we don't want you to write lyrics anymore.

POPOFF: And would you agree that the title track is the heaviest song on the album?
LAWSON: Sure, it's heavy, and it's another one that you can tell was kind of written for the concert stage, and it's something that fans could really get behind. I think at this point in their career, often the title track is exactly that. The title track is often a real anthem, but I guess that goes back to "Let There Be Rock," where, that's the statement of the record. Actually, "T.N.T." and "Dirty Deeds" too. And what's real interesting is that they put it way at the end of the album, as a kind of summation of the whole record.
FRASER: I really liked that one, because to me that was a really good rocker. Plus, it's a good range for Brian. Again, you could picture the live audience singing along to that; I really like the chorus in that song.

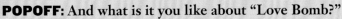

Deutschlandhalle, Berlin, April 30, 1996.

POPOFF: And what is it you like about "Love Bomb?"
LAWSON: Musically, that's got some pretty interesting guitar things going on, but unfortunately, the lyrics are just moronic. But there's just a little bit of interplay between Angus and Malcolm that stands up for me on the album. I don't think any of the leads or solos on here approach the stuff that they were doing in the mid-seventies, when they were really working together. Angus and Malcolm were just a terrific team back then, even all the way up to *For Those About to Rock*—they're great guitar records. Here, overall, not as interesting, but on that track there are a few things going on.
FRASER: I thought "Love Bomb" could've been a single, because of its pop feel. I thought it was a cool departure, without them leaving what they are.

POPOFF: From your vantage point, what did you see in terms of the guitar dialog between Malcolm and Angus?

FRASER: Sometimes Angus would mirror Malcolm's part higher up the fretboard and sometimes he'd add a little lick in the middle of the riff, so they're not always playing exactly the same parts. But they're always complementing parts. And then for any leads, Angus would overdub those, obviously. But Angus had a little bit more room, with Mal holding it down. He had a more room to be a bit more experimental and move around the fretboard a little more.

But Mal and Ang, they were always prepared coming into the studio. They knew what they wanted to do. They'd say, "Okay, here's the song" and they would teach it to Phil and Cliff, and then fifteen minutes later we would be recording it, kind of thing. They'd play it from a cassette first so they could hear the overall direction of the song. Sometimes Cliff would write down notes, like D, C, D, whatever. Phil would just listen once and he would kind of get it. Sometimes there would be drum machine. Sometimes Mal would play the drums, and they would just record it in either Malcolm's little home studio or Angus's home studio or wherever they happened to be at the time. And they would piece stuff together like that, and throw it on a cassette. It's funny—it was always on a cassette [*laughs*].

POPOFF: And would they provide any sort of direction to Phil?

FRASER: Yeah, they would sometimes say, "Hey, Phil, can you do a fill going into the chorus here?" Or, "Hey Phil, could you hit your left crash as opposed to your right crash, going in here?" There would be little things like that. But Phil was kinda given to his own devices. He's such a really good thumper. Kick, snare, kick, snare . . . and he's got this thing, the way he does his high-hat, that not many guys can get that down. It's simple, but it's got a groove to it. A lot of guys, when they do that type of high-hat thing, it's really straight and robotic, whereas Phil has almost got an R & B groove in him. Kick and thump and kick and snare. And where he places his cymbal crashes, I love too. Everybody always hits on the one and the three or whatever, and Phil, sometimes he does it on the two and four, which is not always the normal case. I love that about Phil too.

POPOFF: Is he usually pulling out his hair trying to get a good drum sound? Obviously, it was pretty tough on this album.
FRASER: Well, actually, it's mostly me pulling my hair out, trying to get the sound [*laughs*]. Phil would help us, and he has a really good tech guy that he's had, probably since the beginning, Richard Jones, and it would be Richard and me out there trying to get it together.

But we all knew what sound we were after. It was just a matter of getting it. We would have about six snare drums, and the difficult thing with Phil is because he's such a heavy hitter, quite a lot of times the snare head wouldn't last through a whole take. So we had to get a certain snare sound that would still sound fresh at the end of the take [*laughs*]. So we were changing snares. There would be probably about three out of the six drums that we could tune and get them sounding very similar. But after one take—and sometimes we would like to do three or four takes a row—they would finish, and they would say, "Okay, let's roll the tape again," and go right away.

And we couldn't change the head, because changing the head on the snare drum takes about seven or eight or ten minutes. So we would just change the whole snare and away they would go, and then we would get the takes that way. So it got a bit hairy at times. And it's only because Phil hits so hard. His toms and kick would last a lot longer, but the snare drum, it would be beat by the end of the song.

POPOFF: And finally, what does the *Ballbreaker* album cover say to you?
LAWSON: I think for a band not really known for great album covers, like *Blow Up Your Video* and *The Razors Edge*, *Ballbreaker* presents quite a striking image. I mean, it's sort of part comic book, but it's realistic looking. To me, it really captured the essence of an AC/DC record—you got power, you got electricity, you got a sweaty duck-walking Angus. It's just a really great graphic and an image. Like I say, it looks like part illustration, part photo. But the design of it, the graphic, is just tremendous. It's just a great image for them. Probably one of their best covers, really.

STIFF UPPER LIP

with **RICHARD BIENSTOCK** and **RICH DAVENPORT**

All songs composed by Angus
Young and Malcolm Young

Personnel: Brian Johnson—
lead vocals; Angus Young—lead
guitar; Malcolm Young—rhythm
guitar, backing vocals; Cliff
Williams—bass, backing vocals;
Phil Rudd—drums

Released February 28, 2000

Recorded at The Warehouse
Studio, Vancouver, Canada

Produced by George Young

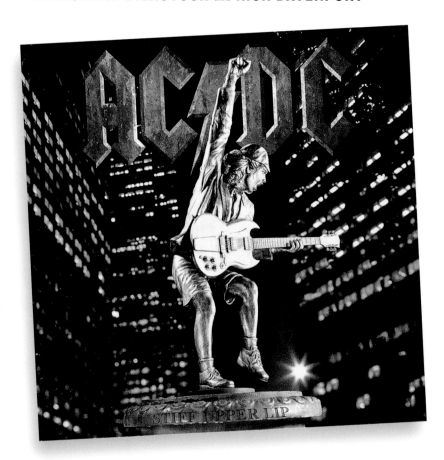

Well into the throes of their sleight-of-hand
semiretirement, AC/DC keeps them guessing with
their third album of what will amount to five in twenty-five years.
But on some of those five—*The Razors Edge*, *Black Ice*—they
made them count. Not exactly so on *Stiff Upper Lip*, where the
band blush with modesty, plunking politely in the proverbial
matchbox, George Young producing them as if they are sunk in
comfy chairs around a warming fire.

The net effect evokes Foghat in the eighties, but more
pertinently Status Quo in the eighties, the idea that so many

permutations of boogie rock explored must eventually give way to a turning down of the guitars and the reconfiguring of the licks into what, in both cases, amount to elegant and compact rock 'n' roll bonsai trees shaded by earlier planted oaks, Rubik's Cube combinations of boogie pop, palm-sized origami sculptures cut and folded from the original blueprints.

And so we get "Meltdown," "Hold Me Back," and "Can't Stand Still" as the worst offenders, which is not that many, but they're all in the first half of the album, souring the memory circuits. With the rest of the record, the vestige of that idea remains through the album's quaint George Young production job, but at least the songs are written around more typical AC/DC riffing, producing the classic grooves of the title track, the swaggering shark that is "Safe in New York City," and then all manner of buried hidden gems toward the end, such as the Stonesy and unwinding "Satellite Blues" (a single, not that you would ever know) and closing duo "All Screwed Up" and "Give It Up," which each create at least three- or four-foot-high walls of sound, significantly high enough to keep the sheep penned.

In shorthand and 'DC vernacular, *Stiff Upper Lip* is considered the band's bluesy album, but let's also proclaim it the least hard rock and, as I've alluded to elliptically, the poppiest, at least since the pre-consciousness debut. Nonetheless, a level of intellectual intrigue is conjured in the way that the band incongruously Frankenstein so many boogie licks—and I do mean licks, brief references, not riffs—to pop writing and arranging, resulting in an album of maturity and experimentation from the band most associated with relentless sameness.

So in the same sly way, the band can retire without letting on they've marbled throughout the record all manner of new ideas through a process of deep-tissue massaging those ideas into a record summarily

OPPOSITE: *Stiff Upper Lip* is considered the band's bluesy album, but let's also proclaim it the poppiest.

BELOW: Club date at Munich's Circus Krone Club, June 17, 2003.

denigrated as lacking in new ideas. And given that few fans and tastemakers would make the effort to notice, *Stiff Upper Lip* would stall at single platinum, slowed by a polite panning suitable to the record's polite playing.

POPOFF: General question: What is the personality of *Stiff Upper Lip*? What is its tone or vibe versus, say, *Ballbreaker*?

BIENSTOCK: Part of the reason I picked *Stiff Upper Lip* is because I don't necessarily think it's a great AC/DC record, but I wouldn't exactly compare it with any of their other records. It stands out as an anomaly, and I would imagine it's one that people tend to forget about. And part of that is I don't think it sounds like any other AC/DC record and it certainly doesn't sound like *Ballbreaker* and it doesn't really sound like *Black Ice* either. And a lot of that, to me, is the guitar sound. I think it's got a great guitar tone, but it's very muted. It's probably their least heavy album. I don't know if that was intentional, but the guitars are super clean, and that's one of the things that I love about it.

DAVENPORT: For me, it's one of the absolute best with Brian Johnson. My favorite AC/DC album is *Powerage*, and this to me . . . people tend to view *Back in Black* as the most celebrated of the Brian era, while *Highway to Hell* is the most celebrated Bon album. Using the same comparison, you could say *Back in Black* is Brian's equivalent to *Highway to Hell*, for his era, and even though they're definitely not the same, I would say that *Stiff Upper Lip* is the Brian Johnson–era *Powerage*.

POPOFF: So what do you like about it?

DAVENPORT: What struck me about it . . . they hadn't done an album for five years, and personally, I don't mind *The Razors Edge*, but I found it overproduced for that style. It's the tail end of the eighties, and producers are covering everything in reverb. And for me, that's not what AC/DC sound like. On *Ballbreaker*, I thought the guitar sound was a bit funny. I don't know what Rubin had done, but there's a way that the guitars are EQ'd and something about the frequencies that sounds different from classic AC/DC.

Stiff Upper Lip just grabbed me straightaway. The title track itself establishes the nod factor; it just gets you nodding and tapping your foot without even thinking about it. It starts with that bluesy little riff and Brian singing it in his lower register. If you know the Geordie albums, he does have

Stiff Upper Lip got you nodding and tapping your foot right out of the gate.

a very extensive range. So it grabs your attention that he's singing lower— not many AC/DC songs where he does that. And when it kicks in, it's just a classic AC/DC groove. And, obviously, they're working with George Young again. They'd worked with Bruce Fairbairn, and he was lined up to produce *Stiff Upper Lip*, and he wanted to do it, but then he passed away. And personally, no disrespect to Rick Rubin and his work on *Ballbreaker*, but I think George captured the classic AC/DC sound, but as it was in 2000. The band doesn't change much, but recording technology has changed. But I think he captured the natural sound of the band right through.

Plus, it's a real feel-good album and it sounds like they're having fun. It sounds laid-back. When I first heard it, my overall impression was they don't need to make another album at this stage in their career. They're huge. And this sounds like they've made an album that they enjoyed and had fun with, and they put that out.

POPOFF: But I recall at the time, *Stiff Upper Lip* was not that well received. Plus it's only gone platinum, a drop since the huge sales comeback they had enjoyed with *The Razors Edge*.

Stiff Upper Lip World Tour, Entertainment Centre, Sydney, January 31, 2001.

BIENSTOCK: Yeah, the record itself just wasn't that popular, and none of the songs were that popular on their own. But at the same time, the band was hitting their stride as being . . . I mean, they've always been huge, but I feel like post-*Ballbreaker*, they became this unbelievable concert draw and playing stadiums all over the world. They'd hit that point where they were sort of wholly accepted as a classic arena rock 'n' roll band. It didn't really matter if what they were doing was new at the time. People loved the idea of AC/DC around that time. Maybe they didn't even know they had a new album out. People didn't really care about that side of the band.

And I remember that record being pushed very hard. In *Guitar World*, we did stories with them. They made themselves available more than they do now. And clearly, with the album cover—that bronze statue of Angus—they created this iconic thing. Angus already had that, but it's very in-your-face. It's like, these guys are the greatest, and they used that on stage and everything. So they were building up that AC/DC legend. And the funny thing about it, it worked and it was all true. But on the flipside, the album itself didn't contribute to that at all. It essentially didn't live up to the weight of all this other stuff.

Stade de France, Paris,
June 22, 2001.

POPOFF: To be fair, Rich, personally, I think some of the most contentious songs are sequenced too far to the front, and that may have affected fans' opinions of the thing.

DAVENPORT: Yeah, they are. Perhaps you could question the running order of the album. "Meltdown" and obviously "Hold Me Back," they're blues-based riffs, they follow bluesy chord progressions, and there are the major and the minor pentatonic scale, and these are more major, much more cheery, upbeat riffs. I personally like them. It's possibly not the best running order. There maybe could've been a couple of the heavier songs at the start of the album, and that would've won more people over. "House of Jazz" has a slow buildup and "Hold Me Back" is mainly bass drum all the way through. Personally, I don't mind because I like the songs, but it took me a few plays looking back, and about the second and third play, it grabbed me.

POPOFF: Richard, any comment on Rich's assessment of the guitar sound on the record? Where do you stand?

BIENSTOCK: I'd agree to an extent. I felt like AC/DC in the eighties and nineties had gotten a bit heavier and more distorted in terms of their tones, just because that's the way bands sounded. In the seventies, they were a little cleaner. And so I do feel like bringing George Young back into the mix, maybe there was a bit of this thought toward searching for that early-days tone. And the truth is, I don't think they got that tone at all. But I think maybe in searching for that cleaner tone, they wound up on this new tone that you hear on this record, that you certainly don't hear in the other records.

POPOFF: Okay, now I think most fans would agree that the title track was a highlight, and perhaps *the* highlight, of the album. Plus, it was one of the record's three singles.

BIENSTOCK: I love that song; I think that's one of the greatest latter-day AC/DC songs. That's the video where they're riding around in the Hummer. I love that opening riff that Angus does, which highlights that super-clean tone that I'm talking about throughout the record. But the way Angus is playing in that intro, it's kind of classic AC/DC, but he's doing a sort of hybrid picking thing where he's not just using the pick, but he's got his picking fingers going on as well. And he actually does that in a lot of songs on *Stiff Upper Lip*. You can hear that approach at the beginning of both "House of Jazz" and "Hold Me Back." It's not that unique, but it contributes to that lighter sound. And the fact that he's doing it in a bunch of the songs, it creates a comparatively mellow AC/DC. Yeah, he's definitely using his fingers more as opposed to his pick. Plus, he's turning down the gain, which also contributes to the overall different feel.

POPOFF: And why that title, *Stiff Upper Lip*?
DAVENPORT: In an interview, Angus mentioned that he was stuck in traffic somewhere, and it just struck him how lips were identified with early rock 'n' roll. Like Elvis with his sneer, and Mick Jagger with his . . . I think Bette Midler said he had childbearing lips. And Angus thought, if he shoved his lips out, they were probably bigger than Elvis's or Mick Jagger's. And he remembers that there's that famous photo on the cover of *Highway to Hell*, where he's curling his lips. And obviously the innuendo about things being stiff [*laughs*], which ties in as well. But that's what he had said, that he'd made that connection of lips with rock 'n' roll.

POPOFF: Richard, you mention the Hummer. So here they are trapped in traffic on a skinny Manhattan street. For "Safe in New York City," they're playing in what looks like a blocked-up Lincoln Tunnel, and then for "Satellite Blues," they are in a very high-tech-looking spaceship, which for all intents and purposes, looks like a train or car tunnel. On the cover, Angus is surrounded by skyscrapers. This is the band's New York album!
BIENSTOCK: You're right, and it doesn't really work for AC/DC does it? Yeah, "Safe in New York City," they're parked in the tunnel. Which, like I say, is kind of weird. When you really think about it, it's not their type of video. I don't know where that was coming from. I mean, for that song you see that connection. But "Stiff Upper Lip" isn't the type of song that seems . . . it's sort of incongruent with the video. It doesn't sound like the type of song you should play on a street in New York City. Maybe they were just out of ideas.

POPOFF: "Safe in New York City" is one of the faster and heavier and more menacing sound songs on this weirdly cheery record, right? Plus, it was issued as a single.
DAVENPORT: That's one of my least favorite AC/DC songs. I was really disappointed when I saw them live on that tour, and that was the only song they played from the album. They've got far more imaginative riffs. To me, that was a bit of a stock riff, and not helped by the way the vocal follows the riff. And as a single track, I just did not see it. There are a couple of single choices—not very often—where you think why on earth did they pick that

one? "Danger," the first single from *Fly on the Wall* is one and this is another.

POPOFF: The terrorist attacks of 9/11 occurred about seven months after the album came out, and there's this single, "Safe in New York City." It's an odd topic for a song, and then I understand the track was added to the list of songs banned there, briefly, as cutting too close to the core of what happened.

DAVENPORT: Yes, as for the lyric, Angus had said they'd been in New York and overheard people say that they felt safe in the city, in contrast to the reputation it had in the seventies. And right at the end there's the line, *I feel safe in a cage in New York City*. So it's like, I'm safe where someone can't get me. They threw that in, which I thought that was a bit of a telling statement.

And yes, there was what was called the Clear Channel memorandum, this long list of songs their radio stations shouldn't play. I think anything that referenced the city . . . there were a few other AC/DC songs that were put on that list, like "Shot Down in Flames," "Hells Bells," "Shoot to Thrill," "T.N.T." The same thing happened here in Britain at the time of the first Gulf War. They banned things like "I Just Died in Your Arms Tonight" and "I'm on Fire" by Bruce Springsteen. Anything that could suggest war or conflict or imagery that would relate to someone losing their life tended to be sort of banned at that time.

"Safe in New York City" was briefly banned on New York radio.

BIENSTOCK: I lived in New York City through all of that, and that was never a song that people . . . it's not like after 9/11 that you would hear "Safe in New York City" and people were viewing it as some sort of signifier of what had gone on. It wasn't like Bruce Springsteen's "The Rising" or anything like that. It didn't have that mainstream recognition. If you were in a rock bar or there was a DJ spinning rock stuff, you would start to hear that song more after 9/11. So like, in the small world of hard rock and AC/DC, the song definitely did take on a bit more prominence. But as far as it being put on that list, I felt like most people didn't know what the hell the song was anyway. So it wasn't making that much of a wider impact.

POPOFF: What about this idea that the guys were poking fun at mayor Rudy Giuliani's claims of having cleaned up the city?

BIENSTOCK: I've never heard them say anything to that effect. And with AC/DC, obviously, you never expect that they're really commenting on anything societal or political. It's possible. I know we did an interview with them around that time, and Angus was basically saying that he remembered being in New York, and people were always talking about how safe it was. And that was probably an effect of the Giuliani thing. But in classic sort of AC/DC fashion, I don't think he was making that connection. To him, it was like, "Oh, people are saying this to me, that New York City is not necessarily a bad place."

Now musically, it's interesting, because that one is a good example of what I was saying. It's exactly as you just describe it—menacing—and yet to me it still feels muted. It's mean and it's fast, but it's not a full-throttle, full-on song. It's almost like prowling and coiled instead of just being balls out. And on that record, that was sort of the height of their aggressiveness, and yet it was pulled back compared to what you usually get from AC/DC.

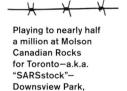

Playing to nearly half a million at Molson Canadian Rocks for Toronto—a.k.a. "SARSstock"— Downsview Park, July 30, 2003.

POPOFF: I really do believe the saving grace of this record is the presence of some good tracks in the back half, such as "All Screwed Up."

DAVENPORT: Yes, I agree. This is the one where the chord progression drops an octave, after the initial chords. Plus, they're playing triplets, groups of three, over a 4/4 beat. And if you're looking for an example of Angus and Malcolm playing separate octaves, this goes right back to the likes of "Baby Please Don't Go." Malcolm is playing the riff below on the guitar, and Angus is playing the same riff at the high end. And what I like about that one is, when you get to the chorus, they kind of turn that initial riff into a chord progression. They add a couple of chords onto the end of it. You get the same riff, but they go somewhere else, which makes it more melodically interesting.

BIENSTOCK: "All Screwed Up" has that interesting harmonic type of thing going on where that single note riff, the guitar and bass are playing it together. Again, it's not anything like, "Oh my God, I can't believe a rock band is doing that." But it's not something AC/DC usually does. I mean, obviously, the guitar and bass play riffs together all the time, but that's specifically a very melodic line, and I can't think of another time in an AC/DC song where the guitar and bass are synced up on a melodic type of motif that closely.

Angus and Malcolm jam with the Rolling Stones at SARSstock.

OPPOSITE: The hallmark of some of AC/DC's great riffs is the amount of space between the beats. This starts with Malcolm's rhythm guitars.

POPOFF: But that "matchbox" quality established earlier is also maintained near the end, with songs like "Come and Get It," which isn't helped by having another forgettable song title.

BIENSTOCK: I totally agree—a lot of these songs are sort of hard to remember. I feel that's why the album gets overlooked too. "Give It Up," "All Screwed Up," "Can't Stand Still," "Can't Stop Rock 'n' Roll," "Come and Get It" . . . there's all these songs right next to each other on the record and they're very generic-sounding song titles [*laughs*]. You know, a friend was asking me, what album is "Give It Up" on? And you think, I don't know, maybe it's toward the end of *Fly on the Wall*. AC/DC has a tendency—especially in the Brian Johnson years—where you can't really remember what's on the second sides of the records, especially by the song titles. And I think *Stiff Upper Lip* has that problem, when you get into it.

But the songs themselves are pretty cool. "Come and Get It," in the pre-chorus, Angus is playing like seventh chords, which is not that big a deal, but in AC/DC world, you don't really hear Angus play seventh chords. It's like major and minor chords. It's not even major and minor chords—it's power chords. But just throw in that seventh, and, well, that's a little bit different.

Plus the backing vocals, that's a little different for them too. They've always done those great sort of gang backup vocals. And "Come and Get It" is one of the only ones where it's just one voice, which I don't even know if that's Angus or Malcolm. But I can't think of another song where you have a background vocal where it's just one of them doing something like that.

POPOFF: We'd be remiss if we didn't talk about the third track that the band picked as a single, "Satellite Blues."

DAVENPORT: One of the album's great tracks, and quite unsung. There's an absolute AC/DC trademark to this one. The hallmark of some of the great riffs they've written is the amount of space between the beats. This starts with Malcolm's rhythm guitars. If you think about the verse of "You Shook Me All Night Long," there are big gaps between the chord stops. Same with "Let's Get It Up," and with "Satellite Blues," we've got that again. It reminds me a little bit of "Start Me Up" by the Stones. It's quite an unconventional rhythmic pattern that makes up the riff. If you listen to maybe a thrash band, they're playing every beat to the bar, if you could divide it into four, eight, or sixteen; every beat is emphasized with the rhythm guitar. Whereas with AC/DC, with the four beats in the bar,

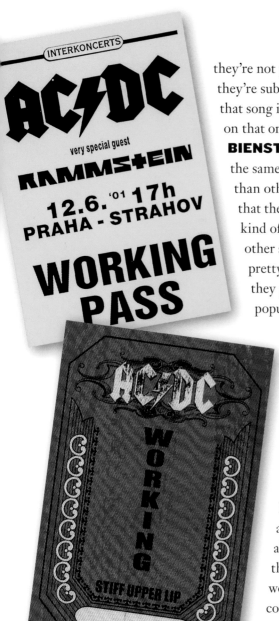

they're not playing exactly on beats one, two, three, and four—they're subdividing it and leaving big spaces in between and I think that song is a great example of that. Great growling backing vocals on that one as well.

BIENSTOCK: Great song. With AC/DC, every song is sort of the same but a little different, so some will come off a little better than others. And that's one, for whatever reason, perhaps the way that the chorus is set up, that's a really good song. But it's also kind of lost on the record, showing up later, surrounded by some other stuff. But I think of it as this lost classic. People who are pretty knowledgeable about AC/DC, they know that song, but they probably wouldn't know where it came from. It wasn't popular. They might think it's a nineties song. It's kind of known and unknown.

POPOFF: It's easy to forget that every one of these songs is credited to Angus and Malcolm. Subconsciously, one thinks of these as the views of Brian, our beloved, longtime lead singer.

DAVENPORT: Personally, I think they lost a little something when Brian stopped writing the lyrics. Brian had done an admirable job with a near impossible task. Because not only was Bon Scott a great singer, he was a really beloved character among the fans. And he was also a heckuva lyricist. And so you've got a triple threat there. And for Brian to fill even perhaps one of those roles would've been a big achievement. I don't think it's fair to compare the two, but I think Brian did have a flair with lyrics. Angus and Malcolm do come up with some good stuff, but I tend to pay less attention to the lyrics since Brian stopped writing them.

POPOFF: And why did Brian stop writing lyrics?

DAVENPORT: Well, there's all sorts of rumors. *The Razors Edge* was the first album where Angus and Malcolm wrote all the lyrics. And Brian said in an interview at the time that he was going through a divorce, so they wrote them, and he was happy that he didn't have to come up with them. There's been the suggestion that he's been frozen out in one way or another, or that it might be a publishing thing. They're such a clannish band [that] you don't honestly know what's going on behind the scenes. And you know, he wrote some cracking songs for a National Lampoon soundtrack two years ago. Cliff was writing as well. So he obviously can still write. Apparently he wrote a musical, on Helen of Troy, which has never appeared. I thought Brian was a really capable lyricist.

POPOFF: Last track on the album, "Give It Up" is a personal fave. Any thoughts?

BIENSTOCK: That one has a little bit of that *Flick of the Switch* vibe, or it sounds like a less amped-up version of "Shoot to Thrill" or something. I feel like there are a few songs at the end of the record that kind of harken back to earlier AC/DC, that being one of them. I think also "Damned" sounds like something that could've been on the second side of *Flick of the Switch* or something. It's very dark and straightforward and . . . sort of forgettable [*laughs*]. But it sounds like an early-eighties AC/DC song to me.

One more I'd like to mention, "Can't Stand Still" is almost like a mellow version of "Thunderstruck." It's the same exact kind of intro riff, with the pulling onto the open string and moving around on the fretboard. But it's just not nearly as aggressive as "Thunderstruck." It's that same open-string pull-off to the B string type of thing that makes "Thunderstruck" sound like a stadium anthem. But here it's a completely different vibe. You know, this whole album, with AC/DC, there are all the little subtleties. Because at the end of the day, if you could listen from far away, it just sounds like an AC/DC record. But for people who really love them, for those who really like to pull the songs apart, they'll find that is a different-sounding record for the band.

POPOFF: Finally, odd question, but what is the role of ol' Phil Rudd on this record?

DAVENPORT: I love his playing on it, and as usual it's so sparse. At the beginning, there's a couple of his trademark thumps where he comes in, and in fact right at the beginning, not even a single thump. Like Brian says, "I was born with a stiff" . . . nothing—and it's classic. And I think he's a big part of that song's groove and a big part of the classic AC/DC sound.

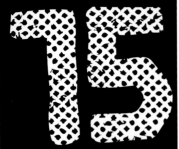

All songs composed by Angus Young and Malcolm Young

Personnel: Brian Johnson—lead vocals; Angus Young—lead guitar, slide guitar; Malcolm Young —rhythm guitar, backing vocals; Cliff Williams—bass, backing vocals; Phil Rudd—drums, percussion

Released October 17, 2008

Recorded at the Warehouse Studio, Vancouver, Canada

Produced by Brendan O'Brien

BLACK ICE

with MIKE FRASER and BILL VOCCIA

Close to nine years since the band last offered us a studio record, *Black Ice* had no business being this bright and aggressive and kicked up the arse with life. Neither *Ballbreaker* nor *Stiff Upper Lip* pressed pedal to metal like *The Razors Edge*. Indeed, the long-lasting AC/DC lover could only hope for a further rounding of the edges that comes with the unfurling of old age, a process that just might render us a small and charming experience to which we could at least crack a smile and sip a wee dram in salute.

But no, whether it was Brendan O'Brien's influence at the production helm or a spring of step caused by 2003's Rock and Roll Hall of Fame induction, or maybe even a switch of labels from Atlantic—home since the beginning—to Sony, the planets had aligned. Malcolm and Angus, to every fan's delight, were serving up song after song, fifteen in total, of mostly cranked, cantankerous part-hardy hard rock, all of it recorded with sizzle and snap, lest the more mature experiments get left behind.

The O'Brien piece is intriguing, for in O'Brien one gets a younger generation—like a Nick Raskulinecz with Rush or an Andy Sneap with Accept—quietly fed up with their employers' slide into old-man music and finds a diplomatic way to summon the fire of some earlier period. Apparently, O'Brien was aiming for some incongruous cross between *Dirty Deeds* and *Highway to Hell*, but arrived closer to engineer Mike Fraser's assessment, namely *The Razors Edge*, because of the tempos, even if I would argue the comparison comes from the smack of the drums and the crash of many crash cymbals.

But I wouldn't deny that *Black Ice* achieves a bit of a *Highway to Hell* vibe either, because if you nudge a few percentiles more organic from *The Razors Edge*, that's where you land. And for the most part, across the album's fifty-five minutes (the longest running time of any AC/DC album), there's ample ornery riff rock. Even deep into the sequence, with songs like "Spoilin' for

OPPOSITE: Combine a strong back end with clear winners like "Big Jack," "War Machine," and the irresistibly Stonesy "Rock 'N' Roll Train," and you've got a full-on album.

BELOW: The *Black Ice* tour opener, Wilkes-Barre, Pennsylvania, October 26, 2008.

a Fight," "Wheels," "Rocking All the Way," and the menacing album closer (for those counting, that's the last three title tracks as some of the heaviest on their respective albums), AC/DC never let up. There's dimension, there's shade, some slide guitar, a bit of *Stiff Upper Lips* blues, but it's all arranged with hard guitars driven home by Phil Rudd, cymbals everywhere, open high-hat, have a drink on me.

Combine a strong back end with clear winners like "Big Jack," "War Machine," and the irresistibly Stonesy "Rock 'N' Roll Train," and you've got a full-on album and a half of double-shot tumblers lined up for throwing down, served up fully eighteen years since AC/DC last felt like a band that was going to get you into some deep trouble.

POPOFF: So set this up for me. What is it like for one of the band's biggest fans to get a new AC/DC album in 2008?
VOCCIA: Well, I remember that it was a long time since their previous album. So I was definitely excited to hear it at the time. It was hard to find details, myself and a lot of fans; we were hoping that they might've gotten Mutt Lange back to do the production.

But they brought in Brendan O'Brien, and I thought he did a fantastic job. And the fact that Mike Fraser was involved also plays a large part in that, and he does a great job mixing their sound. The guitar parts really stand out and the drums are very crisp; you can hear everything very nicely on the album.

A lot of people thought it was too commercial in the sound, but I don't really think it's a commercial-sounding album. I believe they wanted to do a real rock album, with a *Let There Be Rock* or *High Voltage*–type sound, but a modern-day version of what they did in the seventies. Whereas *Stiff Upper Lip* and *Ballbreaker* were bluesier and not as guitar-driven. And sure, it's an AC/DC album with real straightforward rock 'n' roll, with a lot of guitar riffs. And the way the guitars speak to each other—back and forth, each side, Malcolm's parts and Angus's parts, the way they gel on the album—was just really magical.

POPOFF: It sounds like the writers in the band, Malcolm and Angus, used their time wisely, working separately and together over a lot of years, to come up with these songs.
VOCCIA: Yes, I'm sure that they had a lot of song ideas or guitar riffs lying around for quite some time. AC/DC have always been a heavily private and secretive band, so it's difficult trying to find out specifics about what they're

doing, and they're not telling you anything about what they're doing. It's sometimes easier to find out stuff about aliens invading the planet than it is to find out anything about AC/DC. But sure, it was a long time going, and there were rumors that there were health issues going on with Malcolm at the time in-between, a heart scare, and Cliff had hurt his hand at one point as well and didn't play for eighteen months. They needed time for his hand to heal and that added to why they waited so long to get into the studio.

POPOFF: But no signs of Malcolm's unfortunate dementia, confirmed in late 2014?

FRASER: I don't think there was at that point, no. You know, looking back on it all, there were a few little points where now you say, "Oh, okay, I see." Like maybe Mal forgetting to bring his coat to the studio. Angus would say, "Didn't you bring your coat?" "Oh, no, I didn't. I forgot." Little things that you wouldn't think anything about, but you look back on it and you go, oh, what if that was the beginning of it?

Conseco Fieldhouse, Indianapolis, Indiana, November 3, 2008.

POPOFF: Why do we see Brendan O'Brien in the production chair?

FRASER: You know, Brendan is a very musical guy. Really good guitar player. And I think the band wanted to branch out with somebody who would be a little more hands-on, than, say, Rick was. I know since *Stiff Upper Lip*, they had pulled their brother George out of retirement to do that record, and I think they tried to get him again, and he says, "Nah, nah, I'm retired. I don't wanna do it." So they maybe went down a list of producers and found one like Brendan—"Hey, this guy's really good, he's getting popular, he's a musician, he understands, let's give him a try."

POPOFF: So part of the mandate, new producer or not, is also that we do this in Vancouver and we're doing it with Mike?

FRASER: Yep, I think they got hooked on that. Well, they love Vancouver, for one. They love the restaurants, the ambience, and the fact that in Vancouver most of the people would leave them alone. There are the

(continued on page 222)

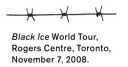

Black Ice World Tour,
Rogers Centre, Toronto,
November 7, 2008.

(continued from page 219)

autograph hunters who would figure out their time that they'd leave the studio or leave the hotel and sort of inundate them. But in Vancouver, maybe because there are so many films being shot here, people aren't always walking down the street, "Oh, look at this!" So they kind of got left alone. They're quite comfortable here in Vancouver and the studios are really good. So, yeah, any time we had a choice, Vancouver was the first choice.

VOCCIA: I hear the band chemistry at this point was going well. They were recording at Bryan Adams's Warehouse Studios. Apparently, the writing and recording sessions for the album went really well. Another thing I'd like to say, Brian Johnson's vocal performance on that album is really significant, which is another key highlight for Brendan O'Brien—he was really able to get a great performance out of Brian Johnson on that record.

POPOFF: And how were the tones captured? What gear are they using to get that nice balance between clean and dirty?

VOCCIA: Angus and Malcolm always would've used classic Marshall amps, Marshall heads, mostly. There are some times when Malcolm was using Wizard amplifiers as well, but yeah, I believe on *Black Ice*, they were using original Marshall amps, straight in. They don't use effects pedals. Just two amplifiers where you drive a tube amplifier to get that tone, and that's where the real rock 'n' roll guitar tone is. They would typically be using those twenty-five-watt Greenback Celestion speakers and the Marshall cabinets to give it that crunch. Malcolm is always using his original '63 Gretsch Jet Firebird, and Angus would be using various Gibson SGs.

FRASER: Yeah, Malcolm uses a, I believe it's a four hundred–watt Marshall bass head, because he uses his Gretsch guitar, and his sound is very, very clean. There's hardly any distortion at all on it. There's no pedals. Part of their sound that we worked hard to do is you have to use the shortest guitar leads that you can. So, you know, basically a ten-foot, nine-foot lead, into the guitar head, and then a very short speaker cable, again, under a ten-foot speaker cable. And that helps retain the sound of the guitar. As soon as you start using these long guitar leads, the sound coming from the guitar slightly degrades. So that's how you get these crisp, certain kinds of guitar sounds.

And for Angus, he uses a one hundred–watt Marshall, for his rhythms, and no pedals at all, and again, short guitar and speaker leads. And then when he goes to do his solos, he's got a fifty-watt Marshall head that he uses most of the time. So the first couple of records I did with them, they would bring truckloads of Marshall heads and Marshall cabinets and all that, on each record, and at the beginning of the record, we'd spend two days going through combinations. You know, Marshall head A into cabinet B. Okay, Marshall head B into cabinet C. And we'd just try out all the combinations. And over the years, we always ended up with the same two or three guitar heads, and maybe three or four of the cabinets were the best combinations. So, the latter records I worked on, they only brought those. No sense going through all the other stuff again.

POPOFF: Generally, in a rhythm track, what is Angus doing and what is Malcolm doing?
FRASER: Well, Malcolm is the rhythm master, and out of all the guitar players I've ever worked with, I think he's gotta be the number-one guy. Just his sense of rhythm and tempo, he's like a metronome. He's just so good at the feel and the tempo that the song needs to be at. So his parts, as I said, are very clean. But because it's through a four hundred–watt bass amp, it's quite punchy and kind of hits you in the chest, almost like a kick drum. And he's really good at playing dynamics on that guitar, because it's clean. He sits, he plays it soft, and it'll really quiet down, but when he bangs it, like I say, it'll hit you like a kick drum.

Whereas Angus's sound is a little bit more overdriven. So you've got one guy holding the tempo down and really getting the groove going, and then Angus can be a bit wilder, playing the same chords, but more open and . . . I don't want to say sloppy, but with some sludge to it, you know? And the combination of those two make the guitars sound huge. Everybody says, "Oh, well, how many times do you double track?" and all this. It's not—it's one Mal on one side and one Ang on the other side and that's it for their guitar sound.

POPOFF: So the album gets done, but we hear this great song, "Rock 'N' Roll Train," as an advance single, two months before the album comes out.
FRASER: Yeah, well that one, they've always got *the* song on one of their albums, and you knew right away that was going to be *the* song. We all knew it as "Runaway Train" right up until, I think, even when we mixed it. And I don't know, management or label said there's already a song called "Runaway Train." So we can't use it. Or if we use it, we have to do this or that, so it was decided right there and then to call it "Rock 'N' Roll Train."

VOCCIA: They were originally going to call the album *Runaway Train* too. The album cover was going to be that famous train crash picture, but they found out it was used already for Mr. Big's *Lean Into It.* So Angus said, "You know, let's do something unique and different here." That's when he started tossing around *Black Ice* as the title, which I found unusual, although it grew on me. And so that became the title track, which is my favorite on the album—just a really great guitar riff in that. But that title came from Brian, where, in Northern England, when he was younger he would often wipe out on his motorbike on black ice, or what he referred to as a glazed frost.

POPOFF: Verging on heavy metal once again for the boys with that one, as well as "War Machine."
VOCCIA: I wouldn't necessarily say heavy metal, but yeah, hard rock with in-your-face rock riffs with powerful guitars and choruses and loud drums. But they're not really too much different in intensity than a song like "Ballbreaker." And "Spoilin' for a Fight" is actually quite similar to "War Machine" in that Malcolm and Angus are playing two different guitar parts, but playing to one another, complementing each other.

AT&T Center, San Antonio, Texas, December 12, 2008.

The magic of AC/DC is, number one, the creativity they put behind some of those riffs. Some people may say that they are basic guitar riffs. But being a guitarist in an AC/DC tribute band, I've seen a lot of guitar players try to play certain AC/DC songs and they don't play them right. Certain chords can be heard different ways, and they're playing the chords wrong.

But tone also plays a huge part in their sound, as well as the way Angus plays, which is very powerful, with a lot of force and feeling—the way he bends the notes, it's not something just anybody can learn. And he knows enough when to play and when not to play too much, to make the song work.

POPOFF: And do they ever use alternate tunings?
VOCCIA: No, at least not on purpose [*laughs*]. On some of the old albums, certain songs may be out of A440 tune, but they have typically been an A440-tuning band, although I think on the last couple of tours, they were tuning down a half step to accommodate Brian Johnson, to make it easier on the vocals.

POPOFF: But there is an AC/DC "first" on this record: slide guitar, on "Stormy May Day," which is in fact front and center throughout the song. I guess some call that slide on "Badlands," but . . .

FRASER: Yes, when we were sort of working that song up—because a lot of times, the song ideas would come in and all the other bandmembers wouldn't have ever heard this—because AC/DC never rehearsed in the studio. So Mal and Angus would say, "Okay, here's the next song we're doing," and we'd play Angus's cassette tape or whatever he had of the song, the demo. And then everybody would be, "Oh, okay, yep, yeah, A, D, A, C," whatever.

So we're working through the song, and then Angus I believe was noodling around doing a slide or something, and Brendan says, "Hey, that's great, let's do that." "Oh, what? You can't put a slide on an AC/DC record." And we all said, "Well, why not? It's all you guys." So I thought that was really cool. To me, it was sort of like the moment when Bruce added a horn section to Aerosmith. How do you put a horn section on a rock band? "This is how you do it," you know? So I thought it added a neat little dimension to AC/DC without all their fans going, "What?! This isn't AC/DC." I think a lot of the fans really enjoyed that moment.

And with a song like that, you can get a visual. In fact, for "Stormy May Day," I'm pretty sure it was even raining the day we were recording it. We've got windows all around the studio and it's one of those gray, drizzly days. So when I hear that song, that's what I envision, you know, windshield wipers on your car. There's not many AC/DC songs you get those sorts of visualizations. They're all about, hey, this song is great, let's go down to the bar, let's go party with my friends or whatever. But that's sort of an introspective song where, when you hear it, everybody can add their own imagery to it.

POPOFF: Once again, these lyrics are credited to Malcolm and Angus.

FRASER: Yes, when they sort of pulled it away from the singers, Bon and Brian, it became a joint thing. But one thing I noticed with *Black Ice*, Angus seemed to have a little more say in the lyrics. So, again, in retrospect, you think maybe something was already happening with Mal, and maybe Angus was taking on more of that role. For instance, the lyrics on "Black Ice" were Angus, and Mal would help him a bit on that. But they were sort of Angus's ideas. He had this notebook. It was funny, on the last record we did, *Rock or Bust*, I got to see his little notebook, and it's this notepad, maybe three inches thick, and it goes right back to '75, '76 [*laughs*]. And I thought, wow, would I know a lot of people who'd loved to have a thumb through this thing.

POPOFF: How about some of these other tracks on here?
VOCCIA: "Rock 'N' Roll Dream" is a great tune; Brian is very soulful in that song. Whether it's coincidental or what, but thinking back now on Malcolm's situation, maybe that was kind of about him, you know? Singing about the last time I'll be in a rock 'n' roll dream. It's a sad thing to think that, but maybe they knew what was going on at the time, recording the album. Maybe that's what the song meant, maybe not, but it's a sad thing to consider.

"Anything Goes" is uncommonly poppy for them, but I thought it was a good song, catchy. It definitely achieves what they were aiming for, which is probably to write a single. A lot of people I know didn't really care for that one much, but I don't know, it's not terrible. "Wheels" is apparently like a Brian thing, because of his car racing and stuff. And, of course, "Stormy May Day is the first and only time that we ever heard Angus play slide guitar on a song, and it's too bad that they didn't play that one live.
FRASER: "Stormy May Day," "Big Jack," and "Anything Goes" I thought were departures away from the normal AC/DC thing. But Brendan was really good at respecting their legacy and not pulling it too far away. First time I heard the songs, I thought, oh, this is okay, but they grew on me because it was still the band, and yet a bit of a departure. I thought, "Hey, this actually sounds neat; it's not the same old song again kind of thing."

"Spoilin' for a Fight" was really cool, and lyrically, it's sort of that Glaswegian AC/DC thing, where you grew up spoiling for a fight. And "Rocking All the Way," that's what they do and that's what they love doing. No matter what they're doing, they're rocking all the way. And actually "Money Made" was another one that I thought was a bit like "Big Jack" and "Anything Goes," a departure but in a cool way, a little more sort of R & B, and more B, than the R [*laughs*]. And "Rock 'N' Roll Dream" had a nice lilt to it.

But, you know, I think "War Machine" is my favorite on the record. "Rock '' Roll Train," you know, is going to be the single, but "War

Machine," just with that *War machine!* gang vocal, it's sort of the "Hells Bells" of this record. It had that dark rock thing to it.

POPOFF: "War Machine" is a good one for backup vocals. How had that function changed in the Brendan O'Brien years?

FRASER: On background vocals, we used the other guys. Brian very rarely gets in there unless it's more of a gang-type situation, because his vocal is so identifiable. Even if he is singing with four other guys, all you would hear is Brian [*laughs*]. So we always asked him to sit out. Cliff is probably sort of the next best singer in the band, so Cliff does most of the background vocals. And then they add Malcolm in there. Just because Malcolm's got that different, real kind of gravelly voice. And then we'd just do a few multitracks of that to create a background sound.

So that's usually the way it goes. When we did the records with Brendan, he's a really good singer too, so he would jump in there and add to sort of the sing-ability of the background vocals. And then on the last record, *Rock or Bust*, because Mal wasn't around at all, we made Angus get in there. Because Angus has got that similar sort of gravelly voice as Malcolm. And Angus doesn't sing, or never has sang, so it took him a bit to coax him in there. But he's all over the record now singing, and actually I think he quite enjoyed it.

POPOFF: As we've alluded to before, what we wind up with in the end is the longest album of AC/DC's career—and no one complained.

FRASER: Usually when you do a record, you do a couple songs extra. Sometimes when they would release a record, they would add an extra one for Japan, that kind of thing. Or they would save one for different packaging later. But by the time of *Black Ice*, that was not really the normal thing to do. People were tired of the longer records. But we did all the songs, and the decision was, hey, let's just go with them. Let's just put them out. Why hold these ones back? "Which ones do you want to take off?" And nobody could really decide.

VOCCIA: I was surprised by that, because AC/DC albums were always short. Which is sometimes good where it leaves you wanting more, or the band has something to save for the next album. But I was pleasantly surprised. I like the way the album flows. Every track, one after another, the way the tracks are lined up on the album, they just flow nicely, one to the next. I can listen to the album straight through. What they came up with here was a solid rock album with structure and order and flow that made for a pleasurable listening experience.

ROCK OR BUST

with **ROBERT LAWSON** and **MARK STRIGL**

1. Rock or Bust   3:03
2. Play Ball   2:47
3. Rock the Blues Away   3:24
4. Miss Adventure   2:57
5. Dogs of War   3:35
6. Got Some Rock & Roll Thunder   3:22
7. Hard Times   2:44
8. Baptism of Fire   3:30
9. Rock the House   2:42
10. Sweet Candy   3:09
11. Emission Control   3:41

All songs composed by Angus Young and Malcolm Young

Personnel: Brian Johnson—lead vocals; Angus Young—lead guitar; Stevie Young—rhythm guitar, backing vocals; Cliff Williams—bass, backing vocals; Phil Rudd—drums; Brendan O'Brien—backing vocals

Released November 28, 2014

Recorded at the Warehouse Studio, Vancouver, Canada

Produced by Brendan O'Brien

And so we arrive at the last AC/DC record in our journey, but will it be the last? If it's not, only two things will have happened. Brian comes back and makes the next one legitimate, or we learn something new and surprising about Angus—that he will risk the legacy with a messy and anticlimactic close.

Rock or Bust is messy in itself, but only a little bit: first, in that Malcolm is gone; second, in that it's the shortest AC/DC album ever; and third, because what's left inside its tiny thirty-five-minute frame is not all that great. I much—*much*—prefer *Black Ice*, but who cares what I think? I mean, I guess it stands for something, but fortunately for our conclusion, *the band's*

CHAPTER

16

conclusion, I find myself being at least a little swayed by the enthusiasm of my speakers on the subject, Mark Strigl and Robert Lawson.

But I had lots of enthusiasm to spare when "Play Ball" was issued as an advance single, what with that complicated little verse riff and classic finger-plucked chorus. Even the whole "play ball" concept, along with the association with Major League Baseball—it was all good, with this sports thing being kind of new for the band, at least with this amount of directness.

And I have no issue with Stevie Young being there, nor his playing or Angus's playing. Heck, I've owned those Starfighters albums their whole lives. But I find *Rock or Bust*'s production a little hysterical and wiry, and the songs stolid, stodgy, a little dour of melody—I mean, it's slim pickings finding much joy here beyond the "Play Ball" chorus.

OPPOSITE: Both Phil and Cliff were on board for the recording of *Rock or Bust*, but Phil, just by the skin of his teeth. Near the end of the tour, Axl Rose would step in for a tossed Brian.

BELOW: *Rock or Bust* is the shortest AC/DC album ever, and what's left inside its slight thirty-five-minute frame is not all that great. Oh, and Malcolm's gone. ANZ Stadium, November 4, 2015.

But why should there be joy? The band's quiet patriarch, Malcolm Young, has been retired due to an early-onset dementia diagnosis, the first one of those I can recall in rock, making it all the more striking and singular. The dynamic becomes much like the Who, with Angus playing Pete, and Brian suddenly becoming the unchallenged co-leader, like Roger. Both singers, for complex reasons, are not the writers in their situations, but the ravages of age have left a pair in each band standing alone.

Of course, both Phil and Cliff were on board for *Rock or Bust*, but Phil, just by the skin of his teeth, and then he was summarily dismissed right after. Near the end of the tour, which saw Axl Rose stepping in for a tossed Brian (already essentially wrecking the ending as far as I'm concerned, although Axl did a killer job), Cliff, the healthiest looking one, announced by video his own retirement.

And so as we do the math, as I write this, officially there is one classic lineup member left in AC/DC, and that would be Angus, who has said so little over the years, he hardly seems like a leader. Although, hey, in theory, the entire and quite legitimate *Rock or Bust* lineup could conceivably make another record. But if it is indeed the end, I, for one, am convinced it's on a bit of a droop with this record. But like I say, I'm being swayed a bit back to the middle through the arguments of my two AC/DC experts, Mark and Robert. Thanks for that, guys—I dearly want to love AC/DC's last album, and your examination into the nooks of crannies of *Rock or Bust* has helped in that regard.

POPOFF: **What kind of record is *Rock or Bust* compared to *Black Ice*?**
STRIGL: Pretty similar for me, but because of everything that was going on with Brian leaving and Malcolm no longer in the picture, I probably listened to it more. I remember going to Walmart and buying the Walmart-only *Black Ice*, but I was actually a little more excited about *Rock or Bust*, because it seemed like there was something going on, the dynamics were changing, and sometimes change is good. Because of Malcolm leaving and AC/DC being in the news a lot, the Phil Rudd scandal that was going on, my curiosity was piqued and I probably spent more time listening to *Rock or Bust* than *Black Ice*.
LAWSON: It's hard to get my head around this concept, but here's the thing: after forty years, AC/DC make an album without their leader, the guy who is the heart and soul of the band. They make a record without him, and what happens? It's one of the strongest records they've done in like thirty years. There's no way that this should work. Like, how do you make an AC/DC record without Malcolm Young? You can't. And they did.

POPOFF: What do you like about it? I prefer *Black Ice*, so I'm really intrigued.

LAWSON: Well, there are a few touches that went against the grain of the cliché that AC/DC puts out the same record every time, or have put out the same record fifteen times.

And I wouldn't say there's a lot of post–*Flick of the Switch* AC/DC records that I go back to too often, but this is one of them. For example, "Miss Adventure" is interesting because you can really hear the interplay between Stevie and Angus, which demonstrates that he's a good and very natural fit; that could have been Malcolm playing those parts.

And before the record even came out, we have the first single, "Play Ball," which I first saw—and probably a lot of people did—used as a trailer for postseason Major League Baseball. So if you love AC/DC and you love baseball, that's a really interesting mix that hadn't happened previously. This is a neat marriage. Basically the song was used as in a trailer to promote the postseason, after regular-season had finished, and this was like the theme song for it. AC/DC has always been a global band, but somehow this went a long way to strengthening their ties to something that was very American.

And a funny thing about that song, the guitar solo, at least the second half of it, is pretty similar to the one in "Shot Down in Flames." Another example of them recycling, right off the start, is on the title cut, "Rock or Bust," which starts like "Nervous Shakedown," and that guitar pattern continues through the whole song. And every time it comes up, I don't see how you cannot think, "Wow, they're doing the riff from 'Nervous Shakedown'" [*laughs*].

POPOFF: And for the record, why isn't Malcolm around?

STRIGL: I guess it was announced a couple months before *Rock or Bust* came out that he was suffering from dementia and was no longer going to be involved. It seemed like a tragedy for someone so young, sixty-one at the time, to be suffering from dementia. But his condition was kept private for quite a while before that because AC/DC has always been a very guarded band. Leading up to that, all we really knew was that he fell ill and was no longer in the picture. There's been rumors that he's in a nursing home and he's just not there mentally anymore.

POPOFF: And how about Phil Rudd? What was his situation?

STRIGL: Phil Rudd's story was a little more entertaining and not quite as sad, although I guess they're both sad, depending on how you look at it. But right as the album was coming out, November of 2014, he was charged with almost doing what they sang about in "Dirty Deeds"—twice in fact. One of those charges was withdrawn and one was dropped, but he was convicted on pot and meth charges. For a guy his age, it sounded like he was living quite an excessive, hard life.

LAWSON: Also, before he even got to the album, it was reported that he was like ten days late for his sessions. So far that Brendan had another guy ready to step in and play drums on the album. So Rudd almost lost his

Grammy rehearsal, Staples Center, Los Angeles, February 6, 2015.

opportunity to play on the record. Obviously, the guy's got some personal demons. But this record cycle represents a real major shift in the lineup, in almost every position. Malcolm is not on the album and he's not on the tour. So our main guy is out. Phil Rudd does the album, but he's out of the tour. Before the end of the tour, about two-thirds the way through, Brian is out. Now, before this whole tour wraps up, Cliff Williams announces that he's out! So we're really running on fumes here. Unless the next release is another archival release—which this band does great jobs of—who is left? You're going to have just Chris Slade and Stevie Young, along with Angus.

POPOFF: Back to the record, what does Brendan O'Brien bring to the situation?
LAWSON: As I've talked about before, AC/DC value trust, and now they've got a guy they can trust; they built a relationship with him through *Black Ice*. Obviously, they're happy. *Black Ice* was successful and they're going to go back to him. With the other records, you've got George and Harry for so long, then you've got Mutt Lange for so long. They did a couple records by themselves; they don't bounce around. When they like someone and they trust somebody, then they're going to stick with them. But this one, to me, sounds more like their early George Young/Harry Vanda records than anything in a while. It definitely doesn't sound like a Mutt Lange AC/DC record.

POPOFF: And this is the third album in a row—and fourth out of the last five—that they record in Vancouver.
LAWSON: If anything, again, they liked being comfortable. They don't like surprises. And even with Malcolm out, Angus is a real stickler for things being the same. And I wouldn't be surprised if there was going to be another record, . . . Brendan O'Brien would be there.
STRIGL: Vancouver's been a hot spot for many bands. Aerosmith, the Cult, Metallica, Bon Jovi, and Mötley Crüe have all recorded there. I only know from having visited Vancouver a few times that there's something magical about that town. All the way from Portland up to Vancouver is such a just a beautiful place, and I feel like it just really peaks there in Vancouver with that city set in such a scenic, gorgeous place right on the Pacific. You do feel there's a magic in the air and I can't help think that being an artist that the vibes are great. I've heard there's a lot of great strip clubs too [*laughs*].

POPOFF: Okay, what are some of the highlights on this record for you? Again, I dearly want to like this record more—take me on a tour!

STRIGL: Sure, well, as the record gets going, it tends to get better and better in my opinion. "Sweet Candy" is one I like: that's a powerhouse of a song. I love the way they kind of pay a little tribute to Jimi Hendrix at the beginning of it, with that "Foxy Lady" kind of thing, where he cranks up the distortion and rubs the strings. It's very Hendrix for the first ten seconds. With "Dogs of War," I feel some of that old fire come back, especially on the opening where you hear Angus's vocal, saying, *Dogs of war*. It almost brings me back to the "Dirty Deeds" or "T.N.T." And then it just kicks into a really great song.

LAWSON: I agree, and "Dogs of War" is really different for them, kind of an atmospheric track. It reminds me of "The Mist Is Rising" by the Joe Perry Project. It starts with just a little bit of backward guitar, which in "The Mist Is Rising," and goes through the whole song. And it has an excellent guitar solo.

And with Angus singing like that, in the really old days, Malcolm was doing a lot of that. It was on the *Highway to Hell* record where they were really introduced the idea of gang vocals by Mutt. So it's like four or five guys all chanting the same thing. But on those early records, it's usually simpler, and it's cool that Angus steps up to the plate to replace Malcolm here, who was leading in that regard.

"Rock the House" has kind of a Zeppelin riff through it, which I think is unfortunate; AC/DC are known for creating some of the classic guitar riffs of all time over the years, and now they're doing a Zeppelin thing. That's like a step back for them. But "Hard Times" is a pretty interesting track, kind of a dark and dirty little number, which I like.

STRIGL: I love "Hard Times" and I'll tell you why. On that song you really hear this vulnerability in Brian's voice, which is not as strong as we remember it and constantly still hear it every day when the radio plays *Back in Black* songs, whether it's "Shoot to Thrill" or "You Shook Me" or "Back in Black." You hear the songs over and over again, and his voice is on fire on that record. But here there's a vulnerable side to his voice. It's rough in the beginning and there's some cracking, and there's a real feel to his voice.

This is Brian Johnson, 2014—he's not that young guy anymore. And knowing what happened afterward, with Brian leaving AC/DC, made this song even more emotional for me. I hear his voice and it's wobbly, on the

beginning. It reminds me of how I love Johnny Cash's voice on those last few records with Rick Rubin. That showed a different side to him. And I think "Hard Times" gives us a really nice moment that I don't think we get anywhere else from Brian. That makes that song really special.

And I also just love the way the solo kicks in, because they do this thing where they throw these two chords in there that makes it sound like they're going to go to this other key for the solo, but then they bring it right back to the original key. It's clever and it's cool.

LAWSON: Another interesting one is "Rock the Blues Away," which has got a nice little descending guitar riff, but it also has this really neat stomping kind of glam rock feel. Which is new for AC/DC. And if they had pushed it a little bit more in that direction, it would've been like a Slade-style number, even Geordie for that matter. You know, all they had to do was increase the stomp a bit and add some handclaps; it really sounds like they're

Coachella Valley Music and Arts Festival, Empire Polo Club, Indio, California, April 17, 2015.

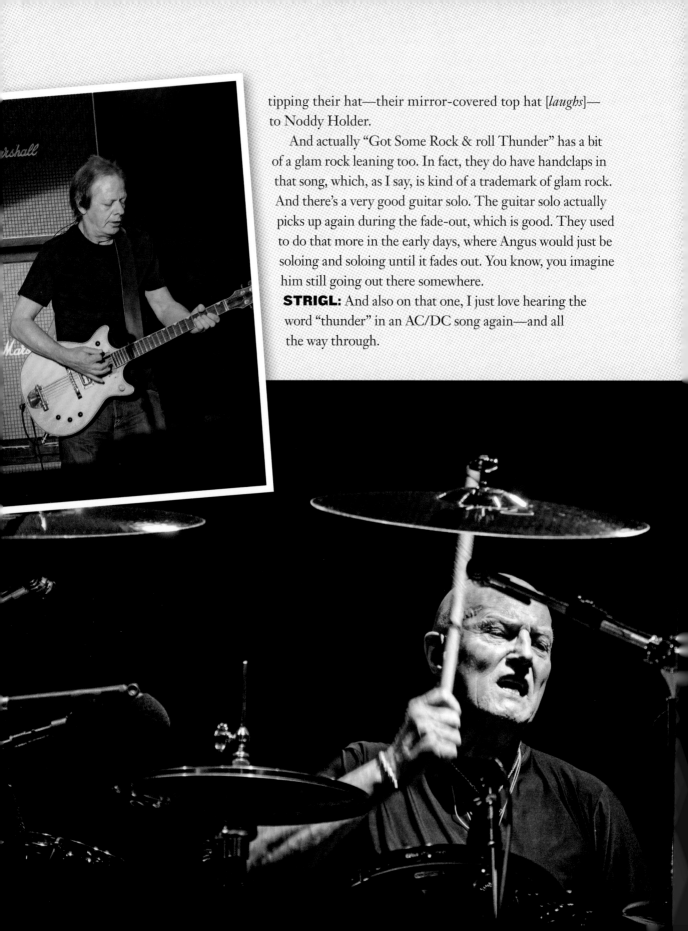

tipping their hat—their mirror-covered top hat [*laughs*]—to Noddy Holder.

And actually "Got Some Rock & roll Thunder" has a bit of a glam rock leaning too. In fact, they do have handclaps in that song, which, as I say, is kind of a trademark of glam rock. And there's a very good guitar solo. The guitar solo actually picks up again during the fade-out, which is good. They used to do that more in the early days, where Angus would just be soloing and soloing until it fades out. You know, you imagine him still going out there somewhere.

STRIGL: And also on that one, I just love hearing the word "thunder" in an AC/DC song again—and all the way through.

POPOFF: Mark, what are your thoughts on Stevie?

STRIGL: Yes, so we have Stevie Young brought in to cover rhythm guitars, to fill the shoes of his uncle, Malcolm. He seemed like the obvious choice, because he had done touring with the band back in the late eighties. I first saw him back on stage with the band when they did the Grammy Awards, and played "Rock or Bust," the title track, and "Highway to Hell."

I thought that was such an incredible moment, to see Brian and Angus at the Grammys, Brian, and I mean, Stevie fits in perfectly. The average Joe watching that might not have even known that that wasn't Malcolm. They might not have even known who Malcolm is. They just fixate on the visual of the guy in the schoolboy uniform with the guy wearing the funky hat and singing, and that's AC/DC to them. But Stevie was perfect. And I thought the performance at that Grammy Awards, bringing him out publicly like that, was such an awesome moment. I'm all for him. If you're gonna bring anyone in, it's gotta be him.

POPOFF: And we've asked this of a lot of our speakers throughout the book, but what is your assessment of what Angus brings to the band— and the world of rock—as a guitarist?

STRIGL: Angus's characteristic is that he's completely from the heart. He's running directly into Marshall cabinets, with his Gibson SG. And when you really listen to it, some people are like, wow, they're such a hard rock band. Back in the late seventies, they even referred to them as a heavy metal band. But when you listen to his playing, there isn't that much distortion on there. He's not playing clean, but like Jimmy Page, it isn't a crazy overdrive. I love Van Halen, but there's flange, heavy, heavy distortion, Echoplex, all sorts of stuff—and that's the heavy metal way.

But Angus, no, straight into the amp, not even maxing out the distortion. He's getting the distortion more by just playing so loud. That's one of the things he did—he played so loud. And because he was playing so loud, the pickups on his guitar would capture the sound coming out of his amp. So there would be this weird, like, looping, bleeding thing going on, that would add to his sound. But barely any effects at all. And there's no one like him, which is mostly from his fingers—it's the way his fingers touched those strings. And that's why when you see an AC/DC cover band, it's usually not very good. You can play those same notes, but they never sound the way Angus plays them.

POPOFF: And what do you guys make of these songwriting credits, with Malcolm in on every song?

LAWSON: Well, it's valid, because there is some recycling going on in this record, which apparently is how Malcolm gets co-writing credits on the whole record. The whole record is credited to Angus and Malcolm, and it turns out that a lot of the songs are from earlier ideas, leftovers, older riffs that they had worked on together. I doubt Malcolm is really the fifty percent songwriter on these songs, but I'm sure part of it is just a family thing to help take care of him. But he definitely earned some of it.

STRIGL: There's a lot about the record that makes me wonder if they were out of ideas. Because, sure, with Malcolm credited as a songwriter on the record, you've got to think they were just going back and taking scraps that they had left on the cutting-room floor throughout the years, and kind of pulling them together trying to make songs. And I think sometimes that works on this record and sometimes it doesn't. And also it's the shortest studio record they ever put out, which also kind of supports the theory that maybe there weren't a lot of ideas.

LAWSON: But I like that. It's true that it's the shortest, but I like to think of it as just very concise. Everything just kind of gets in and out, which I think is a good way to do it. And for guys who in the past had a little bit of trouble getting a whole album's worth of strong material, it's good to keep it short and sweet.

POPOFF: Now this maybe ascribes too much significance, but if "Emission Control" is the last song we ever hear from AC/DC, how capably did the band make their exit?

LAWSON: "Emission Control" is interesting—sort of a slow, groovy funk song, which is very different for them, and then they've got these backing vocals that get a little too close to later Def Leppard territory for me. Like I say, Mutt Lange kind of introduced the gang vocals to AC/DC, and I thought that was fantastic. The band's sales on those albums show that a lot of people did as well. But on this particular song, I thought, "Oh boy, okay, let's stay away from the Def Leppard/Mutt Lange–style vocals."

So it's great to end the record with a bit of a new thing. It's "Okay, wait, what are we doing now? Could this be a new direction?" Probably not. But unfortunate, as I say, for me are those backing vocals. That kept the track from being as interesting as it could be. And it's a weird artistic choice too, because when you hear that kind of slow, funky rhythm, a rumbling groove like that, well, Def Leppard don't have any songs that sound like that, so why would you think of putting that kind of vocal on it? There's no precedent for that.

POPOFF: And what about panning out to the whole album? How does *Rock or Bust* stand as the last AC/DC album ever, if that's what it turns out to be?

LAWSON: I think that as a last record, this is a good way to go out. I rate it an eight out of ten, which is higher than I've rated an AC/DC record in many, many years. So I think they are really going out on a high note. And I'm surprised that it's so good, without Malcolm being there, and hearing about the trouble behind the scenes with Phil Rudd being ten days late to the

Brian's last show with AC/DC. Sprint Center, Kansas City, Missouri, February 28, 2016.

sessions. I imagine during the recording, that Brian was fine. There's certainly nothing wrong with his performance on the record. It's just when the hearing issue came up for him, while the tour was going on, that led to his downfall.

POPOFF: Well that's an interesting point, because *Rock or Bust* is sure to be a record that represents a number of endings. But none is more mysterious than that of Brian Johnson's. Malcolm's is undoubtedly more tragic, but Brian's role in the band has always been shrouded in mystery.
STRIGL: Yes, and as background, there was something on *Howard Stern*. Brian was on with Howard Stern a number of years back, and he mentioned there that because of driving race cars—not because he stands next to the loudest guitar player in the world night after night—but because of driving race cars, his hearing was messed up. But there was, at that point, no indication that this was going to affect AC/DC in any way.

And I mean, what all of us conspiracy theorists believe, and think is quite possible, is that there was something more, or at least in addition to this hearing loss thing going on with the band. We do know now that there really was. And, you know, they weren't playing two shows, night off, two shows, night off. They were on the road, they were playing stadiums, but they were only doing two or three shows a week, which has got to be really expensive, to keep a stadium production on the road when you're only playing two, sometimes three times, a week.

So there was speculation on the Internet that this may have played into it. And, you know, as far back as *The Razors Edge*, when suddenly Brian wasn't getting a songwriting credit anymore, that there was something going on with him, these last, well, almost twenty years at this point, right? Where he had fallen out of favor with the inner workings of AC/DC, namely Angus, and most possibly Malcolm, at some point.

And to me, this hearing thing is . . . he complained to Angus about the hearing, and judging front what Jim Breuer revealed—and then backtracked on—something happened that pissed them off, and basically they sent Brian home, and, like Jim Breuer said, left his luggage on his driveway. I mean, that's not the way you treat somebody you're happy with who has a medical issue.

OPPOSITE: Playing out the string with Axl. Madison Square Garden, New York City, September 14, 2016.

BELOW: Set list for *Rock or Bust* show, Philips Arena, Atlanta, Georgia, September 1, 2016.

Rock or Bust PYRO
Shoot to Thrill
Hell Ain't a Bad Place to Be
Back In Black
Rock 'n Roll Thunder
Dirty Deeds Done Dirt Cheap
Rock 'n Roll Damnation
Thunderstruck
High Voltage
Rock 'n Roll Train
Hell's Bells
Given the Dog a Bone
If You Want Blood You Got It
Live Wire
Sin City
You Shook Me All Night Long
Shot Down in Flames
Have A Drink on Me
T.N.T.
Whole Lotta Rosie
Let There Be Rock
ENCORE
Highway To Hell PYRO
Riff Raff
For Those About to Rock PYRO

OPPOSITE: Final night of the *Rock or Bust* World Tour—and final AC/DC show ever? Wells Fargo Center, Philadelphia, Pennsylvania, September 20, 2016.

And you know, Brian Johnson, to me, always seemed like, even though he was the lead singer in the band, I felt like while I wasn't old enough to have seen Bon live, from the videos I've seen, he always seemed like more of an equal on stage to Angus. Whereas to me, Brian Johnson always seemed like he would stand slightly off to the side from Angus, and it was almost like an Ed McMahon–to–Johnny Carson vibe there. That's totally diminishing, and I probably shouldn't go there. But just in the presentation, it seemed like Brian was always so respectful of not only Angus, but just the legacy of AC/DC. He just seemed like he had stepped onboard this crazy ride known as AC/DC, he was enjoying it, but he was also trying hard to not tarnish it. And I think he did an excellent job. I really have so much respect for the guy.

POPOFF: I've heard stories of how even before *Black Ice*, he'd have a hard time getting those guys to return his calls or pick up his calls.
LAWSON: Yes, well, I'm not sure how much people know about that, but that is something that was rumored years ago, that the band were trying to get him out. And I wonder when they took away the lyric writing from him, if that was a way of maybe trying to force his hand. I can only speculate why, but I think Brian's performance on this last record is nothing but top-notch. You know, he's had some good times and not so good times vocally on some of the records. And on *Rock or Bust*, he sounds really engaged with all the material. I think it's just kind of testament to the man's character that in some ways it doesn't seem like he's that wanted in this band, and yet he's still happy to be there. You gotta think that he's one of the main reasons that for millions of people, AC/DC is their favorite band in the world.
STRIGL: I saw them in Giants Stadium early on in the tour with Brian singing, and I said to my wife at that time, "I think this is the last time I'm ever going to see AC/DC in my life." And it was an amazing, beautiful experience, really spiritual in a way. I just had this feeling that maybe they would never come around again. It was just one of those things. I was wrong, though, because then they came back around. They played Madison Square Gardens, sold it out. They had actually canceled the date, and then they rescheduled, after Axl was on board, and it was one of Cliff's last shows with the band. And to me, something about it seemed like a new beginning as opposed to an end. And whether or not it ever happens, I believe that Angus is not done. I don't know if they will continue on with Axl or whomever, but to me, it just doesn't feel like it's the end for him.

ABOUT THE AUTHOR

Martin Popoff has penned sixty-nine books on hard rock, heavy metal, punk rock, classic rock, and record collecting. He has also contributed to *Revolver*, *Guitar World*, *Goldmine*, *Record Collector*, bravewords.com, lollipop.com, and hardradio. com. Martin has been a regular contractor to Banger Films, having worked on the award-winning documentary *Rush: Beyond the Lighted Stage*, the eleven-episode *Metal Evolution*, and the ten-episode *Rock Icons*, both for VH1 Classic. Martin currently resides in Toronto.

IMAGE CREDITS

ABOUT THE PANELISTS

RICHARD BIENSTOCK: is an editor with *Guitar World* and *Guitar Aficionado* magazines. He is also a musician and journalist whose writing has appeared in numerous US and international outlets, including *Billboard*, rollingstone.com, *Classic Rock*, and *The Village Voice*. He is the author of three books and most recently co-authored *Kurt Cobain: Montage of Heck*, the companion to the award-winning documentary of the same name. He penned the liner notes to AC/DC's 1978 live album, *If You Want Blood (You've Got It)*, as part of Epic's 2003 reissue campaign of the band's catalogue, and has had the pleasure of interviewing Angus, Malcolm, and Brian several times over the years.

PHIL CARSON is best known for his long and distinguished tenure as a senior Atlantic Records executive from 1968 to 1985. He was instrumental in signing AC/DC to the label in the mid-seventies and worked closely with the band, as he did with both Yes and Led Zeppelin. After leaving Atlantic, Carson formed a management company where he guided the careers of Robert Plant, Jimmy Page, Motörhead, Yes, Paul Rodgers, Asia, Foreigner, and Ben E. King.

Hailing from Detroit (Rock City), Michigan, **MARK CICCHINI** can be heard discussing hard rock and metal each week on the No. 1 Kiss-themed podcast *Three Sides of the Coin*. In early 2016, *Three Sides of the Coin* surpassed over two million views and is fast approaching the three million mark. Cicchini has loaned out his vast musical archive for various projects, including Kiss' *New York Times*—bestseller book, *Nothin' to Lose*, VH1's *Ultimate Albums* episode on Kiss' *Alive!*, the deluxe CD reissue of Kiss' *Love Gun*, Billboard's *Kiss Alive Forever* book, Martin Popoff's *Epic Ted Nugent* book, and many more print magazines and online publications. Mark has been a diehard AC/DC fan since the late seventies and can boast a most impressive collection of vinyl, CD, eight-track, and cassette recordings of the rarest of the rare that AC/DC has to offer. Also, Mark has been playing the drums for over forty years. His band, Left for Dead, are currently recording their sixth CD due out in the spring of 2017. Lastly, Mark has had to suffer more than a few discussions on the virtues of Phil Rudd versus Neil Peart. For the record, Mark sides with Phil.

RICH DAVENPORT is a UK-based radio DJ, music writer, musician (with the Blackmail Snaps), and stand-up comedian, and has been a fan of AC/DC since the age of eight, when, like Angus Young, he was still in short pants. In covering the band for radio and magazine features, Rich has interviewed the band's former drummers Phil Rudd and Simon Wright, Tony Platt (engineer on *Highway to Hell*, *Back in Black*, and *Flick of the Switch*), Tony Currenti (session drummer on the original Australian *High Voltage*), Irene Thornton (Bon Scott's ex-wife, author of *My Bon Scott*), and Andre Jacquemin, Geordie producer, and the man who lent Brian Johnson the train fare to come to London for his AC/DC audition. Of note, not only is Rich a distinguished contributor to this book, but the author collared, cajoled, and absolutely trusted him to perform an expert peer review of the complete text.

From humble farm roots in rural Minnesota, **DAVID ELLEFSON** has come a long way, literally and figuratively, to conquering stages around the world as bassist of thrash metal titans Megadeth. Revered for his unique, hard-hitting playing style, and unwavering dedication to his musical craft, Ellefson has woven a vast professional tapestry as a bassist, songwriter, record producer, clinician, and author. As a member of Megadeth, he has been awarded ten Grammy nominations, countless gold and platinum records, and toured the world for the better part of three decades. In addition to Megadeth, David has lent his playing and writing abilities to several other recording and touring projects, including Soulfly, F5, Temple of Brutality, Altitudes and Attitude (with Frank Bello of Anthrax), and Metal Allegiance, the supergroup formed by Mark Menghi with David, Mike Portnoy, and Alex Skolnick, releasing their eponymous debut in 2015 on Nuclear Blast Records. Ellefson, who holds a bachelor's degree in business marketing and continues to lecture on a variety of music- and business-related topics, has also ventured out into other related forays, as president of record label EMP Label Group (Ellefson Music Productions) and with his own coffee brand, Ellefson Coffee Co.

MIKE FRASER's name is as synonymous with recording and mixing records as Gibson is to the guitar world. The artists he has recorded and mixed are a veritable A to Z of the who's who in music. From AC/DC and Aerosmith to Van Halen and Zeppelin, Mike's killer ears and easygoing manner have established him as a legendary engineer and mixer in many genres of music that span an enviable thirty successful years. "Fraze," as he's affectionately known by his musical cohorts, boasts the much-envied position of engineer and mixer to iconic rockers AC/DC. Fraze has recorded and mixed five CDs and many projects in between for the much-loved Aussie group, including massive worldwide hit, *The Razors Edge* (which includes "Thunderstruck," one of the band's biggest anthems), along with *Black Ice* and the recent *Rock or Bust*. Other happy clients include Rush, Metallica, the Blood Brothers, the Cult, Airbourne, Elvis Costello, Franz Ferdinand, Chickenfoot, Joe Satriani, Led Zeppelin, Norah Jones, Zac Brown, the Dan Reed Network, Theory of a Deadman, the Trews, Russell Crowe's 30 Odd Foot of Grunts, Slipknot, Mötley Crüe, Amen, Bryan Adams, Terri Clarke, Corrosion of Conformity, Marianas Trench, the Blue Man Group, Ozzy Osborne, and Bad Religion. Audio and full credits can be found on Mike's website, mikefrasermix. com. Mike lives and works in Vancouver, Canada.

JAY JAY FRENCH (born John French Segall, July 20, 1952) is an American guitarist, manager, and producer. French is most famous for his role as the founding member and one of the guitarists of the heavy metal band Twisted Sister. Being an avid runner, French has also completed two New York Marathons, in 1981 and 1986. As a guitar player, manager, producer, and executive producer, French has sold more than 20 million albums, performed in thirty-four countries, and performed live more than nine thousand times. The seeds for French's musical life were planted in 1963, when he attended his first concert, seeing the legendary folk group the Weavers in Carnegie Hall. But as he so passionately states in this book, "I will tell you this about AC/DC. They are the only band except McCartney left on this earth that I will stand up for, for the entire show. The last time I saw them, I stood for the entire two hours, two-and-a-half hours, and my girlfriend was like, 'You're like a little kid.' And I go, 'Yeah, because if I don't have that, I have nothing left.' And that is what AC/DC can still do for me."

MICHAEL HANNON is Columbus, Ohio's gravel-throated, beer-drinking, bass-playing rock 'n' roll dog. From Geffen's shoulda-coulda band Salty Dog, whose sole release has been reissued twice and sold over 300,000 copies, to being the touring bassist with Dangerous Toys for two hundred shows on their marathon *Pissed* tour. Hannon then went on to front the fifteen-year overnight underground sensation act American Dog, who not only released seven studio albums, three DVDs, did fifteen European tours, countless Midwest dates, and a Japanese tour, but were also the recording and live band for Waysted vocalist Fin Muir and backup band for Ted Nugent band singer Derek St. Holmes. Throughout all of this, Hannon has played stripped-down, mean, and dirty rawk, with more than a little AC/DC in the sound. Michael first saw AC/DC on the band's *Let There Be Rock* tour in Wheeling, West Virginia—with UFO opening—and has since seen them more than twenty times, either with Bon, Brian, or Axl fronting. Hannon feels that AC/DC, Motörhead, Alice Cooper, and Ted Nugent are the greatest rock 'n' roll artists of all time, and if you disagree, you probably aren't drinking enough.

Multi-instrumentalist **PAUL KEHAYAS** has more than two decades of composition, performing, and production experience. His music has been featured in a variety of award-winning feature films, documentaries, and television programs, including *Satan Lives*, *Manson My Name Is Evil*, *Super Duper Alice Cooper*, *We're Savvy*, and *Rock Icons*. Paul is a lifelong fan of AC/DC and once played drums in an AC/DC cover band, with a guitarist who dressed up as Angus Young, and a vocalist who had no formal training, thereby being the most unique AC/DC cover band ever to grace God's green earth (Willowdale, Ontario). He now plays in the Hollow Earth.

ROBERT LAWSON is a Toronto-based music collector and archivist with thirty years of experience working in record stores. Since 2012, he has maintained the music and movies website thissideofthetracks.ca, where he writes album essays, concert reviews, and articles about various cult movies. He is the author of *Razama-Snaz! The Listener's Guide to Nazareth* and a forthcoming book about Cheap Trick. Bon Scott is one of his top ten rock vocalists of all time and AC/DC's *If You Want Blood (You've Got It)* is on his list of top ten live albums. Yes, he is that guy who makes lists . . . so many lists.

JOEL O'KEEFFE is lead vocalist and guitarist for unquestioned keepers of the Australian rock 'n' roll flame, Airbourne, who received the Metal Hammer Golden Gods award for best debut album, upon the release of *Runnin' Wild* back in 2008. The band's fourth studio album, *Breakin' Outta Hell*, was released in 2016 on Spinefarm Records.

Drummer **PHIL RUDD** issued his debut solo album in 2016. Entitled *Head Job*, the album finds Phil and his trio grinding their way through hard-boiled songs that sound like a cross between Rose Tattoo, Angel City, Motörhead, Hanoi Rocks, and the New York Dolls. Rudd is also known as the immaculate timekeeper for AC/DC, having played with the band from 1975 to 1983, and then again from 1994 to 2015. In his private life, Rudd has a weakness for big boats and fast cars.

ROBERT SIBONY is a Toronto-based session drummer, percussionist, composer, producer, and lifelong AC/DC fan. Over the years, he has shared the stage and studio with the likes of Sean Lennon, Esthero, Troy Sexton (Stomp), Bob McBride (Lighthouse), Rich Chycki (Aerosmith, Rush, Mick Jagger, Pink), Roger St-Denis, Reza Derakshani (Peter Gabriel, Madonna, Branford Marsalis), Kush, Liberty Silver, Max Webster, Billy Newton Davis (the Nylons), Thomas Wade (country music artist, songwriter for Celine Dion), the Second City House Band, and Banda DA (EMI Brazil), performing at Roy Thompson Hall in October of 2014. Sibony's many accomplished performances drew attention from a number of industry companies, resulting in endorsements from Yamaha, Sabian, and Rimshot Drumsticks. For Yamaha's fortieth anniversary concert, Sibony was invited to perform on drum set alongside Ndugu Chancler (Miles Davis, George Duke, Michael Jackson) who played congas. Robert has also appeared on *Jimmy Kimmel Live!*, MTV, Much Music, and HBO's *The Chris Rock Show*.

MARK STRIGL is a television producer/writer, musician, podcaster, father, and husband. He has studied and followed hard rock music for over thirty-five years. He founded Talking Metal in 2005. He has been an avid fan of AC/DC since the age of eleven, when his friend exposed him to the *Back in Black* album. Mark's long-form TV production work has included *The Rosie O'Donnell Show* (where he was part of an Emmy Award–winning team), MTV's *It Came from the '80s Part 2: Metal Goes Pop*, VH1's *8-Track Flashback*, VH1's *Legends*, VH1's *100 Most Metal Moments*, Fuse's *Talking Metal TV* series, VH1's *That Metal Show*, and VH1.com's *That Metal Gear*. Mark is also known for producing and writing promos for such clients as WeTV, IFC, USA Network, Notional, Broadway Video, Syfy, Chiller, Cloo, A&E, FYI, and TruTv. Mark has released numerous CDs under the name Captain T. He has performed with such bands as Ronin and Hollywood Superstars. He hosts his own podcasts and runs the Talking Metal Digital podcasting network.

BRAD TOLINSKI was editor in chief of *Guitar World* magazine for over twenty-five years. He is the author of two best-selling music books, *Light & Shade: Conversations with Jimmy Page* (Crown) and *Play It Loud: An Epic History of the Style, Sound, and Revolution of the Electric Guitar* (Doubleday). Brad has had a long association with AC/DC. He wrote the official liner notes for both *For Those About to Rock* and *Flick of the Switch*, and wrote the program notes for their induction into the Rock and Roll Hall of Fame. Tolinski is currently hosting a music-oriented talk show for AOL Build and producing live stream events at the legendary heavy metal club, St. Vitus Bar in Brooklyn for his company, Backstory Events (backstoryevents.com).

BILL VOCCIA has been a diehard AC/DC fan and collector for nearly forty years and possesses one of the world's largest and most comprehensive AC/DC memorabilia collections. In 2010, Bill was hired by Sony Music Entertainment to manage AC/DC's official website (acdc.com) for several years. Additionally, Bill was involved in many AC/DC promotional campaigns and contributed to the AC/DC site's web design and was involved in a variety of other projects focused on the band. Bill has also been a freelance music author and contributor to several publications, having authored articles about AC/DC in *Goldmine* and *Record Collector* magazines, and contributed to several other book publications. He hopes to pen his own AC/DC book—likely about collectibles—sometime in the future. Bill also pays tribute to his all-time favorite guitarist, Malcolm Young, in his tribute band Live Wire: The Ultimate AC/DC Experience (acdctributeband.com), based out of the New York metro area, but touring worldwide.

Manchester-based New Wave of British Heavy Metal legend **SIMON WRIGHT** came on board as drummer for AC/DC in time for the *Flick of the Switch* tour, subsequently playing on the *Fly on the Wall*, *Who Made Who*, and *Blow Up Your Video* albums, touring those records around the world as well. Wright has also drummed for the likes of Dio and UFO and his current gig is with progressive metal wizards Operation: Mindcrime.

COMPLETE AUTHOR

BIBLIOGRAPHY

Fighting My Way Back: Thin Lizzy 69–76 (2011)

The Deep Purple Royal Family: Chain of Events '80–'11 (2011)

The Deep Purple Royal Family: Chain of Events through '79 (2011)

Black Sabbath FAQ (2011)

The Collector's Guide to Heavy Metal: Volume 4: The '00s
    (co-author with David Perri, 2011)

Goldmine Standard Catalog of American Records 1948–1991, 7th Edition (2010)

Goldmine Record Album Price Guide, 6th Edition (2009)

Goldmine 45 RPM Price Guide, 7th Edition (2009)

A Castle Full of Rascals: Deep Purple '83–'09 (2009)

Worlds Away: Voivod and the Art of Michel Langevin (2009)

Ye Olde Metal: 1978 (2009)

Gettin' Tighter: Deep Purple '68–'76 (2008)

All Access: The Art of the Backstage Pass (2008)

Ye Olde Metal: 1977 (2008)

Ye Olde Metal: 1976 (2008)

Judas Priest: Heavy Metal Painkillers (2007)

Ye Olde Metal: 1973 to 1975 (2007)

The Collector's Guide to Heavy Metal: Volume 3: The Nineties (2007)

Ye Olde Metal: 1968 to 1972 (2007)

Run for Cover: The Art of Derek Riggs (2006)

Black Sabbath: Doom Let Loose (2006)

Dio: Light Beyond the Black (2006)

The Collector's Guide to Heavy Metal: Volume 2: The Eighties (2005)

Rainbow: English Castle Magic (2005)

UFO: Shoot Out the Lights (2005)

The New Wave of British Heavy Metal Singles (2005)

Blue Öyster Cult: Secrets Revealed! (2004)

Contents Under Pressure: 30 Years of Rush at Home & Away (2004)

The Top 500 Heavy Metal Albums of All Time (2004)

The Collector's Guide to Heavy Metal: Volume 1: The Seventies (2003)

The Top 500 Heavy Metal Songs of All Time (2003)

Southern Rock Review (2001)

Heavy Metal: 20th Century Rock and Roll (2000)

The Goldmine Price Guide to Heavy Metal Records (2000)

The Collector's Guide to Heavy Metal (1997)

Riff Kills Man! 25 Years of Recorded Hard Rock & Heavy Metal (1993)

See martinpopoff.com for complete details and ordering information.

INDEX